The Social Vision of
William Blake

The Social Vision of
William Blake

MICHAEL FERBER

PRINCETON UNIVERSITY PRESS

PRINCETON, NEW JERSEY

Copyright © 1985 by Princeton University Press
Published by Princeton University Press, 41 William Street
Princeton, New Jersey 08540

In the United Kingdom: Princeton University Press
Guildford, Surrey

All Rights Reserved

Library of Congress Cataloging in Publication Data will be
found on the last printed page of this book

ISBN 0-691-08382-7

This book has been composed in Linotron Baskerville

Clothbound editions of Princeton University Press books
are printed on acid-free paper, and binding materials
are chosen for strength and durability

Printed in the United States of America
by Princeton University Press
Princeton, New Jersey

12⁰⁰

54287

CONTENTS

PREFACE

Are not Religion & Politics the Same Thing? Brotherhood is Religion.

The present book had its origin in my attempt to understand this line from Blake's *Jerusalem* (57.10). It is not a particularly remarkable line, I admit, nor does it offer readier access to the mysteries of Blake than fifty or a hundred others from the same poem, but it struck me with unusual force when I first read it twelve years ago. I no longer remember what I made of it then, but I know I brought to it some intense feeling about religion, politics, and brotherhood. It was not long before reading *Jerusalem* that I had gone to the Arlington Street Church in Boston and turned in my draft card in a "ceremony of resistance" to the Vietnam War along with two hundred other young men who I felt were my brothers. We were part of what seemed a whole generation that took upon itself an original rethinking of what it meant to be political and religious in America, and how it might be possible to revive a failing democracy through organizations based on brotherhood—and, later, on sisterhood. In various ways and on various registers Blake had been a presence in our culture, or more often our counterculture, and I had always admired his lyrics and designs, but it was only after I had experienced moments of fraternity like the one in the church that Blake spoke peculiarly to my condition. I began to read him with new questions and expectations.

I am hardly the first to have taken Blake seriously as a social and political thinker or visionary, but those who have done so have always been a minority among his students and disciples. As George Orwell said of Dickens, Blake is well worth stealing, and occultists, Neoplatonists, Cabalists, Jungians, and even orthodox Christians have all tried to make off with him. Perhaps they are each entitled to keep a portion of him, but I think his "staminal virtue," as he would say, belongs to none of them. No doubt I will press my own claim too far in the pages that follow, but I do so partly as a corrective to these reductions and sanitizations, partly, as well, to see what certain unlikely features of his work will yield when pushed. I cannot deny a motive to steal him back and enlist him in the present phase of the cause he joined in his own day, the politics of spiritual fraternity.

Perhaps uniquely among western nations, America preserves the close conjuncture of religion and politics that was normal in Blake's England. One need think only of the revival of rightist fundamentalism in the 1970s and the more recent rise of "left evangelicalism" and Catholic peace activism. Many of the ideas and programs of the secular left in Europe have found a wide following in America only in a religious framework, and America's strong resistance to Marxism and socialism, even at their most moderate, has much to do with their supposed "atheism." In trying to account for this rejection of secular socialism, Robert N. Bellah writes, "one may wonder whether, if Karl Marx had studied a little less at the feet of David Ricardo and a little more at the feet of William Blake, he might not have had a far more powerful impact on English-speaking intellectuals."[1] Marx would not have been Marx if he had, of course, but Bellah's point about Americans, if not about all English-speaking intellectuals, seems right. Taken seriously as a visionary socialist, Blake offers something crucial to the heart of a movement for liberation and social justice—to its mind, too, but especially to its imagination, verve, and courage. No theory of history and society, no strategy of political change, can provide it, and without it no theory or strategy will usher in a society much better than the one we now have.

A similar claim might be made for Shelley or William Morris, for Thoreau, Martin Luther King, Dorothy Day, or Robert Merton (Merton's great spiritual pilgrimage began with a dissertation on Blake), but Blake's very difference from ordinary modes of thought, his difficulty, his combination of poetry and visual design, his archaic biblical diction, all confer a certain distinction on him. There is no need to plead for him in any case, for he draws ever larger numbers of readers. There is also no need, of course, to choose Blake to the exclusion of anyone else; too much has gone wrong with every kind of society on earth for us to be dogmatic as to where we garner wisdom or courage.

It is thus no help to the cause when Marxists, or those who think they are Marxists, make Blake over into another Marx, or a proto-Marx. That, too, is theft, and no less a flattening of his prickly particularity than the opposite claim, which would have Blake wandering only through the streets of his mind, thinking only about eternity or his anxieties as a poet. There is nothing very Marxist in the attempt to make Blake into another Marx, and in any case we do not need another Marx. We need Blake. Although Blake often sounds like the young Marx, who was himself a Romantic poet before he turned to philosophy and economics, it is their complementarity, even their conflict, which is valuable, not their resemblance. So I agree with E. P. Thompson when he says, "If I had to devise my own pantheon I would without hesitation place within it the Christian antinomian, William Blake, and I would place him beside Marx."[2] Side by side, they can argue it out in what Blake called "the severe contentions of Friendship," and so can we.

In Blake one thing leads to another in an endless network, and I soon felt far from my original subject. Often when I felt farthest from it, however, one more step brought me back into the midst of it. That led to the problems of presentation most Blake scholars seem to have wrestled with: where to start, where to stop, what to leave out. As the book grew, moreover, I found I was synthesizing, or at least making ample use of, the two preeminent works on Blake, Northrop Frye's *Fearful Symmetry* and David Erdman's *Blake: Prophet Against Empire*. In common with every other student in the last thirty years, I learned to read Blake through Frye's wonderful book, and it has partly inspired the integrating gestures, the use of analogues, and perhaps even the tone of my own. The trouble with Frye's book is that it is almost too wonderful: it is so thorough an internal elaboration of Blake that it dazzles and intimidates as much as Blake himself does. What is needed is an external elaboration, a study from one or several external standpoints that will not submit to the blandishments of Blake's seemingly unified vision, but will hold it at sufficient distance to "comprehend" it—as a cultural object of a certain sort, in a certain context, at a certain historical moment.

David Erdman's masterly study of Blake's historical context and allusions is indispensable to any attempt to do that. I have borrowed heavily from his erudition while paying only scant returns with a discovery or two of my own. Erdman's book is ordered chronologically, whereas I have tried for larger integrations of Blakean ideas than would have been possible had I bound myself to the order in which his works were produced. In exploring a series of themes like brotherhood, liberty, labor, and history, I have dwelled on Blake's two completed epics, *Milton* and *Jerusalem*, but have drawn freely from every phase of his career. I have also tried to be somewhat more introductory than Erdman and have presumed a little less on the part of the reader. This book remains demanding, however, and anyone who has been good enough to read this far should be sure to have gone at least once through all of Blake's poems before deciding whether to continue.

My attempt to "integrate" Blake, incorporate Frye and Erdman, and still appeal to the inexpert reader began at one point to swell the book unmanageably. I was drawn, too, to Jean-Paul Sartre's inspiring ambition to "totalize" his subject with "a supple, patient dialectic," an approach that would acknowledge the particularity or specificity of a poet-painter while accounting for him by inserting him in a series of mediations, "regressions," and cross-references.[3] A glance at Sartre's enormous yet unfinished study of Flaubert sobered me up, however, and I would now be content if what I have written could serve as materials toward a totalization of Blake, and if I have avoided the premature closures and reductions that come of forgetting that Blake lived when and where he did, knew certain people but not certain others, hated war during a war-crazed time, made little money, had a dear brother who died, spent a lot of time engraving copperplate, and the like.

In getting this book down to reasonable proportions I have left out several chapters of sustained "close readings" of whole works (texts and designs), which ought to be the proof of the pudding. These will probably go into a second book.[4] I have also had to be selective in singling out themes to explore, and I have compromised between those that are most central and those that have not been much discussed by others. More important as a focus, however, is the concept of ideology, which I introduce in the first chapter. Ideology has many theoretical difficulties, and in crude hands it has led to crude literary criticism, but in recent years in better hands it has shown its subtlety and fruitfulness. It is just about the only category adequate to the task of mediating between social history and literary or aesthetic meaning. It is not the master key to Blake, but without it certain doors of perception will not open.

The remaining seven chapters press the notions of totality and ideology less heavily than chapter one does, since I wanted the themes to be drawn out with a certain autonomy and thoroughness before being folded back into the Blakean whole or referred to the social context, but at many points they link up with each other and with the opening argument. I may at times have indulged a suggestive and digressive tendency on my part, but it seemed more honest to let things unfold as they seemed to demand and to trust the reader, as Blake did, to make the connections, rather than to tie things up and click them shut with my governing theoretical premises. Life is short, and Blake is bottomless. I have done my best, however, to bring out the social and political bearings of each topic, and that is a large part of ideological analysis. Ideological analysis, in turn, does not exhaust the meaning or value of Blake's social and political vision, which at several points, as I shall argue, pitches beyond ideology into something more critical, universal, and true.

All eight chapters, finally, are more or less independent of one another and may be read in any order with little loss. Their sequence is not entirely arbitrary, nevertheless: the argument is intended to accumulate toward Blake's own attempt at totalization, which I call *apocatastasis*, or the restoration of all things. If my first chapter seems a categorical net to catch a rare and eccentric species, my final chapter may be taken as a humble acknowledgment of the vastly braver and more ambitious striving of my subject to comprehend everything that has ever lived.

SEPTEMBER, 1984

WASHINGTON, D.C.

ACKNOWLEDGMENTS

The author of a book so "woven with his life" and so long in the weaving ought to thank every one of his friends and everyone who influenced his thinking, but he would get small thanks if he did. So I will limit myself to those who directly helped me, either with ideas about Blake or comments on the manuscript.

Warner Berthoff took on faith that I had something worth saying about Blake and cheerfully agreed to supervise my dissertation at Harvard; for that and many years of friendship and support I owe him my greatest debt. To Zachary Leader, my fellow graduate student and "Blakemate," I am grateful for a very careful reading of the whole book and many wise suggestions. David Erdman also read the book, at two stages, and helped me think my way out of several confusions. I owe more thanks than I can express for the deep encouragement of Nancy Schwartz, and for the doors she opened to ways of thinking I would have missed without her. Staughton Lynd and E. P. Thompson offered salutary criticisms of part of the manuscript and reoriented my thinking at crucial points. And Anne MacKinnon, with great editorial skill, made me look with disenchanted eyes at my often casual and clumsy sentences.

I am also indebted to Susan Arnold, Harry Bracken, Jeremy Brecher, Noam Chomsky, Jill Cutler, Margaret Ferguson, Brooke Hopkins, Will Kirkland, Edward Mendelson, Jeffrey Merrick, Harold Pagliaro, and Alan Trachtenberg. For the errors and follies that remain despite all this good advice I alone am to blame.

I am also grateful to the Morse Fellowship Committee at Yale University for giving me a year free of other tasks.

An earlier version of chapter three appeared in *PMLA* for May 1978.

ABBREVIATIONS

E	David V. Erdman, ed., *The Complete Poetry and Prose of William Blake*, Commentary by Harold Bloom, 5th ed., rev. (Berkeley: University of California Press, 1982). All Blake quotations are from this edition.
Bloom, "Commentary"	Commentary in E
A	*America: A Prophecy*
Eur	*Europe: A Prophecy*
FZ	*The Four Zoas*
J	*Jerusalem: The Emanation of The Giant Albion*
M	*Milton: A Poem in 2 Books*
MHH	*The Marriage of Heaven and Hell*
NNR	*THERE is NO Natural Religion*
U	*The Book of Urizen*
VDA	*Visions of the Daughters of Albion*
VLJ	*A Vision of The Last Judgment*
PL	John Milton, *Paradise Lost*

The Social Vision of
William Blake

1

The Concept of Ideology

For the past fifteen years or so English and American scholars have been catching up with the Continent in their theoretical discussions of the concept of ideology and its application to literature. A good deal of their work has been to translate, interpret, and extend the major theories: those of Georg Lukács (especially during his brief phase around 1922 as an independent Marxist), Antonio Gramsci, the Frankfurt School (Theodor Adorno, Walter Benjamin, Herbert Marcuse), Jean-Paul Sartre, and French structuralist Marxists such as Louis Althusser. In England, almost alone, Raymond Williams has been patiently working out his own theory of "cultural materialism"; he has now incorporated it with the work of younger English thinkers and of Europeans like Lucien Goldmann.

In the hands of "vulgar" orthodox Marxists ideology could break butterflies on the wheels of history; thus Wordsworth was "objectively" a reactionary petit bourgeois whose poetry expresses only the nostalgia of a doomed and marginal class, and so on. But ideology has been rescued from reductionists and given greater conceptual reach and subtlety by heterodox thinkers who have, on the whole, taken their young Marx with their old, absorbed Weber and Freud, felt the pressure of anti-Marxist critiques, faced up to Stalinism, and retained their love of literature. That theoretical problems remain, and that effective use in any concrete case demands a great deal, are no excuses for ignoring ideology any longer.

If universities—and in America, at least, it is mainly there that literary theory is produced—are to live up to their name, some such coordinating and cross-disciplinary notion as "ide-

ology" will have to come into use. It is indispensable for con-
necting the conventions of literature, in form and content,
with the experience and interests of groups in society. The
connections may be very complex and densely "mediated,"
but without such a way of trying to connect literature to its
place in the social totality, literary history will remain anec-
dotal and claustrophobic. And without a grasp of the power
and persistence of ideology, even in literature departments—
the "departmentality" of universities, in fact, being a major
ideological force—we risk falling prey to ideology in our own
literary theories. We find today, for example, the widely prop-
agated idea, born in part of the very desire to break out of
the confines of a department or discipline, that everything is
a text and that reading is the basic mode of human compre-
hension. It begins by taking what used to be called "works,"
a word with its own presuppositions, and naming them "texts,"
founding thereby a certain kind of critical activity which, how-
ever rich and brilliant it sometimes is, forgets what it erased
in its opening gesture. To take the object as text is to fail to
take account of its nontextual features. This school's next
move is to globalize "text" to include not only other forms of
culture but all of history and even nature. One hardly needs
to say that this is not the same as situating a text or work in
a larger context (the normal use of "context" invites this text-
model); it is to assimilate the context under terms set by texts.
There are even "Marxist" versions of this textual imperialism,
according to which a text "produces" meanings, or ideology,
or even the reading subject itself. It is not to deny their power
if one points out the kinship of such theories to the ideology
of Melville's "sub-sub-librarian" and the division of whales into
folios, octavos, and duodecimos. In Blake's words, they "view
a small portion & think that all, / And call it Demonstration"
(J 65.27-28).

The task—if this needs to be said—is to study everything
and fit it all together. To put it practically, it is to learn some-
thing of the different planes of knowledge and how they
intersect, to respect the integrity of an object or event in cul-
ture while trying at the same time to "explain" it, to trace its
nearer ramifications and at least acknowledge the farther

ones, indeed, to gain a standard of near and far in relevance, and to accept and enjoy the communality of scholarship. To put it negatively, the task is to avoid the twin temptations of premature synthesis and chronic analysis, the hypertrophy of a single method or set of terms and the noncommittal pluralism of insulated approaches. The concept of ideology, of course, is not immune to overgrown pretensions, but I will try to live up to my brave words and offer a definition and defense of it, if not as a sovereign conceptual key, then as a useful coordinating or regulating idea.

Blake presents some special problems. Faced with his heroic efforts to hammer his eccentric and multifarious thought into unity, those of us who take Blake seriously may become what we behold, and do the same with our own critical commentary. Northrop Frye's well-titled *Fearful Symmetry* is the greatest example of Blake's contagion, greatest in being most Blakean in its formal spirit and intuitive understanding, though for those reasons losing some of the distance proper for critical leverage. In other critics Blake seems to have magnified the general tendency to methodological exclusiveness; they have unified their commentaries by finding one or another outside standpoint from which to pry him up, and so we have the series of one-dimensional contractions of his work to Neoplatonic, Cabalistic, or Swedenborgian sources or to Jungian, Freudian, or Marxist analogues that have made the Blake shelves in the library so unbecoming to behold. A reaction against such books has set in, and many Blakeans are now content modestly to labor in their patch of the common field and leave to future generations the gathering in. Much of the ground for their work and my own has been cleared magisterially by David Erdman; his own caution before grand generalizations certainly warns me sufficiently. It is my impression nonetheless that some of the careful studies of this or that minute particular have come up against limits not surpassable by tying the particulars together link by link, as it were; rather, the particulars demand a multiplanar organizing interpretation to situate them properly. Blake's own example of persisting in folly also remains before us, and life is too short to await all the returns before trying to assess him. I am one, too, who believes Blake can make an essential contribution to the vision and program we need in order to reconstruct the damaged societies of the world, and we do not know how much time will be given us for that work.

Blake may seem peculiarly resistant, finally, to a specifically ideological analysis. His difficulty and eccentricity kept him even from readers of his own time who shared his social status and political allegiances; his effect on readers now, even after all the scholarly attempts to attach him to familiar traditions, begins with the strong impression that he is like nobody else in the world. That his idiosyncrasies will test any comparative or triangulating method, however, is no reason to shrink from trying it. Rather the opposite: his obvious orneriness may help keep the method honest, and his very difficulty may be the best place to begin.

* * *

We may distinguish at the outset the ideology of a social class, the ideology of an individual, and the ideology of a work.[1] There is nothing simple, however brief our labels might be, about specifying the ideology of a social class, for classes are always changing their characteristics as the structure of the economy changes, merging older classes, splitting into new ones, struggling against competing ones, and so on. Their ideologies change similarly, blending, fissuring, hardening, and absorbing new experiences. Among complications there are the permeation of an underclass's ideology with crucial features of the ruling ideology, as in the wide acceptance of the middle-class values of self-help and individual upward-mobilism by a working class for whom only concerted action will bring progress, and the reverse process, no doubt weaker, the "trickling up" of democratic and populist traditions, which may limit the options of the ruling elites, or at least force them into hypocrisy. The history of Christianity from its plebeian provincial origins to its adoption by the patricians and over-lords illustrates this permeation in both directions, and it reminds us too of another factor, the "drag effect" or conser-vatism of ideology, its persistence after its appropriate social

basis has altered, as well as the persistence of archaic insti-
tutions in the base itself. There are different tempos of change
in culture, all bearing complexly on each other.

One component of class ideology we may call aesthetic ide-
ology: a body of conventions, genres, styles of discourse,
themes, and notions of the artist's function and means of
making art. One of the most important studies in aesthetic
ideology is Ian Watt's *The Rise of the Novel*; whether or not he
has got them right, Watt is making the sort of connections
between the common life of a social class and the forms and
styles of its literature only seldom attempted. Another ex-
ample would be Lukács's effort to correlate the shift in mode
from "realism" to "naturalism" in the French novel with the
bloody class war of 1848. Within the region of aesthetic ide-
ology we might want to distinguish an ideology of artists, a
slant or bias in favor of the producers of works that express
overall the ideologies of the classes that sponsor and consume
artworks. To give a charming if obvious example, in the *Od-
yssey* the role of the bards is more or less what it probably was
in reality—to sing at aristocrats' tables and memorialize the
deeds of their ancestors—but we can detect a whiff of "bardic
ideology" in the special protection they are granted, Odysseus'
deep response to one of them, and the bardlike traits of Odys-
seus himself.

From these kinds of class ideology we should distinguish
an individual's ideology, which may be a very complicated
affair. As Sartre memorably put it, "Valéry is a petit bourgeois
intellectual, no doubt about it. But not every petit bourgeois
intellectual is Valéry."[2] The biographical point of insertion
into class ideology is mediated at the very least by the family,
itself a changing historical institution but with certain features
that may cut across class lines and persist over centuries. More-
over, some individuals rise or sink in their class affiliations,
or they serve another class and identify with it, or they think
for themselves and reflect on their own situation and may
rebel a little or a lot, and so on. I do not want to suggest that
a measure of objectivity or "truth" is beyond reach, nor would
I confine it solely to the very abstract "science" that some
French Marxists say is the only realm free of ideological con-

tamination. But ideology touches all experience, and the sense of having transcended ideological illusions is very often itself an illusion born of the clash of two or more of them. Yet such a clash may also genuinely remove illusions, I would argue; Blake's peculiar insight into ideology, which we will note throughout this book, may owe a good deal to the conflicts to which his social position exposed him.

Finally, I think it makes sense to say that all literature has an ideology, or components of an ideology. Some Marxists, as I mentioned earlier, would prefer to say that literature *produces* an ideology, a way of putting it that seems to bring out the active process of reading, but that also seems to assign that activity mainly to the text itself—as if by being so good as to read it a reader becomes putty in its hands—rather than distributing the determining activity between text and reader as co-producers of the "ideological effect." I suspect too that this parlance is itself a product of a new desire for rigor among Marxists who are restating aesthetic theory in terms of production, Marxism's founding concept. But we may leave aside this refinement; it will do for now to say that all literature "has" an ideology.

To put it simply, literature has designs on us, palpable or not, and those designs have social bearings, however remote. All literature teaches, even if it claims only to delight. In fact, the claim only to delight not merely is false but has a fairly evident ideological ring. Certain highly self-conscious works, deliberately critical of prevailing ideologies and alert to their social bases, might make an exception to this rule, though of such works it might be truer to say that they project an anti-ideological viewpoint that is itself partly ideological. So one might argue of James Joyce's *Ulysses* that, while its many narrative stances and styles seem to sweep away all Archimedean points from which to comprehend, or at least speak about, the world, the careful continuity of its "realistic" level beneath all the devices, and the final surfacing of that level in the seemingly artless soliloquy of Molly, endorse after all the standpoint of "life," of empathy, of realism, of something like Albert Camus's anti-ideological decency, whose ideological features are not hard to discern.

Perhaps, too, certain very short works, such as sonnets or haiku, do not carry much of an ideology, perhaps only fragments or gestures vaguely consonant with more than one, yet we can see that the very *forms* of sonnet and haiku trail little ideological clouds from their former uses in courtly games, their conventional sublimation of desire, or their equally conventional adumbrations of satori. The apparent purity of some forms of art, ritual, and game, it could be argued, serves precisely to ratify as Olympian and objective the way of life of a leisured group with very particular interests. There are, in any case, ideologies of form, or ideologies *in* form. For Shakespeare to write a play about a merchant-adventurer, a Jewish usurer, a soldier of fortune, and an heiress "richly left" in the form of New Comedy in the "scapegoat" subgenre is to organize obviously political and economic material into a form in which love and "nature" always successfully bring about a social renewal and resolution, a universal pattern of action and value governing anything-but-universal interests or positions.

The ideology of a work is combined in complex ways with the ideology of the author. Marx and Engels themselves anticipated modern suspicions of the intentional fallacy in their praise of the reactionary Balzac. We might say there are artistic methods and conventions with enough momentum of their own to transform the conscious and unconscious attitudes of the artist, and that even if the form, to put it simply, does not undermine the manifest tendency of the content, it may by "foregrounding" it put it at a distance sufficient for scrutiny and critique. Althusser speaks (somewhat mysteriously) of the "internal distantiation" of art, a retreat that lets us see "the ideology from which [the work of art] is born, in which it bathes, from which it detaches itself as art, and to which it alludes."[3]

Not only forms, of course, but discrete, seemingly innocent stock objects, characteristic human types, and historical individuals may gather an ideological nimbus from their changing contexts in real social life as well as in extended ideological argument. The name "Milton" might mean a safe religious writer or a republican and regicide, according to what asso-

ciations a context triggers. Why does Blake make his hero Los
a blacksmith? One factor might have been an aura of sub-
versiveness or at least political loquacity that higher classes
sensed in real blacksmiths. They might, to borrow Fredric
Jameson's term, have been potential "ideologemes" ready for
activation, seconded by older traditions about the volcanic
Vulcan, in a particular narrative context. Certain highly spe-
cific, seemingly neutral systems of thought may gain, or lose,
a political edge. Along with the associations of blacksmiths, it
would be interesting to know why Jacobins like Thomas Hol-
croft and Blake's friend Henry Fuseli were seriously inter-
ested, as Blake was, in Johann Kaspar Lavater. Was there
something we can meaningfully call "left physiognomy"?
These are examples of the sort of thing I shall pursue in this
book, though often I will only raise them as questions.

I have been slowly backing into a definition of ideology. I
will use the word to mean a set of related ideas, images, and
values more or less distorted from the "truth" (which pre-
sumes some grasp of the way the social totality really works)
through the impact on it of the material interests, conscious
or unconscious, of those who believe and propagate it, insofar
as they are divided from one another in classes with conflicting
interests. That is a Marxist definition, though it is not the
latest model. There are other definitions that might be pre-
cipitated out of Hegel or Weber and that deny the priority
of material conditions, and there is Karl Mannheim's more
positivist and relativist theory that denies any privilege to the
standpoint of the proletariat. I would defend the materialist
clause, but gratefully accept from Weber some sense of the
"elective affinity" of certain beliefs with certain ways of making
a living, and from Hegel the idea, partly assimilated by Marx,
that the false is the partial and the true is the whole. I think
it is no longer true, however, if it ever was, that the industrial
proletariat is in the best position to grasp the truth of the
social totality. (I am not sure who is, however. Mannheim says
scholars and intellectuals are, but then Mannheim was a
scholar and intellectual.)

Any *theory* of ideology must assume the existence of a mean-
ingful totality in which all material, social, and cultural objects,

events, and forms find their specifiable "places" and in which there is no such thing as an autonomous feature or level entirely free of the impress of the social whole. Ideology is one domain in culture, and it bears the marks of its continual emergence from and reimmersion into its social environment. Any particular ideology can be understood, and its pretensions or "self-understanding" debunked, by following these marks back to the social formations that gave rise to the ideology and that the ideology in turn reinforces. The pretensions of ideology are usually two: first, a claim to universality, as I mentioned earlier, which typically depends on the "naturalization" of something social and the exaltation of a part into the whole, and secondly, the very claim to be autonomous or *audessus de la mêlée* that a theory of ideology must assume to be impossible. What the Germans call *Ideologiekritik* can proceed "immanently" by working out the consequences of the ideology's premises until its absurdity is glaring, and extrinsically by showing that the world, if not heaven, has more things in it than are dreamt of in the ideology, things indeed which generate that ideology or condition it. Non-Marxist theories can do this, too. They all practice what Paul Ricoeur calls a hermeneutic of suspicion and offer explanations for the features they suspect. The oldest example of *Ideologiekritik* on record, if we exclude the Old Testament attack on idolatry, goes back to Xenophanes in the sixth century B.C. He was even a materialist. He wrote: "The Ethiopians say that their gods are snub-nosed and black, the Thracians that theirs have light blue eyes and red hair." And if horses or lions had hands, he added, they would draw pictures of horse-shaped or lionlike gods.[4]

Having established ideology's pedigree, I conclude these preliminaries by noticing the tendency in some recent theories of ideology (particularly Althusser's) to so expand its range that it covers all experience and all thought (except the "science" of Marxism itself). It is said that the acquisition of language, any language, draws the child into a realm of illusory subjectivity (the effect, in part, of deictic pronouns like "I"), and it is on the notion of a subject that all ideologies are erected.[5] Whatever interest this theory may arouse it is not very useful for a historian or a literary critic who wishes to site literary works in their time and place. Language may breed illusions, but it is better not to call these illusions ideological unless we find a different term for the particular illusions that arise from and ratify the unequal divisions of society. I would rather use a word like "culture" to refer to structures of thought and feeling shared throughout a society, such as "English" and "Christianity." The ways diction and syntax may be manipulated for ideological effect are well worth studying,[6] and so are the ways Christianity has been enlisted in reactionary, revolutionary, and moderate causes. The ruling ideology may permeate these cultural terrains, but it does not own them, and they have enough inherent inertia or momentum to keep them from turning entirely plastic at ideology's touch.

2

Blake's Ideology

At centennial celebrations of the Glorious Revolution of 1688, many a toast to liberty and the rights of Englishmen was followed by another toast to that revolution's philosopher, John Locke. "Locke" was a regular feature of the rhetoric of liberty. When the Dissenting interest preached parliamentary reform it did so in the name of its "holy of holies," the Great Liberator.[1] Addressing the Society for the Commemoration of the Revolution a year after the centennial, the Dissenting minister Richard Price adduced a list of Lockean rights that included the right to cashier governors. Burke indignantly observed that he was not slow to justify the recent French Revolution by an English precedent, and Price was no doubt aware that the revolutionary *philosophes* had been admirers of Locke. In 1794, when the artisan Thomas Hardy, founder of the London Corresponding Society, was on trial for treason, his lawyer Erskine appealed to Locke as an advocate of the very reforms Hardy had been indicted for trying to obtain.[2]

To give a later example, in *The Examiner* of June 10, 1810, the liberal Leigh Hunt wrote that "it was Locke, and such men as himself, who, in teaching us to give up our mental liberty to no man; but to prefer even the consciousness of independence to a slavery however worshipful—To such a man as Locke, therefore, every Englishman owes love and reverence."[3]

It was in the centennial year of 1788 that Blake engraved a set of twenty-seven aphorisms on three groups of tiny plates, of which two share the title "THERE is No Natural Religion" and the third is called "ALL RELIGIONS are ONE." Their main target is John Locke. Throughout Blake's works—as throughout the present book—Locke's name comes up (sometimes joined with Bacon's and Newton's) as a sign of all that Blake despised in the realm of thought. We are so familiar with his hostility to Locke that we acquire a sense of its historical oddness only with difficulty. But odd it surely was in one who at least peripherally joined the circle around the bookseller Joseph Johnson, which included Thomas Paine, William Godwin, Mary Wollstonecraft, and Dr. Price; who may have come from a Dissenting family himself;[4] who was trained as an engraver by "republican" antiquarians and Miltonists; and who, as a London artisan, almost certainly knew and felt sympathy for radical reformist organizers like Hardy.

BLAKE, LOCKE, AND DISSENT

The first step in situating Blake's thought, then, is to measure it against the ideology of the Dissenting interest, with which Blake shared most political goals (liberty and reform of Parliament, support for the French Revolution) but few epistemological and theological assumptions. To Dissenters he no doubt seemed muddled and quaint; to him they must have seemed weak and compromising, bound too tightly to the premises of "sensation" and "natural religion" to think their way to genuine liberty. "Locke" is the site of the problem, and we must look again at what the name meant in Blake's day.

For one thing, the thrust of Locke's theories was not as unambiguously radical as his admirers might imply. The *Two Treatises of Government* (1690) was rightly taken as a rationale for the removal of James II, the exclusion of his son the Catholic Duke of York, and the summoning of William of Orange. It justified the right of rebellion against the sovereign when he grievously violated certain rights such as property, and it defined those rights as natural and indefeasible, belonging to individual men by a right of nature more fundamental than any positive or man-made law. Such ideas are liberal enough, but it is also clear that Locke himself carefully circumscribed their application and probably never intended the majority of the people to consider themselves participants in the decisions of the nation.

Locke's right of property includes the right to acquire all you can through your own labor (and your labor can be alienated to acquire property for someone else), and the social contract that protects it in effect guarantees its unequal distribution as well. Nothing, moreover, requires a proprietor to use his property for the good of the commonwealth, as tradition and the older natural-law theory demanded.[5] Conservative gentry could, and did, invoke Locke as sanction for strict penalties against poachers, tenants in arrears, and disrespecters of enclosures.

In the colonies the *Two Treatises*, though cited by revolutionaries, was probably not an ideological force for independence. An early supporter of the revolution, Peter van Schaack of New York, decided after carefully studying it that the provocations of the British government did not warrant revolution after all.[6] Locke's political theory, in short, was sufficiently broad and vague to inspire or sanction opposite positions; as E. P. Thompson summarizes, "In the 1790s the ambiguities of Locke seem to fall into two halves, one Burke, the other Paine,"[7] An "anti-Jacobin" of that time put it clearly, and not altogether implausibly: "Price, Priestley, Rousseau, Paine, could justify on the principles of Locke, their own visionary doctrines, pregnant with consequences so mischievous to society and so different from what Locke himself intended."[8]

One of the ambiguities in the Lockean theory of natural rights was the uncertain meaning of "inalienability."[9] An inalienable right, some said, is a right that can only be renounced willingly, like a piece of property, but this interpretation was unsatisfactory to the more radical spirits of the Dissenting community. Some rights, they claimed, cannot be bartered for others when parties enter into a social contract. Richard Price argued in this way as he extended the older cause of religious liberty to the more radical one of civil liberty. He warned against "the folly of *giving up* liberty in order to maintain liberty," as traditional social contract theorists would have it.[10] It is not that society works best when some rights are retained, we might say, but that a human being cannot surrender them and still be human. Liberty is essential to one's moral capacity, and "the grand lines and primary principles of morality are so deeply wrought into our hearts, and one with our minds, that they will be forever legible."[11] Among the inalienable or ineradicable rights are the right of conscience and the right of revolution. The New Hampshire constitution of 1784 stated it concisely: "Among the natural rights, some are in their very nature inalienable, because no equivalent can be given or received for them. Of this kind are the RIGHTS OF CONSCIENCE."[12]

Neither in his early aphoristic tracts nor in his later poetry does Blake have much to say about natural rights or any other subject found in the *Two Treatises*. His attack on Locke is almost entirely focused on his epistemology, and at first glance it would seem to have nothing to do with politics or moral matters. But the view that there is a chasm between matters of fact and matters of value, known to modern analytical philosophers as "Hume's Guillotine," was not widespread in the eighteenth century. How you come by your ideas, many believed, has much to do with your rights and duties toward God and man. Some Dissenting thinkers were certain they could see the connection between the doctrine of sensation and what they held to be an inadequate theory of natural rights. They criticized, as we shall see, some of the same points of Locke's epistemology as Blake did.

Locke was much better known for his *An Essay on Human Understanding* than for the *Two Treatises*, both published in 1690. Indeed, the latter appeared anonymously—Locke acknowledged it as his own only in a codicil to his will—and its later reputation was partly a reflection of the fame of the author of the *Essay*. The *Essay*, despite refutations by George Berkeley and revisions by David Hume, was the most influential epistemological and psychological treatise of the eighteenth century, the point of departure for nearly all serious discussion of the nature of the mind.

The "tendency" of the *Essay*, like that of the *Two Treatises*, was, in its context, liberal or progressive. The early reaction to the *Essay* by Bishop Stillingfleet, William Sherlock, and others was fueled by the implications of Locke's critique of innate ideas for faith and morals, for the social order. Innateness was the only sure foundation for belief in God and knowledge of good and evil. The principles listed as innate by Locke's contemporary critics were, of course, formulations, often theological, of the dominant ideology; for example, there is a God, God is all-powerful, He that made me should govern me, I must worship and venerate God, I must honor and obey my parents, and (even) my private parts must be covered.[13] Locke's attack on innateness, it was felt, acted as a corrosive that ate away these props of hierarchical society, despite Locke's belief that many of them could be reestablished on sounder, more rational principles.

Having done its work against these traditional views and on behalf of an emergent entrepreneurial class who wished to be free of feudal and state restrictions, Locke's empiricist principle, whereby the mind is born a blank slate and all knowledge is a product of sense impressions (and of mental operations upon them), encountered in the mid-eighteenth century a critique from the left by some of the same Dissenters who revamped his doctrine of natural rights and who had doubts about unbridled commercialism. Against Locke's belief that self-evident truths were evident to the reason, which compares, contrasts, and derives by induction, James Burgh argued that "self-evident truth is not collected, or deduced, but intuitively perceived" by an active and direct faculty.[14] Price was more explicit than Burgh in his denial that sensation and reflection are the sources of all our ideas, for we have an active faculty that gives rise to new ideas, "the power within us that *understands*; the *Intuition* of the mind."[15] In a set of vivid expressions akin to those Blake used later, Price wrote that the passive faculty of sense "lies prostrate under its object" and "must therefore remain a stranger to the objects." Sense "sees only the *outside* of things."[16] Such expressions, of course, have moral and political connotations,[17] and it was largely against the moral thrust of Locke's epistemology that the Dissenters, like the bishops before them, directed their fire. But while Stillingfleet held on to the notion of innate ideas engraved in the mind (a view that ultimately made the human mind passive, before God if not before external nature), Price spoke of an "innate light" or an "eye of the mind," not unlike the Inner Light of the Quakers, that can directly intuit moral truths.[18] Locke grounded morality on a calculation of probable pleasures and pains and on obedience to a law that will maximize pleasures; Price's faculty could perceive morality "without making use of any process of reasoning."[19] Thus man had a measure of independence from his environment. He was not just a creature of his circumstances but in part a creator of them. And among the conditions he was able to free himself from were the laws and customs of an oppressive, hierarchical England. Locke was unable to discriminate, according to Price, between an act that is right because it is God's will (as our intuition tells us) and an act that is right because it conforms to *the decrees of the magistrate, or the fashion of the country.*"[20]

A related aspect of Locke's thought reveals clearly the link between his politics and his theory of knowledge. In the *Two Treatises* there are forthright statements of natural equality based on the universal possession of rational faculties. "And being furnished with like Faculties, sharing all in one Community of Nature, there cannot be supposed any such *Subordination* among us . . ." (II.6). Locke's notions about epistemology, however, tend to undermine his reason-grounded egalitarianism. In a later work he stresses natural inequalities in intellect: "There is, it is visible, great variety in men's understandings. . . . Amongst men of equal education there is a great inequality of parts."[21] In the *Essay* and elsewhere he makes clear that because men are not born knowing any truths, moral or otherwise, they arrive at truth by study—by observations and reasoning. This process takes time, and we are not surprised to hear that only a small class has that time. "The greatest part of mankind want leisure or capacity for demonstration. . . . And you may as soon hope to have all the day-labourers and tradesmen, and spinsters and dairy-maids, perfect mathematicians, as to have them perfect in ethics this way."[22] From this "natural" inequality of intellect (quite obviously social in origin) Locke can justify the aristocratic order that in fact prevailed in his day and long afterward. If you are imperfect in ethics, someone else must tell you what to do.

To meet this argument some Dissenters appealed to their notion of a universal capacity to intuit self-evident moral truths, a "common sense" which brought the natural law within the reach of even the meanest classes. Not all of them were prepared to go so far, but John Cartwright, in language that anticipated Paine, swept aside all traditional arguments derived from custom and charters and processes of reasoning in favor of direct intuition: "But a title to the liberty of mankind is not established on such rotten foundations: 'tis not among mouldy parchments, nor in the cobwebs of a casuist's brain we are to look for it; it is the immediate, the universal gift of God."²³

The complexity of the intellectual world of Dissent finds an epitome in the friendship of Price and Joseph Priestley. They were both Unitarian ministers and courageous political reformers, but they disagreed on many theological and epistemological points. Priestley was in some ways the more radical and modern of the two, being a scientist, a materialist, a monist, a mortalist (like Milton) as to the soul, and a Socinian as to Christ (that is, one who believes Christ was human). He was much closer to Locke than Price was in his theory of knowledge, denying innate intuition and ascribing all knowledge and even all action to the environment; despite his devotion to civil liberty he was a necessitarian (like Godwin), taking all action as mechanically determined by nature and ultimately by God. Scientific mechanism and a residual Calvinist predestinarianism combined to drain Christian liberty of most of its meaning. "The work of conversion and reformation," he wrote, "takes place according to the usual course of nature."²⁴ One can imagine Blake bristling at such a comment and agreeing with Price's general complaint that Priestley neglected the work of the Holy Spirit, the indwelling "Con-Science" of the free Christian.

When Blake read Price's famous sermon about France, on the other hand, one can imagine him making mental annotations like "Uneasy" or "Price here too priestly!" He would agree with the direction of Price's opening thought, which is to define the "country" we are to love as "not the soil or the spot of earth on which we happen to have been born; not the forests and fields, but that community of which we are members"—what Blake would call the Universal Brotherhood but Price tends to confine to those "bound together by the same civil polity." The Unitarian does point out that Jesus never even mentioned love of country but preached "that UNIVERSAL BENEVOLENCE which is an unspeakably nobler principle than any partial affections," such as Burke's for his little platoon, but Price makes the common-sense concession that "our regards, according to the order of nature, begin with ourselves; and every man is charged primarily with the care of himself." To this Blake might have said, "True, and so much the worse for the order of nature, with which Christianity has nothing to do." For Price Christianity crowns a rational and natural order of the spirit, though the crown may come from higher and deeper sources than Priestley conceives. For Blake Christianity shows the rational and natural order to be an illusion, and indeed the realm of Satan, whom Price unknowingly worships as the "Governor of the world."[25]

Though they mention him little, the Dissenters of the Pricean sort have the position of David Hume for their target as well as that of Locke.[26] Hume was a rigorous empiricist in philosophy and a Tory in politics, and if the argument sketched by Price is correct it is no accident he was both. Hume went beyond Locke in denying that we can know that our knowledge comes from outside ourselves, but he steered around solipsism by invoking a rather suspect "feeling" that there is in fact an external world which we more or less truly reflect.[27] He was less equivocal in his environmentalist ethics. A frank relativist, his guillotine between "is" and "ought" allowed no logical entailment of values from our perceptions of the world by any faculty whatever. "This is good" means "This is approved of," and what is approved of is an empirical question. One could say that for Hume, then, principles of morality *are* statements of fact. It is the case that certain acts and things are approved of in one's milieu or environment, and since there is no rational way to negate or transcend one's environment one might as well relax and adopt prevailing custom as one's moral norm.

One might add here that Locke and Hume both considered

the Negro race and the other colored races to be inferior to the white, and both considered slavery and the slave trade justifiable. It has been argued recently that Locke's rejection of innateness rather surprisingly *facilitated* his ideas about radical inequality;[28] it is clear, in any case, that the Quakers, most emphatic about the Inner Light, were in the forefront of the abolition movement. The long speech against Lockean views of the mind by Blake's Oothoon, who among her other roles speaks for the Negro slave, may be less the digression it has been held to be.

Whether, as seems likely, Blake was aware of these arguments of Price and other Inner Light radicals or not, his fierce attack against Locke's theory of knowledge is, like theirs, inextricably linked to his radical social and political beliefs. We need not agree with Blake or Price, of course, but it may help us understand them to dwell for a moment on the plausibility of connecting an empirical epistemology with ethical relativism and political conservatism. It is not the usual view. Bertrand Russell, granting that Hume was a Tory, suggests that the contrary connection, the more natural one, was simply broken in Hume's case. "But after the time of Kant, when German idealism began to influence English thought, there came to be again a connection between philosophy and politics: in the main, the philosophers who followed the Germans were conservative, while the Benthamites, who were Radical, were in the tradition of Locke."[29] By "Germans" Russell seems to mean Fichte, Schelling, and Hegel, not the liberal Kant.

Russell's spiritual godfather John Stuart Mill, despite his attraction to Coleridge, was quite explicit in his dislike of innatist or intuitionist doctrines and their social implications:

> Now, the difference between these two schools of philosophy, that of intuition, and that of experience and association, is not a mere matter of abstract speculation; it is full of practical consequences, and lies at the foundation of all the greatest differences of practical opinion in an age of progress. The practical reformer has continually to demand that changes be made in things which are supported by powerful and widely spread feelings, or to question the apparent necessity and indefeasibleness of established facts; and it is often an indispensible part of his argument to show,

how those powerful feelings had their origin, and how those facts came to seem necessary and indefeasible. There is therefore a natural hostility between him and a philosophy which discourages the explanation of feeling and moral facts by circumstances and association, and prefers to treat them as ultimate elements of human nature; a philosophy which is addicted to holding up favorite doctrines as intuitive truths, and deems intuition to be the voice of Nature and of God, speaking with an authority higher than that of our reason. In particular, I have long felt that the prevailing tendency to regard all the marked distinctions of human character as innate, and in the main indelible, and to ignore the irresistible proofs that by far the greater part of those differences, whether between individuals, races, or sexes, are such as not only might but naturally would be produced by differences in circumstances, is one of the chief hindrances to the rational treatment of great social questions, and one of the greatest stumbling blocks to human improvement.[30]

This is an impressive argument, but it is essentially negative. To the extent that human improvement is a matter of removing obvious stumbling blocks Mill's philosophy may be essential. Some stumbling blocks are not obvious, however, and in fact nothing can be strictly defined as an obstacle until the path of improvement is itself defined, and for that task we need a more positive set of standards. Mill offers us "reason," and with that, it might be argued, we are not much better off than with Locke's laws of association.

Marx and Engels cite the "materialist" tradition of Locke and Jeremy Bentham (and their French followers) as a precursor of communism: "*Owen*, proceeding from *Bentham's* system, founded English communism."[31] In his third thesis on Feuerbach, however, Marx indicates the flaw in environmentalism, however progressive: "The materialist doctrine concerning the change of circumstances and education forgets that circumstances are changed by men and that the educator must himself be educated. Hence this doctrine must divide society into two parts—one of which towers above."[32] In this I think he rightly sees a tendency toward elitism in the tradition from Locke to Owen and Mill. On what values shall we change our circumstances and educate our educators? Marx himself may not have provided a sufficiently rich idea of human nature to serve as a standard, but he shares with Blake and Price, as opposed to both Locke and the innatists Locke attacked, a sense of human nature's active, creative power. To remember that people make themselves and their world may not answer the question of the kind of people and world we want, but it will at least warn us away from the solutions proposed or imposed by the managers of our social and natural environments.

Enough has been said, I think, to suggest at least the complexity of the question of the political "tendency" of an epistemology; it also shows that the pattern prevalent in nineteenth-century England does not prove a relationship of entailment between a critical and radical political theory and an empiricist theory of knowledge. As for Blake's day, while it is true that the three most influential radical writers, Priestley, Paine, and Godwin, were in some sense empiricists and materialists, it is also true that many equally radical thinkers were not. Probably the majority of the artisans and poorer classes of "radical London," if they stopped to think about it, were innatists in an older Christian sense, and yet saw no difficulty in finding grounds for stoning the king. The point is that, while innatism may have affinities with conservatism, quietism, and irrationalism if detached from certain other assumptions about human nature, Lockean empiricism has affinities with conservatism, elitism, and relativism when it ceases to criticize superstition and erects an ethic of its own.

The matter is far from settled today. The debate is still lively between the radical anarchist Noam Chomsky and the elitist "liberal" B. F. Skinner over the wealth or poverty of humanity's innate mental endowment, while, in a more familiar pattern, those who assert the heritability of IQ or the inborn "naked ape" character of humankind are hostile to basic social reform. For our purposes, the intellectual problem bequeathed by Locke and Hume to social and psychological theorists of the late eighteenth century may be summarized in Herbert Marcuse's words:

> If Hume was to be accepted, the claim of reason to organize reality had to be rejected. For as we have seen, this claim was based upon reason's faculty to attain truths, the validity of which was not de-

rived from experience and which could in fact stand against experience. " 'Tis not . . . reason, which is the guide of life, but custom." This conclusion of the empiricist investigations did more than undermine metaphysics. It confined men within the limits of "the given," within the existing order of things and events. Whence could man obtain the right to go beyond not some particular within this order, but beyond the entire order itself? Whence could he obtain the right to submit this order to the judgment of reason? If experience and custom were to be the sole source of his knowledge and belief, how could he act against custom, how act in accordance with ideas and principles as yet not accepted and established? Truth could not oppose the given order or reason speak against it. The result was not only skepticism but conformism.[33]

The problem was to find the Archimedean point from which to pry up "experience." William Blake joined Burgh, Price, Cartwright, and others in finding it not in nature or society, which are only aspects of the given "experience" to be overcome, nor even in a transcendent orthodox God, who is just as much "given" as nature and before whom we must lie prostrate, but in man himself, in his inborn intellectual and spiritual power.

We may now see this radical construction and dignifying of the autonomous self or subject as itself an ideological shift appropriate to the phase of capitalism's emergence from a strong, even pervasive, mode of production nonetheless hampered by older social structures (monopolistic charters, mercantilist state intervention, guilds, and so on) into full domination of English society. If Karl Polanyi is right, the last barrier to what Weber called "formally free labor," essential to the complete "commodification" of labor which capitalism requires, fell only with the New Poor Law of 1834, but other traditional barriers had been falling for over a century.[34] The ideological adjustment to this emerging system (and earlier "utopian" anticipations of something like it) entailed a notion of a morally autonomous individual who could alienate his labor power on the free market. It may not matter much whether an environmentalist theory or an innatist theory is pressed into serving the new ideology or set of ideologies; abstractly conceived, the blank slate and the Inner Light could both justify a certain kind of labor, rational activity, and social contract. It may be said of Price, Blake, and the Romantics, however, that they armed themselves in advance, by going back to seventeenth-century radical Christian notions, against the eventual domination of a system that would, as Frankfurt theorists like Marcuse have argued, close off all discourse and experience by denying any basis for an outside standpoint. The Inner Light, too, shines in unexpected places. Blake passionately believed, as I will try to show in chapter three, that man's potential innate autonomy requires for its fulfillment not the "right" to enter into contracts with other isolated selves but the radical mutual interpenetration of others in a total community. However hard that may be to conceive concretely, it absolutely prevents Blake from joining what C. B. Macpherson calls "possessive individualism."

So many Blakean positions nonetheless bear a family resemblance to those taken by the Dissenting interest—the critique of clericalism and mystery, the liberty of conscience, praise of "industry," abhorrence of war—that it is understandable that a Marxist as sophisticated as Terry Eagleton can call Blake a "mythologer of bourgeois revolution."[35] Such a view is not exactly wrong, but even after allowances are made for the necessary brevity of the phrase, "bourgeois" is too misleading to be allowed to stand. What seems universal or mythological in Blake is not merely a projection and generalization of the emergent bourgeois class, which must "represent its interest as the common interest of all the members of society . . . expressed in ideal form," according to Marx's early formulation.[36] Blake does not simply accent the bourgeois worldview in a distinctive way, but draws as well from very different values which, whether or not they are timeless or universal, are larger and older than those of the bourgeoisie, not altogether assimilable to them, and often in conflict with them.

Blake and the Seventeenth Century

The respectable Dissenting interest, established in its academies, scientific circles, Unitarian and Quaker meeting houses, and increasingly in the technologically advanced factories in the Midlands, had a somewhat disreputable plebeian cousin, or nest of cousins, about whom the historical record is far less ample. Both sides of the family took their character from the crucial experience of the 1640s and 1650s, and historians among each might have thought the development of the other had been arrested by the trauma of that time, the high Dissenters by repressing 1649 and displacing their ardor onto 1689, the low radical Protestants by continuing to celebrate 1649 but in displaced apocalyptic forms. How far the threat of government prosecution kept both from speaking their minds deserves to be weighed here, but quite apart from that, the legacy of the seventeenth-century revolution seems to flow in two distinct though not mutually exclusive channels. George Crabbe's "Village Courtship" (1812) describes a village conventicle turning, at the close of its regular service, to a commemoration of the Good Old Cause by unveiling a painting of Cromwell dispersing the Rump Parliament. Millenarian sects survived with surprising tenacity well into the nineteenth century. Quakers, Traskites, Sandemanians, Muggletonians (the last avowed Muggletonian died in the 1970s), and other tiny sects preserved a matrix of language and imagery by which they could imagine the new revolutionary times even if they dared take only occasional and covert action. According to Christopher Hill, "Just as a surviving Lollard tradition contributed to the English Reformation over a century after the defeat of Lollardy, just as a surviving radical Protestant tradition contributed to the English Revolution, . . . so the radicals of the English Revolution perhaps gave more to posterity than is immediately obvious."[37] Most of the sects had meetings in London and all of them found adherents among the artisan class. They were a notable part of Blake's milieu and probably a greater influence on his thought than we have recognized.[38]

Blake's friend and fellow engraver William Sharp nicely emblemizes the intersection of respectable and secular Dissent—he was a leading member of the London Society for Constitutional Information in the 1790s—with the plebeian religious fringe—he joined the Swedenborgians two years before Blake did and later endorsed the prophecies of Richard Brothers and Joanna Southcott.[39] Blake's connection with the Swedenborg Society was brief and he stayed aloof from Sharp's enthusiasms, but he seems to have found more nourishment in the debased overliteralized biblicism of these groups than in the drier and cooler discourse of the Dissenting *philosophes*. Blake's resemblance to the seventeenth-century antinomian tradition has been noted by recent scholars, and the resemblance of even the high Dissenters to it was noted by Edmund Burke, who flailed Price by comparing him with Hugh Peters, chaplain in the Parliamentary army and notorious regicide.[40] It was as if the times had heaved in enormous circles, as Blake put it in *America*, and brought back a revolutionary situation like that of a century and a half before. Respectable Dissent and plebeian sectarianism, the two heirs of the first, having grown at different ideological tempos, were equipped to respond to different features of the second, one to the rational reform of government so as to remove hindrances to personal liberty, the other to the restoration of all things in a new heaven on earth.

In Blake's use of the word "enthusiasm" we can trace the legacy of radical Inner Light Protestantism. Around 1650 the word seems to have been extracted from its Greek context, the rites of Dionysus, and applied more vaguely, and pejoratively, to the radical sectarians then springing up. By mid-eighteenth century a whole library had accumulated of sermons, satires, polemics, and philosophical treatises on (and invariably against) enthusiasm, as part of the reaction to the outburst that had threatened the ruling classes. By then the word had lost much of its precision and came to mean any sort of extravagant or ill-regulated religious emotion. Its earlier use, however, was probably more apt than the anti-enthusiasts realized when they borrowed it from the classics, for some of the more radical believers, denying the existence of an external God, claimed they were themselves "godded" with an inner God: Greek *entheos*, whence *enthousiasmos*, means "engodded" or "full of god." More loosely, "enthusiasm" was often used as a synonym for "revelation," though anti-enthusiasts found it rhetorically more useful than revelation because it lacked the latter's biblical sanction. As the ideology of reason spread during the eighteenth century, the doctrine of natural religion spread with it. Its denigration of special revelation, so hard to regulate, is part of the anti-enthusiastic reaction.

John Locke, as we might expect, articulated and synthesized this ideology as he did so much else. In the final chapter of his *Essay on Human Understanding*, called "Of Enthusiasm," he criticizes enthusiasm not so much for its claim to be from God as for its rejection of reason. There are two kinds of revelation: "Reason is natural revelation, whereby the eternal Father of light, and fountain of all knowledge, communicates to mankind that portion of truth which he had lain within the reach of their natural faculties." Direct revelation from God, bypassing the natural medium, cannot conflict with natural revelation, but only "enlarges" natural reason, and comes, moreover, with credentials to prove to the reason that it indeed comes from God. It is easy to imagine Blake's reaction to this discussion. He would have noticed Locke's strategy in dressing up "sensation" in the phrase "natural revelation," a contradiction *in adjecto* in Blake's worldview but a seductive premise in Locke's, for it allows Locke plausibly to make the next claim that special revelation must be in harmony with it, on the unstated but obvious assumption that God would not contradict Himself. For one like Blake, who denied that God created nature and for whom nature was an impediment to vision, Locke's argument has no force. Locke might have denied special revelation altogether, as eighteenth-century skeptics did, but his concession to Christian orthodoxy is only apparent, since reason remains the judge of revelation's authenticity.

Conviction alone, according to Locke, can give no grounds for belief. "Firmness of persuasion," he headed one section, "no proof that any proposition is from God." Blake replied to this claim explicitly, if a little evasively, in *The Marriage of Heaven and Hell*: "Then I asked: does a firm perswasion that a thing is so, make it so? He [Isaiah] replied. All poets believe that it does, & in ages of imagination this firm perswasion removed mountains; but many are not capable of a firm perswasion of any thing" (E 38). Such a reply is a characteristically Blakean shift from the objective (the "fact" that something is from God) to the subjective (the effects and capacity of belief), a case of his fundamental project of "anthropologizing" religion, much like Feuerbach's a little later. To prove that an idea comes from God is really to show that we believe in a God "out there," for the enterprise of "proving" or "demonstrating" a fact is really the creating of the fact in the first place. Locke asks, "How shall anyone distinguish between the delusions of Satan, and the inspirations of the Holy Ghost?" (IV.19.3). With Locke's answer of rational proof Blake might sarcastically agree, except that what passes the test of rational demonstration can only be the delusions of Satan, the god of this world, "the Mind of the Natural Frame" (E 625), worshipped by the likes of Locke under the name of God the Father. Locke fears that for the enthusiast the source of the supposed light is only his own mind (IV.19.11); Blake cheerfully proclaims no other possible source.

By Blake's day, as a result of critiques like those of Locke, Joseph Butler, and others, "enthusiasm" had come to have a pejorative meaning, and those who were meant by the word chose less tainted terms to refer to themselves. Even Coleridge said that enthusiasm was "always indeed to be deprecated," even if some fine souls had it.[41] Blake, however, applied "enthusiasm" to himself, and in doing so he once again thumbed his nose (a snubby one, as he insisted) at the dominant ideology.

Though we lack his comments on Locke's *Essay* we find in his marginalia to Sir Joshua Reynolds's *Discourses* an irritation at that Augustan's disparaging, and rather contentless, use of "enthusiasm." To Reynolds's high-toned dictum that "enthusiastick admiration seldom promotes knowledge," Blake answered, "Enthusiastic Admiration is the first Principle of Knowledge & its Last" (E 647). "Mere enthusiasm," says Reynolds, "will carry you but a little way." "Meer Enthusiasm," Blake rejoined, "is the All in All!" (E 645). It was evident to Blake "that Reynolds Wishd none but Fools to be in the Arts & in order to this, he calls all others Vague Enthusiasts or Madmen" (E 647).

At least once Blake had a condescending thought about enthusiasts: in a note on Lavater he argued that even if he is superstitious the "poor enthusiast" will be led in the paths of holiness (E 598). He was quite forthright, however, about himself:

Thirteen years ago I lost a brother & with his spirit I converse daily & hourly in the Spirit & See him in my remembrance in the regions of my Imagination. I hear his advice & even now write from his Dictate. Forgive me for Expressing to you my Enthusiasm which I wish all to partake of Since it is to me a Source of Immortal Joy even in this world by it I am the companion of Angels.

(Letter to Hayley, 6 May 1800; E 705)

Emerging from a difficult period two years later Blake proclaimed that "Nothing can withstand the fury of my Course among the Stars of God & in the Abysses of the Accuser My Enthusiasm is still what it was only Enlargd and confirmd" (Letter to Butts, 22 Nov 1802; E 720). In the introduction to *Jerusalem*, addressed "To the Public," Blake appeals for understanding of his enthusiasm and, as he had with other words, restores "enthusiasm" to something like the original Greek meaning it had early in the seventeenth century: "The Enthusiasm of the following Poem, the Author hopes no Reader will think presumptuousness or arrogance when he is reminded that the Ancients acknowledge their love to their Deities, to the full as Enthusiastically as I have who Acknowledge mine for my Saviour and Lord, for they were wholly absorb'd in their Gods" (E 145).

In his Preface to *Milton* Blake does not mention enthusiasm but enlists the synonymous "inspiration" and "Imagination" as his champion against the memory-governed imitation of the classics that infected Milton. Blake's quarrel with Milton, like his dissent from the Dissenters, can be summed up in his charge that in *Paradise Lost* the Holy Ghost is a vacuum (MHH 6). And it is true that, except for the invocations and a reference to the Comforter (12.485f), the Holy Ghost is conspicuous by its absence. There is, of course, an interiorization of much Christian orthodoxy, such as the "paradise within," but the difficulty is that what gets lodged within the upright heart is not, in Blake's view, the Holy Spirit but the voice of the Father, reason. The Christian liberty that burned in the hearts of the radical sectarians of 1650 becomes Milton's "Rational Liberty," a colder thing that speaks of laws and obedience rather than love and forgiveness, or enthusiasm.

Milton moved from Presbyterianism to Independency but

seems not to have gone any further to the left; there is no evidence that he supported the Levellers either before or after Cromwell and the Independents defeated them in 1649, let alone the Ranters, Diggers, or Familists.[42] "Reason" in his moral theology corresponds to the rational rule of the fit though few over the passion-swayed many, to a Parliament of the wise and sober, and even to a Lord Protector. But the word "reason" among the radicals often meant the principle of universal brotherhood or harmony of all "fellow creatures," something very like the Holy Ghost itself. Milton's reason, though internalized, has a component of transcendence, governing like a father over the unruly passions; the radical version was more purely immanent, the ruliness of a soul "godded" with Christ. Milton's reason is authoritarian, the radicals' is democratic.

Blake, then, is the heir of the radical Gerrard Winstanley the Digger (1609–1660+), even though he doubtless never heard of him. This obscure mercer and farmer from Lancashire now has an honored place in the history of both socialism and anarchism.[43] Hearing in a trance the command "Work together; eat bread together," he gathered a group to squat on wasteland in Cobham and farm it ("dig" it) communally. They lasted about a year before the landowners and local residents drove them away. During and after this communal experiment Winstanley published several pamphlets, some of them quite long, such as *The Law of Freedom in a Platform* (1652), which combined theological speculation with political theory.

Winstanley does not deny the Trinity, but the first two persons are taken as preliminary or partial versions of the third. If the Father is a "fiery orbe, or spirit of burning," and the Son is "the light and declaration of the Father," then "the Holy Ghost is a man in whom the Father dwels bodily, which is, Emanuel, God with us, and in and by whom the Father dost manifest his power in doing great works" (131). The historical Son, "Jesus Christ at a distance from thee, will never save thee; but a Christ within is thy Saviour" (113). Blake's Jesus tells us the same thing: "I am not a God afar off, . . . / Within your bosoms I reside, and you reside in me" (J 4.18-

19). "He that looks for a God without himself and worships God at a distance," says Winstanley "he worships he knows not what, but is led away and deceived by the imaginations of his own heart."[44]

"Imaginations," we can see, is used in an un-Blakean but traditional sense, and Winstanley's term for the inner spirit is the antonym, "Reason." "Reason is that living power of light that is in all things; it is the salt that savours all things; it is the fire that burns up drosse, and so restores what is corrupted; and preserves what is pure; he is the Lord our righteousnesse" (104). Reason "dwels in every creature, according to the nature and being of the creature, but supreamely in man" (109). Thus it is not at all like the reason of the eighteenth-century rationalists, against which Blake and the Romantics rebelled; Winstanley also railed against the kind of reason used in "Anatomyzing Divinity" (242), which is reason blinded by imagination. Winstanley's Reason is the Logos or indwelling Christ and is almost exactly what Blake means by Imagination, while Winstanley's imagination is the power of producing fantasies or specters that Blake calls reason. This precise reversal of terms by two radical Protestants neatly illustrates the drastic cultural changes that took place in the century that separated them.

Reason generates specters, according to Blake, mainly because it has divided itself from the totality of the psyche; indeed, reason is the principle of division and separation itself, as the opening of *The Book of Urizen* tells it. From separation comes the sense of self and the will to control what is now separate: Blake's political allegory emerges readily from his psychomachia. So with Winstanley. The selfish imaginings' usurpation of translucent reason leads to greed for things. The primordial creation, which was held by all in common, is now divided up into *meum* and *tuum*, "upholding this particular propriety of *Mine and Thine*" (159); thus are born private property and enclosures.

> And hereupon, the Earth (which was made to be a Common Treasure of relief for all, both Beasts and Men) was hedged in to In-closures by the teachers and the rulers, and the others were

made Servants and Slaves: And that Earth that is within the Cre-
ation, made a common Store-house for all, is bought and sold, and
kept in the hands of a few, whereby the great Creator is mightily
dishonored, as if he were a respecter of persons, delighting in the
comfortable Livelihood of some, and rejoycing in the miserable
povertie and straits of others. From the beginning it was not so.

(252)

"From the beginning it was not so" was the slogan of radicals
from long before Winstanley's day to long after Blake's. Mil-
ton's story of Adam and Eve in the Garden is a rationalized
and artificial derivation of the true original state of mankind,
which both Winstanley and Blake characterize as a brother-
hood of all mankind without the imposition of priest, king,
Lord Protector, or teacher.

Artisanal Dissent

It was noticed in Blake's own day that his ideas were congruent
with much contemporary philosophy in Germany, and indeed
Blake's reputation was secured in Germany before it was in
England. Henry Crabb Robinson, himself interested in Ger-
man thought, wrote a somewhat equivocal appreciation (that
is, Blake was a genius but mad, a romantic cliché bound to
impress German readers) for the *Vaterländisches Museum* in
1810. Much of Alan Cunningham's *Life of Blake* was translated
into German in 1830. Recent scholarship has taken up the
German context, especially the philosophy of Hegel, whose
dialectical arguments often strikingly resemble Blake's.[45]
Blake's critique of religion, though consonant with the En-
lightenment attack on clerical orthodoxy, seems closer to
Feuerbach's "anthropologizing" of religion, as we noted ear-
lier, and to the ideas of the young Hegelian and romantic
poet Karl Marx. Schiller, Schelling, and Novalis could all be
brought into fruitful comparison with Blake, and I shall not
resist trying a few comparisons myself in this book.

I mention the Germans here, however, to suggest another
preliminary vantage from which to triangulate Blake's posi-
tion. If one is convinced that the features Blake shares with
contemporary German thought and with seventeenth-century

English thought are not peripheral or adventitious products of Blake's antiquarianism (though even antiquarianism, as we shall note, has its political point), then an interesting question arises about the possible social basis of the ideological space Blake occupies. We need only remember the notorious "backwardness" of the German bourgeoisie to see the possible coherence of Blake's two sets of affiliations: the tradition of German mysticism and pietism, which corresponds roughly to the radical Christianity of the English Commonwealth, was still alive in the thought of the German counterpart of the English entrepreneurial class who, by 1790, under the faster tempo of industrial development, had largely secularized or abandoned its first characteristic forms of thought. As an emblem of this different temporality we might cite Jacob Boehme, the German cobbler-prophet whose works, translated into English by the 1640s, influenced many of the radical sectarians, including probably George Fox and Gerrard Winstanley, and who had a second, smaller vogue in England at the same time he was profoundly influencing Schelling, Hegel, and others in Germany. Blake was an admirer of this self-taught German artisan; he probably owed his crucial term "Selfhood" to Boehme's *Selbheit*.[46]

I suggest that we can discern—and we should at least seek—an ideological space for artisanal labor and its characteristic social relations, a space intersecting at many points with the worldview of the "middling classes" in general and the emerging entrepreneurial sector in particular, indeed, willing to follow the lead of this emerging sector even where their interests conflicted for the sake of their common struggle against aristocratic privilege, the landed interests, and the old corporations. In 1640, perhaps, the "masterless men" in London and other towns may have been "emergent," powerful enough in various alliances to push a political revolution farther than anyone had thought possible. That may have been their moment. By 1790, artisans could feel a new pressure besides the immemorial struggles with middlemen and merchants—the increasing proletarianization of unskilled rural labor in the factory towns. They nonetheless posed a grave political threat to the Pitt regime and the social hierarchy on which it rested. It was not for about a decade that the regime managed to crush such overt reformist movements as the London Corresponding Society, in part by severing it from the more "respectable" Whiggish sectors that, in their 1640 version, had made so powerful an alliance with it. The sphere of "artisanal ideology," then, if something definable as that is discoverable, would seem to offer another point of purchase on Blake's own ideology.

Blake and most other skilled craftsmen, I think, would have shared the Dissenters' great stress on liberty. They wanted to be free to follow their craft and enjoy the fruits of their industry, as well as to worship as they chose, and they wanted the state to withdraw from religion and the economy. As I shall argue in chapter five, this essentially negative freedom, which we find in so many Dissenters' writings, would not have seemed enough to Blake, as it did not to spokesmen for the L.C.S. and other artisan-based reform societies. For Blake as for the Dissenters, the Beast (when they allowed themselves such archaic language) was state tyranny wedded to religion. Blake's democratization of spiritual vision certainly entailed liberty of conscience, but he could hardly have made laissez faire a foundation of his social ideals, as his insistence on the interdependence of all people attests.

His relative silence about equality might seem consonant with the Dissenters' insistence, in the face of accusations that they were levellers, that equality of condition was not what they sought, but Blake could not have endorsed claims like this from the Manchester manufacturer Thomas Walker: "The rule is not 'let all mankind be perpetually equal.' God and nature have forbidden it. But 'let all mankind start fair in the race of life.' "⁴⁷ However much resentment we find in Blake's notebooks against the unfair promotion of mediocre toadies and the neglect of honest genius, it is not hard to imagine his scorn of this "race of life," not to mention God and nature's putative prohibition. The "career open to talent," however attractive to an industrious unknown, bears in its very term "career" an antisocial connotation. We are not here to run a race against our brothers, but to walk with them and help them along. The real sense of this race is *enrichissez-vous*, that is, greed, the remnants of Christian conscience being relegated to pious charity toward the "deserving poor." Blake appeals both to an ideal community and to what remains of real precapitalist social bonds. And though a London printer or shoemaker might well want to better himself and move up in status (Blake himself sought recognition as "artist" as well as "artisan"), the stubborn growth of benevolent societies and trade unions, in defiance of every pressure to dissolve them, bears witness to the strength of artisanal solidarity and mutual aid.

The virtues of frugality, calculation, and self-command may have been shared by skilled craftsmen, but these must have been modified by the traditions of fraternal generosity and the occasional profligate binge. Blake worked every day of his adult life, but probably his most characteristic demand throughout his poems is to give and receive in spontaneous generosity. "Can I see anothers grief, / And not seek for kind relief" (E 17). We see everywhere in Blake's writings, too, images of unrepressed labor, of work wholehearted, inspired, full of passion and pleasure, to set against the enforced tasks of a cold and calculating Urizen. No doubt Urizen holds sway in this world, but he cannot banish eros from labor in one who denies his assumptions and forswears the worldly prize he offers. Against every kind of repression, from the "religion of chastity" to the enslavement of drudgery, a drudgery he knew well as an engraver of others' designs, Blake is everywhere indignant.

Blake held two other positions highly typical of middle-class Dissenters in their two-front struggle against aristocratic privilege and what seemed the irresponsible fecklessness of the lower orders. In an early phase of his thought, at least, Blake believed that the imperial ambitions of the court and the aristocracy were to blame for England's continual wars, whereas if the mercantile and manufacturing orders had their way England would have peace and prosperity.[48] He may have lost his illusions on this score through the depth of jingoism during the French wars, but he never ceased to denounce the corruption of both manufacturing and agriculture by a war economy, no matter who was responsible.[49] He has a vision

of a past—and future—city of brotherly commerce in which
a charming change is rung on the London Exchange:

They came up to Jerusalem; they walked before Albion
In the Exchanges of London every Nation walkd
And London walkd in every Nation mutual in love & harmony.

(J 24.41-43)[50]

Blake has given his own inflection to the case put forward
by the earliest characteristically bourgeois thinkers (in the six-
teenth and seventeenth centuries) that trade and the arts pro-
mote peace and in turn prosper during peacetime, while it is
princes who make wars. The case rests, of course, as Albert
Hirschman has recently shown, on the power of enlightened
self-interest to quell violent passions; this is the positive side
of the familiar Puritan asceticism and calculation that Blake
so despised.[51] Perhaps what Blake was trying to do was pre-
serve the positive aspect of the bourgeois critique of aris-
tocratic depredation and waste while recuperating the
aristocratic ideals of spontaneous expression of feeling,
magnanimity and openness to friends, and well-rounded de-
velopment of the personality.

It is easy to show, in any case, the extent to which Blake
inherits the Enlightenment critique of superstition and cler-
ical obscurantism, a critique aimed at least as much at the
rural masses, "deprest in dark ignorance" and "bound in the
dens of superstition," as he puts it in *The French Revolution*
(214, 228), as it is aimed at the priests, who "took advantage
of & enslav'd the vulgar" by "Choosing forms of worship from
poetic tales" and pronouncing that "the Gods had orderd such
things" (MHH 11; E 38). In this he is at one with the *philosophes*
and Dissenters as well as the majority of the artisan class of
his day, who, under Paineite influence and prompted by the
manifest corruption of the Church hierarchy, weaned them-
selves pretty thoroughly, and permanently, from theology.

The conclusion to *The Four Zoas*, "The dark Religions are
departed and sweet Science reigns," is, as Geoffrey Hartman
reminds us, an enlightenment commonplace.[52] On the other
hand, Blake's "sweet Science" here was not the mathematics
and statistics of Reverend Price, the chemistry of Reverend

Priestley and Erasmus Darwin, or even the engineering skill of Tom Paine, though the closer science came to the simple workmanship of the "arts of Life" the better Blake liked it. Blake is thinking rather of the "sweet instructions" the lamb gives to the infant and the lion gives to the man of years, the conversation of men with each other and with their work in an arcadia of vocal nature (FZ 71.7). The ideal is "To know sweet Science & to do with simple companions / Sitting beneath a tent & viewing sheepfolds & soft pastures" (FZ 51.30-31) and singing songs, no doubt, that teach and delight. We are closer here to Christian Science than to the bourgeois science of the Birmingham Lunar Society, however closely linked the latter was to radical politics.[53] For Blake faith and knowledge were one. The single vision of Newton and Locke, of Rousseau and Voltaire, enemies of superstition though they may have been, only replaced one confined system of thought with another, equally one-dimensional, system, a system without even the congealed residues of the poetic spirit superstition preserves.

In his disparagement of modern science, I suspect, Blake distanced himself from his fellow craftsmen, but we should not forget the various intermediate stages possible between religious obscurantism and the high road of progressive science, some of them attractive again today to those who fear where this high road has already taken us. Blake's intellectual milieu was peopled by brilliant autodidacts who combined electrical experiments with phrenology, hydraulics with the search for Atlantis, calculations of eclipses with the ten horns of the Beast, fervent dedication to experimental science with fervent confidence in "experimental religion." These homemade syntheses, born of senile religion and infantile science, expressed at their best the beauty and skill, the attention to detail, the harmonizing of disparate realms, and the originality that we prize in any work of an artisan or artist. If Blake's epics sound at times like travel guides, chronicles, or compendia of useful knowledge, we might take the hint and consider the dissertations on Stonehenge, the dimensions of Solomon's Temple, or the lost original language of mankind as literary works, as elegiac epics perhaps, assembled by skilled tinkerers with prophetic visions.

It is obvious enough that Blake's insistent theme of laboring, especially in his epics, sets his work apart from the literature, whether "pre-Romantic" or contemporary, written by Dissenting or otherwise reforming or even Jacobin poets and novelists. There is nothing quite like it among philosophical or political works, either. Before we leave this summary of Blake's affiliations with bourgeois thought, however, we should recall the importance of the labor theory of value put forth by Adam Smith and the Scottish school and its bearing on the artisanal ethos. I am competent only to gesture here. The sort of thing we associate with Adam Smith, and the uses to which he was prominently put by wealthy industrialists who wanted an end to paternalistic and protectionist laws, should not keep us from seeing the moral dimension of the theory and especially its frank account of the injury to the spirit of the laborer that the progress of manufacturing entails. It is most explicit in Adam Fergusson's writings, which were much admired by Schiller.[54] Man becomes a part of the machine he must work with. But behind this, implicitly at least, is a "scientific" assertion that labor—not nature alone, and certainly not the landowners—is the source of all wealth and the measure of all value. We need not look ahead to Marx's development of this assumption into a theory of capitalist exploitation to recognize the revolutionary potential slumbering in the Bible of the mill-owners.

SANS-CULOTTISM

Had Blake lived in Paris instead of London, it is tempting to think, he would have been a sans-culotte; however imponderable that thought may be, it is worth a look at the deeds and ideas of the *menu peuple* who entered so dramatically into French revolutionary politics for two or three years starting in 1792. The sans-culotte was the useful artisan and the true patriot, one who knew "how to plough a field, handle a forge, a saw, a file, to cover a roof, how to make shoes and to shed his blood to the last drop to save the Republic."[55] He also knew how to club together with his brothers into the Parisian sections, expel the moderates, and compel the Constituent Assembly to more militant republican policies.

Hannah Arendt finds the significance of sans-culottism to lie not in its contribution to political thought and practice, but rather in its overwhelming pressure on republican political institutions to find solutions to problems of social misery that cannot be found: the realm of public freedom, newly established on republican principles, was drowned by the hitherto private and unpolitical demands of happiness and prosperity.[56] However that may be, we may find in the sans-culottes' manifestoes and their distinctive practices a sufficiently coherent ideology, and language appropriate to the "ordinary people" of Paris or London, from which we can take bearings to help situate Blake. I must leave this task to those better equipped than I, but I can suggest that one contribution may lie in their promoting the idea and feeling of *fraternité* with great vigor and endowing it with an almost religious significance. The word does not often occur among the revolutionary slogans or titles of the bourgeoisie from 1789 to 1792; only with the rise of the sans-culottes does it gain prominence and join *liberté* and *égalité* in importance.[57] Albert Soboul describes how "the sans-culottes invented a new form of communication—fraternization": "If one Section was threatened by the moderates, the entire general assembly of the neighboring section would move to the threatened assembly, and, in the name of fraternity, the two assemblies would be fused into one by the mysterious ties of the oath and the fraternal kiss, and decisions would then be taken in common."[58] Such "rushing together," as Blake put it in *America*, may have destructured but certainly also invigorated the clubs and sections, which were in fact the first modern appearance of the distinctive and spontaneous revolutionary forms that Arendt so admires, the communes, councils, *Räte*, or soviets that constitute the only genuine "spaces of freedom."[59]

Despite great differences between the social and political patterns of France and England, it is striking that in both countries at virtually the same time the plebeian classes appeared on the public stage in these distinctive forms. In 1793,

Year II of the Republic, the sans-culottes organized several *journées* that forced changes on the Constituent Assembly, while the London Corresponding Society (named after one of its own distinctive forms of fraternity, perhaps modeled on the colonial Committees of Correspondence) held its first open-air meeting in Hackney on October 24, a harbinger of the truly gigantic demonstrations of 1795, where perhaps two hundred thousand gathered to demand parliamentary reform and peace with France. It may indeed have been the first threat of war with France that led to expressions of international fraternity from both sides. "What fused these democratic forces in both countries into a common front of political solidarity," Albert Goodwin writes, "was the issue, on 25 July 1792, of the 'bloody and tyrannous' manifesto reluctantly signed by the Duke of Brunswick as generalissimo of the Austrian and Prussian forces poised for their assault on revolutionary France."[60] Registered tentatively as the "german forged links" of his "London" draft, Blake's feelings about this manifesto are easy to imagine; evident everywhere is his deep belief in the power of brotherhood to withstand the reassertion of tyranny.

"True genius is almost always sans-culotte," a sans-culotte wrote; it is certainly true that among the plebeian radicals of both capitals were plenty of writers, actors, painters, engravers, and printers who had grievances against the privileged of their own trades, those who found wealthy patrons and the solace of the salons while the majority starved in Grub Street garrets. Robert Darnton, from whom I have borrowed the quotation (by Henri Grégore, 1793), has sketched the world of the French "literary proletariat" in the two decades before the revolution. The deep resentments festering among the disappointed geniuses against the literary aristocrats who made a mockery of the "republic of letters" bred a revolutionary rhetoric as well as real revolutionaries with useful skills.[61] In London a comparable set of overlapping groups had been growing in size, and perhaps in resentment, for a long time, caught as they were between two modes of production, or at least of financing—patronage by aristocrats and sales to a middle-class public—with the humiliations, vanities, and displaced class warfare the well-known result. It was the theme of much of the poetry of the age, from Thomas Gray's mute inglorious Miltons to the myth of Thomas Chatterton's death, in Coleridge's phrase, by "bleak freezings of neglect." Blake's resentment blisters pages never meant to see the light. "Having spent the Vigour of my Youth & Genius," he writes in his copy of Joshua Reynolds's *Works*, "under the Opression of Sr Joshua & his Gang of Cunning Hired Knaves Without Employment & as much as could possibly be Without Bread," we must understand his indignation and resentment. He goes on to identify himself with James Barry, poor and unemployed, John Mortimer, despised and mocked, and Fuseli, indignant—republican artists all. Fuseli "almost hid himself"; "I was"—he crosses it off and updates it—"am hid."[62]

In such intersections of artist and artisan, resentment and revolution, patronage and the "people," some of Blake's distinctive positions and much of his "pathos" can be located. Unlike the Book of Revelation, which otherwise profoundly informs his vision, Blake's engraved works are largely free of bitterness and vengefulness; it may be that his genuine belief in forgiveness and reconciliation modulated that bitterness into the mournfulness and indignation that alternate throughout his work, although he had much else, such as the wars with France, to mourn over. His great celebrations of dawn, of spring, of the sun's return to its ancient place, are prompted, too, not only by his visions of a world at peace but by the arrival of the long-neglected genius of the common people into its day of recognition.

CLOSURE

How successful Blake was at hammering together his home-made system is a subject of considerable disagreement. That he was much concerned to create a system no one denies; it is explicitly avowed (by Los, if not by Blake) and implicitly demonstrated at great length. His epic catalogs are only the most prominent sign of this ambition, as well as the most salient symptom, some would say, of his failure. What I want to take up at this point is the ideological bearing of the impulse toward system-making itself, the extent to which Blake became a prisoner of his own system or saw his way clear of it, and the contamination of his system by the one he was fighting.

To turn to the last point first. Blake's arch-systematizer is Urizen, a figure for the faculty of reason become abstract, withdrawn (an early sense of "abstracted") from the company of his fellow mental powers and dwelling in a realm of abstractions, of empty and rigid forms. He can make sense of what comes to seem chaos only by imposing a unitary law upon it; in fact the chaos or void is a creation brought about by his retirement from the eternal plenitude, and his law is a tyranny that reduces the myriad unique individuals to intermeasurable units. Against this Blake pits two related contraries, the unfallen or resurrected state of eternity, only briefly treated, and, at much greater length, the building by Los of a counterculture called Golgonooza, which seems almost the same as the world of art, the sculptures and "visionary forms dramatic" that allude to the very works we read and see them in. When Los says, "I must Create a System, or be enslav'd by another Mans," we sense the danger that he may be succumbing to the enemy, for to fight like one's enemy is to give in to him. Blake quickly adds, as if to forestall this suggestion, "I will not Reason & Compare: my business is to Create" (J 10.20-21); his system, if a system it must be, will have a very different basis.

To fight with the enemy's weapons, however, is the sort of poetic justice that is enshrined in the tradition of defeating the devil with his own devices and that a sense of satisfying literary form almost dictates. Los may have his own system, but like a guerrilla soldier he steals enemy weapons as well:

> by mathematic power
> Giving a body to Falshood that it may be cast off for ever.
> With Demonstrative Science piercing Apollyon with his own bow!
> (J 12.12-14)

"Giving a body to Falshood" is unique to the arsenal of Los and his creative allies: it is enacted in startling literalness in *Milton* (19 and 20), where like a sculptor the poet Milton builds new flesh or red clay on the bare bones of Urizen. It is man-

ifestly a strategy of Blake's throughout his works, the poetic
equivalent of *reductio ad absurdum* in an "immanent" critique
of ideology. But "mathematic power" and "demonstrative sci-
ence" may burn, or freeze, the hands that wield them, however
inspired, and in Los indeed we can find many instances of
despair, rage, momentary tyrannizings, and even an an-
guished collaboration in the original solidification of Urizen's
world. More interesting in our context are the Urizenic traces
in Blake's own work.

Here it is easy to be cavalier and dismiss the catalogs, say,
or even worse the litany of Golgonooza's gates and directions
in *Jerusalem* (12 and 13) as so much Urizenic intrusion upon
a slumbering poetic genius. The bardic barking may sound
too imperious to deserve the name of honest indignation. Of
both sorts of passages a defense can be made; one might begin
by noting how rarely Urizen speaks and how little he seems
to care for details. A nice example, however, of how a Urizenic
form may infect a Blakean content, how the language of rea-
son may abstract or reify a minute particular, lies in the phrase
"minute particular" itself. Occurring some dozen times in *Je-
rusalem* and only there, it has the air of a new discovery Blake
is trying out, and it is quite a good one: it unites in a single
phrase the realms of aesthetics (his annotations to Reynolds's
Discourses praise minuteness, particular details, minute dis-
crimination, and so on), epistemology (from particulars to
generals), politics ("Minute Particulars in slavery"), and reli-
gion ("every Minute Particular is Holy"). It lends itself to
several concretizations, such as the "little particle" or grain of
sand which may grow opaque to the light or open like a jewel
(in turn a metaphor of the human individual), or to the "little
ones" of Jesus' flock (from Matthew 18), Jerusalem's children,
members of the Divine Body, and even Jesus himself as an
infant. The phrase also modulates to "minute articulations"
and "small articles" and from there to "scarcely articulate"
speech and back to the "arts" of life. It seems to entwine every
significant thematic strand of *Jerusalem*, and one could do
worse, after one's first intimidating reading of it, than trace
through all the intersections of metonym and metaphor that
"minute particular" implies. The problem, of course, is that

such a master trope is only a step from becoming a trope of mastery, an imposition of a single idea onto many unique and disparate individuals, which almost confesses its tyranny in its very name, Latin polysyllables smothering honest English little ones (though of course even "little ones" remains a generalization).

What is one to do? The "stubborn structure of the Language" is only a floor, a "rough basement," beneath the collapsing Albion, but Los must build English to keep Albion talking (J 36.58-60).[63] And if Blake is going to talk to Albion at all he must use his language, however corrupted by Urizenic ideology. Faced with later corruptions of the language into a one-dimensional, operational, or instrumental system, modern critics of society have turned to deliberate difficulty, irony, obscenity, and poetry, not to say wordless art or total silence, for both weaponry and sanctuary. For Blake, obviously, the recourse was to art and not to direct statement, but direct statements are in the works, and they raise questions. Troubled by them, Blake may have overreacted on his catalogs of minute particulars, whose significance we can now see as proper names, ungeneralizable, untyrannizable, stubborn, and unique.

Under the influence of Jacques Lacan, Louis Althusser, and Jacques Derrida, some critics now use "ideology" in a wider sense than I have done. For them any system of thought that posits a privileged ground or center, whether in the world or the self, whether an origin, substrate, or final form, is an ideology. In a useful account of Derrida, Jonathan Culler writes that "to grant any principle this privileged status, to make it the prime mover unmoved, is a patently ideological step."[64] "Ideology" here would seem to embrace all systematic thought, whether or not it enters into social conflicts or domination. As Culler's discussion of the *Tel quel* group suggests, it may not be so much the privileging of a principle but the forgetting that one has done so (and Blake's critique of religion comes in here), the witting or unwitting concealment of the founding gesture, that gives a system its ideological character. One would certainly exempt a musical composition even though it "privileges" a certain key, or the system of Euclidean

geometry even though one may not question the five postu-
lates. Indeed, the critical practice of the *Tel quel* group resem-
bles intellectual play, where paradigms are produced only to
be deconstructed and replaced in a *jouissance* of creativity.

Whatever the difficulties with this view,[65] it brings to the
fore features of thought systems or *Denkformen* which are
preeminently, if not uniquely, ideological. Closure, system,
totality: we are taught to suspect these as forms of repression
or exclusion. One of the characteristic tactics of deconstruc-
tion is the surgical extraction of a myth of origins and a proof
that it is circular or endlessly regressive; taken in a wide sense
(from "antecedents" to "epistemological grounds"), "origins"
and their mystifications are undoubtedly a prime ideological
feature.

In Blake it hardly needs to be shown that two realms, ul-
timately the same one, are privileged; that is, by the terms of
Blake's system, setting aside whatever distancing or subverting
effects the form of his work may instill, one cannot think
beyond either the plenitude of Eternity or the Poetic Genius
(Imagination or Holy Spirit). Both are "fountains" or
"springs," sources of everything else. We could stop right here
and discuss what Derrida calls the "metaphysics of presence,"
which Blake shares with western thought, even though Blake
consigns most of that thought to Urizen. He has not escaped
the larger system, however little resemblance his energetic
Eternity of Inner Light bears to Locke's blank slate or the Old
Testament Lawgiver. I think, however, that it is more inter-
esting, more appropriate to Blake, and certainly more specific
historically to take up less abstract and global questions. How,
given these two founts, does the Fall come about? The fact
that there are half a dozen different versions of it in *The Four
Zoas* alone is less an index of that poem's unfinished state than
of the incompleteness of Blake's "system," or possibly a clue
to Blake's real attitude toward the question.[66] Why, in the
light of this, does he begin at the beginning in so many works,
even where plot and genre would dictate entering *in medias
res*? In two copies of *Milton*, for example, Blake expanded the
Bard's Song, which opens the poem, to include part of the
creation story from *Urizen*. Why? Is Blake putting it in the fore-

ground to make us question it? Or is the point less the content of the origin story than its existence—that there is another place or time than this one, however solid and permanent it may seem? In other words, Blake may be making the move necessary to upend the current reigning worldview, and may care much more about doing that than about grounding his own in a consistent way.

To dwell on this point for a moment: at the opening of *Urizen*, Blake's fullest treatment of ultimate genesis, there is no account whatever of Urizen's decision to withdraw. It begins: "Lo, a shadow of horror is risen / In Eternity!" We come to learn a little more of what bothered Urizen about Eternity, but not why it bothered him or why it did so then, if "then" makes any sense in Eternity; it just happens. Blake probably knew enough about the exasperations of Christian theodicy, and of Milton's unsuccessful wrestlings with the origin of evil in *Paradise Lost*, not to spend too much time on it. For the main point, one could argue, is that *The Book of Urizen* is meant to precede and supplant the Book of Genesis, to show its belatedness or secondariness: Genesis is merely a derivative of some ancient source that flows more directly into Blake. *Urizen* takes the story back chronologically several phases earlier than Genesis, which begins with chaos but leaves chaos, and God, too, unexplained; Blake accounts for chaos in all but the initial separation, and leaves Eternity unexplained. The two cosmologies are formally equivalent, but Blake, intervening in a culture that posits chaos as primordial and honors the Creator of nature, wants for complex reasons, some of them political, to set up an alternative that merges the creation with chaos and sets them both against something higher. He wants to induce us, too, to ask a question difficult to entertain among a nation that kicks stones to refute ideas: Why is there nature? The seemingly so solid, primary "givenness" of nature Blake would pry up and deny to the epistemologies and moralities of Locke, Hobbes, and the British empiricist priesthood. And it is a priesthood. From his new Archimedean standpoint the earth of such down-to-earth thinkers shows itself weightless and delusory, an insubstantial pageant conjured up by the "primeval priest," as Blake calls

Urizen in the very first line of *Urizen*, and imposed on the trusting multitude. It takes another twenty-six plates in his long story of the devolution of mankind to get to the obvious starting point of common sense: "No more could they rise at will / In the infinite void, but bound down / To earth by their narrowing perceptions," submitting to the impositions of Newton, they shrink, form laws of prudence, and die. We had to do fearful things to ourselves before we could get to where we took Newton, and Locke, and Genesis, as "original."

It would be interesting to know if in Blake's day there arose a more widespread or intense search for total systems and satisfactory cosmogonies. If, as we have some evidence to argue, the economic and social dislocations then accelerating to industrial "takeoff" were felt as something new, ungovernable, and irreversible, we might expect as responses to them an anxious study of origins. There are certainly plenty of treatises on the origins of inequality, language, national mores, religion, the state, the economy, and everything else, though whether they are proportionately more numerous I do not know. Treatises on the origin of ideas were hardly new, but their number seems to have grown: David Hartley, Thomas Reid, Dugald Stewart, Priestley, Price, and many others produced revisions of Locke and Berkeley, all prompted in part by moral, political, or religious interests. We need only think, too, of Wordsworth's *Prelude* to remind ourselves of the increasingly widespread and intense scrutiny of the origins of the self and its creative powers.

More specifically, the American and French Revolutions, new and startling events both, demanded explanation, while the movement for reform in England, though staved off for another generation, inspired a new scanning of origins and precedents I would call "left antiquarianism." Little more than a boy when the news arrived of Lexington and Concord, a young man during the storming of the Bastille, Blake wrote genealogies, geneses, and generations in large part to comprehend and evaluate the radically new thing under the sun, revolution, even if he used the very recurrence of the sun as a major image. Nothing could make the social sources of his apparently pure cosmogony clearer than the startling first line

of *Urizen* I have just mentioned: "Of the primeval Priests
assum'd power." That line would serve to open a very dif-
ferent poem, set well along in historical times, when, say, the
Hebrews instituted the Aaronic priesthood, after at least two
prior ages of poetic animating and system-forming as Blake
presents them in plate 11 of *The Marriage of Heaven and Hell*.
Priests, in other words, are not primeval, yet here is Urizen,
one of the primeval human powers, behaving like a priest.
There may be a pun on "prime evil"; there are certainly sev-
eral meanings in "assum'd," political, religious, and logical.
One may assume an office legitimately, or, as a "pretender"
(not a bad name for Urizen), one may arrogate or usurp it;[67]
the old theological usage of "assume" as "receive up into
heaven," along with "power" as one of the ranks of angels,
brings out the idea that the primeval priest has taken away
our power and lodged it in the heavens above us; and Urizen
imposes on our reasons a new set of assumptions, the "givens"
we must "take for granted" or be excluded from the elect. If
Blake's ostensible point is that priests reenact the primordial
dislocation of the unified spirit, his premature labeling of
Urizen makes us work the argument backward: from Blake's
very eighteenth-century hatred of priests, whether they are
ecclesiastical officers of Church or Chapel or pontificators of
reason like Locke and Bacon, to his timeless speculations
about the Fall.

LEFT ANTIQUARIANISM

As this book is itself an exercise in it, what I have called "left
antiquarianism" ought to have a place in an account of Blake's
ideological affiliations. Blake served his apprenticeship under
James Basire, engraver to the London Society of Antiquaries,
which had a "somewhat democratically biased interest in the
relics of British history."[68] Among the company was Thomas
Hollis, a philanthropist with Dissenting connections, a "stren-
uous Whig" (Boswell's phrase) who sponsored the production
of seventeenth-century republican classics and helped Mrs.
Macaulay in her *History of England*, the Whig reply to Hume's
Tory version; he also collected relics and portraits of Milton,

whom he celebrated as a republican and lover of liberty.[69] In this, of course, Hollis and the other republican antiquaries were reenacting the politically pointed antiquarianism of their own subject of research: the Society of Antiquaries had fallen into disfavor under James I for raising uncomfortable questions about English history, and much of the ideological preparation for the parliamentary revolution against the Stuarts came in the form of appeals to ancient liberties and customs usurped by innovating tyrants. Sir Edward Coke appealed in 1605 to the "ancient and excellent laws of England" as "the birth-right and the most ancient and best inheritance that the subjects of this realm have"; Milton himself, after an erudite survey of book-licensing, found that "We have it not, that can be heard of, from any ancient state, or polity, or church, nor by any statute left us by our ancestors elder or later," and that its only precedent is the Inquisition.[70]

It is easy to see what was at stake in Blake's day. Burke in his *Reflections* paints the French Revolution as an altogether new thing under the sun, "the most astonishing [revolution] that has hitherto happened in the world," a disturber of the placid condition of the rest of the world, notably England. England has not changed in at least the last four hundred years, and "the present time differs from any other only by the circumstance of what is doing in France." Against the absurd and monstrous spectacle of an infant growing strong enough by moments to wage war with heaven, Burke invokes "the antient permanent sense of mankind" and especially "our *antient* indisputable laws and liberties, and that *antient* constitution of government" which we have "as *an inheritance from our forefathers.*"[71] To reply to all this, Thomas Paine appeals to an even greater antiquity. "The error of those who reason by precedents drawn from antiquity, respecting the rights of man, is, that they do not go far enough into antiquity. They do not go the whole way. They stop in some of the intermediate stages. . . . But if we proceed on, we shall at last come out right; we shall come to the time when man came from the hand of his Maker. . . . Here our inquiries find a resting-place, and our reason finds a home."[72] Paine has nicely combined an "immanent critique" of Burke, outprecedenting the precedent-citer, with his own preferred appeal to nature and reason, which Burke had badly savaged. Burke had indeed stopped halfway in his own history, and could fend off further inquiries into the events preceding 1688 only with a series of outraged rhetorical questions. "Do these theorists . . . mean to attaint and disable backwards all the kings that have reigned before the Revolution, and consequently to stain the throne of England with the blot of a continual usurpation?" Paine answers by calmly proceeding to do so. At least once Burke acknowledges the uncomfortable truth behind royal foundations, but he brings in at the same time his distinctive argument of "prescription," a sanction by time itself, whatever the origin: "the time of prescription, which, through long usage, mellows into legality governments that were violent in their commencement."[73]

The impact of antiquarian polemic is highly visible in Blake. We see it in his near-obsession with universal origins and in his particular claims about, say, the primordial empire of Albion or the authenticity of Macpherson's Ossian. One of the most interesting signs of it lies in Blake's frequent play on the word "ancient" itself, a close study of which would make an excellent entry into his political opinions. In both *The French Revolution* and *America* the word frequents the speeches of the reactionaries—the King of France, the Duke of Burgundy, the Prince of Albion—and carries a largely Burkean resonance. Louis is haunted by the "terrors of ancient Kings" and "ancient darkness," while "the ancientest Peer," Burgundy, summons the "ancient forests" of chivalry, and of Europe, to battle against the Parisian rebels. Albion and his "ancient Guardians" are the keepers of the "ancient heavens" that Orc threatens to rend. In each poem, too, there is an archetype of ancientness itself. The Archbishop of Paris sees an "aged form, white as snow," who is God himself, but weeping out of weakness because he is no longer worshipped by a "godless race." He remains a projection of the Archbishop, but at the climax of *America* the God of Princes, Urizen, also white and weeping, musters enough strength to send an obfuscatory blizzard over England. Such ancientness gives way in each poem, however, and betrays its secondariness to a prior, original antiquity in Paine's sense. King Louis seems to recognize, at the outset, that he and all his ancestors are not eternal and were not first: "the ancient dawn calls us / To awake from slumbers of five thousand years. I awake, but my soul is in dreams." The Bastille contains seven symbolic prisoners; one of them wears an iron mask which "hid the lineaments / of ancient Kings," implying a line of nobility older than the Bourbons, now seen as usurpers, suggesting too the primordial community where all were kings. (This effect is seconded, and complicated, by the appearance of the good King Henry the Fourth.) Like the French *ancien*, which can mean "old" or "former," the English word shifts from "old" to, by implication, "young." In ancient times the world was young; the world renews, Orc returns, "the times are return'd upon thee," and the women of England, among others, break their bonds and "feel the nerves of youth renew, and desires of ancient times" (A 9.19, 15.25).

All of this reminds us how relatively recent is the invocation of the future as a standard of value. The French themselves played Roman parts; they were republicans like Brutus overthrowing tyrannous kings. The pursuit of the new is a modern novelty, and much nostalgia may be found in the theories of modern revolutionaries. It has been argued, I think convincingly, that capitalism is the chief revolutionary force in the world, revolutionary in the modern sense: it overthrows all traditional values, urbanizes the countryside, puts a price on all things and all deeds, and in its "spectacularization" of culture erases the past itself as a significant alternative to the pervasive present. Blake reminds us that an anticapitalist revolution should not try to march more efficiently into the future only to complete capitalism's task, but should restore, in part, what capitalism has obliterated. The role, therefore, of "left antiquarianism" may be more important today than it was in Blake's time, for our times need more reminders of what we have lost.

ART

It was during Blake's lifetime, more or less, that the words "artist" and "artisan" parted ways. Poetry and painting rose in stature and came to be called the "fine" arts; engraving became one of the "useful" arts, and was pointedly left out of the new Royal Academy. Blake was both artist and artisan, and it is possible to see some of the tensions in his ideas and images as products of two incongruent systems of thought. On the question of production, for example, we find both a symbolic earthliness in Los's labors and exalted claims of inspiration from on high. There are passages about joint laborers on a collective enterprise and passages about the loneliness and uniqueness of the creative calling. Set against vatic postures typical of Romantic poets, Blake at times sounds mundane; one imagines him interrupting a rhapsody with a vulgar snort and an "I've got work to do." But no one more than Blake represents the absolute claims of inspiration: "I am Inspired!" his Bard shouts, "I know it is Truth! for I Sing / According to the inspiration of the Poetic Genius . . ." (M 13.51-14.1).

It is interesting to see how these incongruities may affect single passages, and perhaps quite a few passages, that we think of as distinctly "Blakean." The Romantic privileging of the "moment," *das Augenblick*, the auroral glimpse or grasp of higher truth, sits uneasily with "industry" in these lines from *Milton*:

> There is a Moment in each Day that Satan cannot find
> Nor can his Watch Fiends find it, but the Industrious find
> This Moment & it multiply. & when it once is found
> It renovates every Moment of the Day if rightly placed[.]
>
> (M 35.42-45)

We say an idea comes to us, or dawns on us, but this Moment has to be sought for diligently, in the face of Satan, and rightly placed before it will multiply into a day's good work. The "once" in "when it once is found" is a case in point; rightly placed, this "once" resounds oddly but in multiple tones. This is the Moment when "the Poets Work is Done: and all the Great / Events of Time start forth & are concievd in such a Period / Within a Moment" (M 29.1-3). The poet's work here seems midway between mysterious inspiration and workaday perspiration.

We find, or there come to us, similar compromises in the

invocations, as we would expect. *Milton* begins conventionally enough with "Daughters of Beulah! Muses who inspire the Poets Song," but then they are offered an oddly anatomical pathway: "Come into my hand / By your mild power; descending down the Nerves of my right arm / From out the Portals of my Brain." Wordsworth chooses the main region of his song, according to the Preface to *The Recluse*, as "the Mind of Man" or "the intellect of Man"; the *brain* of man would never do. Of course, Blake everywhere corporealizes spirit and spiritualizes bodies, but he brings it in here, I think, as a playful shock. This is humanism with a vengeance. In the preface to *Jerusalem*, finally, Blake gives away the inspiration conceit, or the idea that we are vessels who "can do nothing of ourselves," with an apparently unwitting contradiction: "When this Verse was first dictated to me I consider'd a Monotonous Cadence like that used by Milton & Shakespeare . . ." Considered? While taking dictation? And what sort of "Verse" is this which does not specify its own "Cadence"? Such a passage suggests a conflict, which if better resolved might have produced a clearer parody, between the desire to join the elite who breathe the air of Olympus and the resentful urge to expose them all as pretentious windbags.

Though he may tease some of its conventions, Blake is one of the fountainheads of the Romantic valorizing of art, and what Raymond Williams has said of that privileging gives the best bearings for its social meaning and for the useful correction Blake, when rightly placed, can provide it. "The positive consequence of the idea of art as a superior reality was that it offered an immediate basis for an important criticism of industrialism. The negative consequence was that it tended, as both the situation and the opposition hardened, to isolate art, to specialize the imaginative faculty to this one kind of activity."[74] Something like an ideology of art arose to counter the ideology, and the fact, of the commodification of labor and its products. Around "art" gathered nearly everything that faced extinction: organicism (a social metaphor long before it became an aesthetic one), intuition, harmony of human faculties, joy and creativity in labor, and so on. "Art" cannot bear this burden, of course, and by the end of the century its

defense had grown steadily more extreme, shrill, and inef-
fectual. The reception of Blake by the Pre-Raphaelites, Swin-
burne, and Yeats shows clearly enough the burden put on
Blake himself to symbolize the ulterior realm of beauty, har-
mony, and truth. The aggrandizement and hypostasis of art preserves, how-
ever, a radical moment, as the career of William Morris from
Keats to Marx, or of Georg Lukács from Novalis to Lenin,
should remind us. "Art" can be unpacked and its revolution-
ary content revealed by, among other means, reading back
from it the conflicts that gave rise to it, hedged it in, and froze
it. The usefulness of Blake in this regard is that, even while
erecting cities of art as refuges of his frustrated hopes for the
world, he had such a generous idea of what should go into
those cities and how they should be built that the world never
seems very far away. No hushed tones, dim lights, and incense
in his imaginative Eden, no trembling of veils. Art is no hier-
ophany for the redeemed elect. Blake invites us all in, right
off the street, sets us to "wars and hunting" and noisy debates.
And he does not mind, good artisan that he is, if we lift up
a few curtains and criticize the joinery; he leaves the lights
on; he wants us all to become artist-artisans ourselves.

Something of this message comes across in the very form
of Blake's works. Products of as much direct control by one
person as technology and mortal energies permit, they are
models of the "revealed" society, a society whose social rela-
tions and material productions are lucid and accessible to
every member of it. Complex it may be, but mysterious it is
not, or must not be, lest tutelage and tyranny find veils to
hide behind. Wagner's term *Gesamtkunstwerk* is suggestive
here, if we prise it from his own mystifying notions of the
genius: society is a total work of art, a gathering of arts by a
gathering of artists, an "assembly" in every sense. As Blake
the craftsman can make every aspect of his illuminated po-
etry—starting with copperplate (and I suppose he would have
made that, too, if he had had the time and equipment) and
ending by arranging his colored designs and texts, very often,
in an order unique to each copy—so he imagines a collective

man to unite in his person all of "nature" and culture, including technology, down to the minute particular.

It is easy enough to see the potential mystification in this idea as well, for the collective man who knows and orders everything can be displaced into Providence (labor in your calling and God will provide), an Invisible Hand bringing social benefits out of private pursuits, or a Central Committee that plans and engineers our labors for our own good. Blake himself sometimes lapses into appeals to Providence and Divine Limits, but they are not the essence of his thinking; they are "theological" residues that will yield to radical "anthropologizing" in Feuerbach's sense, though I am not sure exactly how. What a lifelong concentration on producing things in many phases and dimensions has told Blake is that man has made everything and that nothing is "given"; even "nature," as an external datum, is an illusory space betokening only the failure to express human culture.

We often think otherwise, because the natural and social world seems otherwise, but it seems otherwise, it seems "other," because we forget. "All reification is a forgetting," Adorno has said, and it is indeed to modern social theorists, recombining Marx's theory of alienated labor with insights modern art gives into reified or spectacular culture, that Blake's myth of total making most usefully points. Sartre's term "practico-inert," in its honest ungainliness, may improve our vocabulary for the process by which social institutions like the state or corporations or political parties, even the language we speak, no less than buildings and subway systems, are congealed products of past labor whose inertia appears to be an eternal fact. To recover our initiative in the face of the glaciation of social life we need to recollect past attempts to understand it, and draw strength from a language of energy and ratio as well as praxis and practico-inert.

Several implications immediately suggest themselves. The thorough mastery of several interlocking skills is not too far from the idea, and the feeling, of freedom in the positive sense of self-mastery, whose sources in the tradition of Christian liberty I shall sketch in chapter five. The proverbial stubborn attachment of craftsmen to political freedom, understanding Jefferson's yeoman farmer to be among them, may have much to do with the experience of multifaceted work, as well as the social intercourse it often permits or even demands. The same experience, in its stress on clarity and precision, and on knowledge of material things as opposed to "spiritual" or legal doctrines, leads readily to the republican ideal of open discussion and full debate over principles, even to the constitution-making that appealed so much to the French. The "Enlightenment" in a full-blooded sense seems quite at home in the studios and workshops of those who need to know a great deal about things and people, and to discuss them with one another, in order to make a living. Freedom and fraternity, then, two of the master themes of Blake, are bound up in the idea of mastery itself, in the cooperation of many intellectual and manual skills.[75]

The charismatic figure of the craftsman is still a feature of the ideal American mindscape, almost as important as the rural village, and indeed usually a part of it. The do-it-yourself movement, the image of the tinkerer in his shed who invents an airplane (and gets rich) or of the scientist in the lab who cures cancer or defeats the Martians (and gets the girl), and now the new self-help therapies whose metaphors of "body-work" and "alignment of energies" smell of the garage—these we easily spot as mysteries in the negative sense, obfuscations of the real situation, hopelessly beyond such solutions. But they are also deposits of utopia, sublimations of repressed longings precisely for a sense of mastery in one's labor and lucidity and solidarity in one's social life. They are not always arbitrary or reactionary, however puerile the form (one thinks of Luke Skywalker's self-mastery, which lets him summon "the Force" to fight superior technology), any more than the new propaganda of the family expresses antifeminism alone. The figure of the craftsman is a sign of the degradation of labor in real life and one whose power to evoke desire ought to be recuperated by any movement for social reconstruction.

To return once again to Blake's historical moment, it may not be too farfetched to attribute something of Blake's peculiarly prophetic conservatism on the questions of art, labor, and freedom to the condition of the printing and engraving industry. Marshall McLuhan has reminded us that typography was the first mechanization of a handicraft.[76] In an interesting recent study Morris Eaves has shown how the atomization of writing necessary for movable type found a partial parallel in the "dot" and "lozenge" techniques of engraving; Blake, in refusing these newer methods of "blots and blurs" and insisting on the bounding line for his designs, repeats his gesture of refusing ordinary printing for his poems.[77] Despite some innovations in method, Blake was a technological conservative in his own craft. I would suggest that, being a part of the printing and design-reproducing trade, Blake could see a kind of model of the replaceability of parts and the Taylorization of labor that was under way in many crafts but not yet dominant in his lifetime. If the prevalent mode of production in his little sphere was prophetic of the structure of the whole economy, then his reaction against it prefigured later reactions, some of them quite "revolutionary" in thrust, against modern industrial capitalism. Blake's contemporaneity, or what some would call his timelessness, may be partly a resultant of two vectors or tempos, Blake's and his industry's. This is not so different from the double displacement we sense in Blake's kinship with radical sectarians of a century and a half earlier: Blake may speak an older "enthusiastic" language, but those who spoke it in 1650 were at least a century and a half ahead of their time. Some historians have argued that the republican experiment in England was premature; possibly the radicals of 1790, most of them "masterless" craftsmen like the Levellers and Ranters, felt that England has missed its moment in 1650 and must now follow the lead of America and France. If we superimpose these double temporalities, in any case, we begin to do justice to the complexity of Blake's position while gaining some purchase on his relevance to our own time.

A NOTE ON BLAKE'S DIFFICULTY

In Blake's second "Memorable Fancy" of *The Marriage of Heaven and Hell* (12-13), he is dining and conversing with Isaiah and Ezekiel.

I then asked Ezekiel. why he eat dung, & lay so long on his right
& his left side? he answerd. the desire of raising other men into
a perception of the infinite this the North American tribes practise.
& is he honest who resists his genius or conscience. only for the
sake of present ease or gratification?

In his answer to Blake's question, Ezekiel professes a goal so
absurdly out of proportion to its means that its very profession
is a revelatory shock, like the answer a Zen master might give
to a novice, whom Blake would call an "idiot Questioner," in
order to raise him into a perception of the infinite. In chapter
four of the Book of Ezekiel the Lord commands the prophet
to do these things as "a sign to the house of Israel." We do
not learn what happened after he did them; the sign was no
doubt sufficient, and no questions were asked. Blake asks,
however, and the surprise in Ezekiel's reply comes not only
from its sublime absurdity but from its rewriting of the biblical
source. In the original, Ezekiel is to enact an elaborate mimetic
charade with very specific applications to Israel (Israel is to
suffer as many years as the days Ezekiel lies, and so on), but
here Blake, who rejected such outright predictions by a
prophet ("He never says such a thing Shall happen let you
do what you will"), pretends not to grasp the evident meaning
of Ezekiel's play, only the most scandalous parts of which he
seems to remember, and draws from Ezekiel a radical Inner
Light Protestant reading of it. In other words, it is the original
meaning that is really absurd; it is comprehensible enough,
but contemptible. Ezekiel has learned something in the 2,300
years since he died (he knows about American Indians, for
example), just like Blake's Milton, "Unhappy tho in heav'n,"
who undergoes a conversion one hundred years after he died.
    In translating Ezekiel's silent doings into a a speaking pic-
ture, and condensing a text about them into the cryptic wit
of a Zen *koan*, Blake has not only taken Ezekiel's place himself
but invited us to take his own. Blake seems to concede that
his readers may feel like idiotic Israelites unable to see through
Ezekiel's feigned madness, so he kindly stands in for us and
has his personified text give the only answer it will ever give
to the question "Why are you so hard to understand?" To a

real questioner, a Reverend Dr. Trusler, Blake several years later wrote:

> . . . You say that I want somebody to Elucidate my Ideas. But you ought to know that What is Grand is necessarily obscure to Weak men. That which can be made Explicit to the Idiot is not worth my care. The wisest of the Ancients considered what is not too Explicit as the fittest for Instruction because it rouzes the faculties to act. I name Moses Solomon Esop Homer Plato[.]
>
> (23 August 1799; E 702)

Why is Blake so difficult? To rouse our faculties to act, to raise us into a perception of the infinite.

That is one answer, the argument from the side of rhetoric, the art of persuading and moving an audience. Ezekiel gives another, its twin from the side of expression, the manifesting of one's own persuasions and emotions, the sincere utterance of one's inner nature. In having Ezekiel say "genius or conscience" Blake has neatly linked the Romantic values of individualism and sincerity to the older Protestant value of obedience to the Holy Ghost within, itself a revival of the bold speech of the apostles before priest and judge, who in turn were reenacting the forthrightness of the prophets (Ezekiel's obliquity here being something of an exception). Blake frequently acknowledges the temptation to depart from the path of his individual artistic genius to wander after present ease and the gratifications of popularity and money. In the opening address "To the Public" in *Jerusalem*, Blake asks indulgence for his enthusiasm and "this energetic exertion of my talent." That talent, which is death to hide, Blake hid for most of his three years at Felpham doing work at his patron's behest that would be easy and gratifying to his public and profitable to him: that "three years Slumber" made him vow never to abandon for long the expression of his own unfettered genius. Blake's second implicit answer to complaints about obscurity, then, is the Holy Ghost: "I have written this Poem from immediate Dictation . . . without Premeditation & even against my will" (Letter to Butts, 25 April 1803; E 728-29). Complain somewhere else, he could say. Complain, in fact, to yourself, for you are endowed, if you would but rouse it to act, with the Holy Ghost, your imagination.

Adopting as he did the radical Christian heritage of inner-sense biblical interpretation, Blake also adopted a kind of inner-sense canon of privileged biblical books. These, whose literal meanings are already strained by their allegorical burdens, are also the most difficult: the visions of Ezekiel, Daniel, and Revelation; the image-laden Song of Solomon and the Psalms; the dark speculations of Ecclesiastes and Job; the parables of Jesus. Though any passage of the Bible might declare its presence in Blake's work, it is to these that he recurs most often for his central imagery and ideas. The Jesus with whom Blake in serious playfulness identifies himself creates difficult texts like his:

> The Vision of Christ that thou dost see
> Is my Visions Greatest Enemy
> Thine has a great hook nose like thine
> Mine has a snub nose like to mine
> Thine is the Friend of All Mankind
> Mine speaks in parables to the Blind
>   (E 524)

Though this Christ is doubtless a likable rough-and-ready sort of fellow, we may feel somewhat snubbed, even if we do not take ourselves to be the addressee, by the suggestion that we may be not only idiots but blind. We may recall the Parable of the Sower and the division between those who understand and those who do not, "that seeing they might not see, and hearing they might not understand" (Luke 8:12). It is put most harshly in Mark, who has Christ deliberately exclude some of his hearers, "lest at any time they should be converted, and their sins should be forgiven them" (4:12). (Matthew seems to put the burden on the hearers, who wilfully close their eyes.)[78] The parable suggests that Jesus was not, like Blake's Ezekiel, trying to induce a vision of the infinite or honestly following his genius, but was concealing his message for other reasons. John Linnell, who met Blake in 1818 and came to know him well during his last ten years, invoked a snubby Christ to account for him: "I never in all my conver-

sations with him could for a moment feel that there was the
least justice in calling him insane; he could always explain his
paradoxes satisfactorily when he pleased, but to many he
spoke so that 'hearing they might *not* hear.' "79

To invoke another of his precedents, one Blake cites in his
letter to Trusler, we can say that his works, like Christ's par-
ables, are Aesopian, and for the same reason—fear of per-
secution. Satan's watch-fiends, as Blake called them, the spies
and thought-police of an increasingly oppressive England at
war with France, must be thrown off the scent. If oppression,
as Jorge Luis Borges says, is the mother of metaphor,80 it
breeds Blake's "deep dissimulation" as "the only defence an
honest man has left" (J 49.23). "Deep dissimulation" is not a
bad definition of poetry, or of metaphor, and it even seems
to echo Sidney's phrase for poetry in his "Defence"—"honest
dissimulation."81 The paradox in Blake's line and Sidney's
phrase, however, takes us sadly far from Ezekiel's rhetorical
question, "is he honest who resists his genius or conscience
. . . ?" A few years before he wrote that line Blake had been
indicted for sedition, in particular for seditious words spoken
to a soldier who Blake later decided was expressly sent to spy
on him.82 But long before then there is evidence that Blake
was afraid of being misunderstood, or perhaps of being too
well understood, by the public. His one substantial bid for an
audience for his poetry, the relatively accessible *French Rev-
olution* (1791), was set up in type but then withdrawn, very
possibly by Blake himself.83 Booksellers were by then getting
into trouble for selling Tom Paine, but some continued to do
so, and works more obviously radical than Blake's readily
found publishers. Not only writings but radical activity flour-
ished for several more years, culminating in the great dem-
onstrations of the London Corresponding Society in 1795,
though there were also in sedition trials, new laws, and the
suspension of *habeas corpus*. Blake may have been tempera-
mentally timid in "real life," or given to exaggerated fears
bred in isolation from political activism (the episode with the
soldier must have seemed a farcical fulfillment of his worst
personal fears); in any case *The French Revolution* never ap-
peared.84 What did appear grew increasingly obscure in con-

tent and unconventional in format. Blake never again "published" his own writing, in the normal sense of that word. Proper publication and a genuine public had to wait over a century.

In *Jerusalem* Blake seems to portray his own situation in that of Los:

And Los shouted with ceaseless shoutings & his tears
    poured down
His immortal cheeks, rearing his hands to heaven for aid Divine!
But he spoke not to Albion: fearing lest Albion should turn
    his Back
Against the Divine Vision: & fall over the Precipice of
    Eternal Death.

(J 71.56-59)

These lines, and in a sense the whole of Blake's illuminated poetry, are themselves the "ceaseless shoutings" no one but God could hear. We think of medieval monks in their great silent labors "In the studious hours of deep midnight"[85] designing ornaments to the scriptures for the greater glory of God. Blake spoke not to Albion, and it is mainly because friends of his divine vision have with monkish devotion intervened after a century and more to publish him that he speaks again to us, "Children of the future Age, / Reading this indignant page" (E 29), as if we have opened a time capsule. It is interesting, however, that the fear he names here is not for his own safety but for Albion's, as if simply to see the divine vision would be too much for Albion and he would recoil like one who has burned himself and would never again come near it. Can this be what Blake means? There is at least a hint that to turn his back against the divine vision is a euphemism for the official suppression of visionaries like Blake for their seditious utterances. (When Los does speak to Albion earlier in the poem, at J 45.36-37, it is to plead for forgiveness of others.) But if we take it at face value, we see a prophet in a hopeless dilemma. What is an honest man to do? "Honest" means "loyal" as well as "forthright," and Blake's line about deep dissimulation may mean that loyalty to Albion, as distinguished from obedience to king or Parliament, requires

Aesopean language and *samizdat* circulation. It is something, no doubt, to keep the Divine Vision in time of trouble (J 44.15), but a prophet's virtue cannot thrive in a cloister and he must speak, or at least create speaking pictures like Ezekiel's little play.

The solution Blake adopts for his speaking pictures is a compromise. "Tell all the Truth but tell it slant" is Emily Dickinson's advice, and Los and his creator both follow it. After Albion collapses halfway through *Jerusalem* Los does not speak to him again, at least not directly; as he speaks to others or to himself we may imagine Albion overhearing him and stirring in his sleep, but it is finally only the voice of Albion's own emanation, perhaps his conscience, that rouses him and brings him to a recognition that Los is his friend (J 96.22). Blake chooses a language and a strategy of incremental revelations that seem designed to draw the reader in and shut him out simultaneously, or perhaps to winnow out the selfish and resisting side of each reader while gathering the imaginative part for the apocalypse. "The Truth must dazzle gradually / Or every man be blind."[86]

I have gone into the problem of Blake's difficulty as sympathetically as I can, but now we must step back a little and ask what bearing it has on the question of his ideology. Blake's contribution to ideology, or to the reception and emotional integration of ideological beliefs, was negligible in his own day. Supposing he had found readers who had taken the trouble of making sense of him, however, what would the "trouble" itself have signified? I would argue that the trouble is itself anti-ideological in intent and, at least partly, in effect. One of the chief functions of ideology is to smooth and bolster the narrow beds we are forced to lie in, or to conceal the disturbing existence of the Other (whether class, race, or sex) who inhabits the same house and demands recognition as an equal, and ideology must be easily absorbed, repeatable, and anchored in the familiar verities if it is to do so. To work hard at understanding anything having to do with society, morality, or religion is to prompt subversive thoughts. Blake's work multiplies the general tendency of literature, as Lionel Trilling has argued, toward purging and liberalizing the imagination.

You walk into Blake's workshop, pick up the only copy of a small book of copperplate script and designs watercolored by hand, and only half-understand the portentous-sounding first page: "Rintrah roars & shakes his fires in the burdend air." It is as if you are holding the unique sacred book of the primordial wisdom, older than the Bible, which has somehow found its way into an unlikely little studio in Lambeth. If you do not dismiss him as mad, if the respect you have been trained to hold for the Bible, ancient truth, and lowly beginnings of grand events keep you standing and turning the pages, the radicalization of your imagination is then under way. Or so Blake seems to have intended.

You would be struck, at least, with the "quaintness" of Blake's methods. "Quaintness" is one of the categories by which we dismiss older spheres of production while absorbing them into the present system of consumption; it gives commercial value, and Blake's originals sell today at prices greater than their producer's lifetime earnings. His methods in his own day were sufficiently "old-fashioned," and he persisted in his anticommercial folly with such tenacity, that the quaint and charming work in your hands might singe them a little with its "aura." "Aura" is Walter Benjamin's now well-known term for the phenomenon of uniqueness and unconsumable but communicative "distance" in an artifact, its network of connections to its maker, occasion, function, and site, its resistance to the system of capitalist reproduction, consumption, and commodification. The aura of an object seems to "return our gaze" and remind us of a time before the disenchantment of the world by market forces when nature was not alien to spirit, Blake's time of "happy Eternity" when "the Cloud the River & the Field / Talk with the husbandman & shepherd."[87]

Aura and difficulty are independent if mutually enhancing effects—Blake certainly does not seem much easier to read in aura-free mass-produced paperbacks set up in ordinary type and normalized punctuation—and it is difficulty that concerns us at the moment. The inevitable comparison is to the Modernist poets, and at first the assemblies of fragments T. S. Eliot and Ezra Pound shored against the ruin of European culture seem much in the spirit of Blake's desire to rescue every minute particular from oblivion. The labor that readers must perform to understand "The Wasteland" or the *Cantos* is part of their education or *paideuma* in that lost culture. The elitist implication of such an initiation has been clear since these works appeared, but it is not much different formally from the division Blake seemed content to make among his readers, between idiots and those who rouse their faculties to act, or the division Jesus brought between sheep and goats through his parabolic preaching. The esoteric allusions and quotations in foreign languages, the footnotes, the austere elegiac tones of Eliot and Pound seem designed to read us out more than to sign us up, however, and the lost mythical world evoked in the fragments, precapitalist though it may have been, is an ascetic and hierarchical order very far from the radical brotherhood Blake envisaged. "The Waste Land" and the *Cantos* reproduce the fragmentation they bemoan, moreover, and in their self-referential gestures we may detect a note of self-congratulation: this is Culture, we have got it, show the proper humility before its mysteries. Blake commits no such "fallacy of imitative form," as Yvor Winters dubbed it, whatever barriers he may have erected; if anything they arise from the urge to say and show too much too soon, without preparation, as if he knew he would have you only once by the buttonhole and dared not hold back anything essential for your salvation. Here it is, you have it now, go figure it out and then come back and argue with me.

3

Brotherhood

Two metaphors govern nearly all of Blake's formulations of social life: brotherhood and membership. Membership in a body is one of the most ancient images by which individuals have tried to grasp a sense of belonging to a group, and in various forms it is a central analogy in classical, Christian, and modern political thought. Brotherhood is probably an equally ancient notion—certainly brotherhoods are found in many traditional societies—but while the language of fraternity persists into our day, the idea has attracted only occasional scrutiny by Christian thinkers and virtually none by secular theorists. Of the great trinity of liberty, equality, and fraternity there is a vast theoretical literature on the first two, written both before and since the French Revolution, and an even vaster secondary literature, but before fraternity serious discussion nearly halts.

This is not to say that eighteenth-century French theorists, for example, never mentioned fraternity, but they did not treat it as an independent principle with the weight of the other two: it was an adjunct to equality, a variant of the classical notion of sociability, or a vaguely edifying appeal to Christian ethics. Milton's Michael tells Adam of a period of "fair equality, fraternal state," but this state is still "under paternal rule" (PL 12.26, 24): nowhere does Milton lay much stress on fraternity, or even equality. Blake's great enemy Locke discusses the relations between brothers in the first of his *Two Treatises*, but as his object is to refute Sir Robert Filmer's patriarchal doctrines (and implicitly Milton's) he stresses the equality and mutual independence of brothers, not, as Blake does, their bonds, or "fibres." The idea of brotherhood was doubtless embarrassing to the individualistic liberalism that began to dominate political and ethical discourse from at least Locke's day. This neglect of brotherhood, whatever the reasons for it, is frustrating to a reader of Blake who senses the importance and profundity of his treatment of the idea but who would like to take a few bearings from its earlier history before plunging in. I hope I will be forgiven a few amateurish formulations of my own.[1]

For his part, Blake was deeply interested in liberty and fraternity but had almost nothing to say, as we have noted, about equality. There is plenty of evidence that he wished to see a world of equals as strongly as he did a world of free brothers, but most of his cases of inequality (slavery, colonialism, the subjection of women, the Calvinist division of elect from reprobate) he treated as forms of some other evil. Blake's anti-Calvinist universalism, for example, has an egalitarian thrust, but he considered it mainly, as we shall see, in terms of love and brotherhood and their opposites. Perhaps equality bore connotations offensive to his love of the uniqueness, the minute particularity, of each individual. "[S]ince the French Revolution Englishmen are all Intermeasurable One by Another," he wrote to a friend, "Certainly a happy state of Agreement to which I for One do not Agree" (E 783).[2]

Liberty, of course, is Blake's great theme, and we shall devote chapter five to it. In language and imagery inspired by the revolutions of his time as well as by the older tradition of Christian liberty, he celebrates freedom in all its forms, from the rising of Orc to the descent of Jerusalem. It may help us to see the central importance of brotherhood, on the other hand, if we consider it as a correlate or "contrary" of liberty that keeps liberty from veering off into individualistic megalomania and even tyranny or into atomistic withdrawal and solipsism. Liberty and fraternity are not independent principles with competing claims, as liberty and equality are often held to be; they are aspects or implications of each other, sometimes virtual equivalents. Without the other, Blake insists, neither can exist.

Depending on their formulations, the metaphors of brotherhood and membership may cohere or conflict. The idea of fraternity generally tends toward equality, for if we are all sons of the same Father then we are alike in dignity (or abjectness), though some thinkers, following St. Paul (Rom. 8:29), distinguish between elder and younger brothers. The thrust of the metaphor of membership in a "body politic" or *corpus mysticum* may be toward equality or hierarchy. If the structure of the "body" is left vague and the emphasis falls on universal membership in it, then the thrust is similar to that of brotherhood. Coleridge wrote in "Religious Musings":

> 'Tis the sublime of man,
> Our noontide Majesty, to know ourselves
> Parts and proportions of one wondrous whole!
> This fraternises man . . .   (ll.126-29)

If, however, the hierarchical structure of an organism is taken seriously, the metaphor will support a hierarchical view of society. The prototype of this use is Plato's correlation of the tripartite soul with the three classes of the city-state. Another memorable example, one that shows more clearly an ideological function of the metaphor, is found in Menenius' speech to the mob in Shakespeare's *Coriolanus* (drawn from Plutarch) where, oddly, the Senate is likened to the belly. Christian theorists declared the Church to be *unum corpus*, with Christ as its head and the Church officers as its various organs.[3]

Blake likes to ramify metaphors. With his usual thoroughness he associates each of the four Zoas with both a facial and a bodily organ: Luvah, for example, is both the nostrils and the loins, or "reins," of the universal man Albion. Yet Blake declares the Zoas to be brothers, and they are presumably equal; indeed, the attempt by one of them to usurp power over the rest is the usual beginning of Blake's several accounts of the Fall. He avoids, in other words, the consequences of his own organic metaphors even as he elaborates them and passes easily, like Coleridge, from one analogy to the other. He wants not only to maintain the implicit egalitarianism of brotherhood but also to combine the notion of inseparability or mutual dependence with that of love, which neither analogy alone will allow him to do.

The prime source of Blake's ideas about brotherhood, as about so much else, is the New Testament. The early Christian community was really a fraternity with an uneasy relationship to its environing community and even to its own women and children. "Brethren" was the prevalent term of address and brotherly love (*philadelphia*) one of the first obligations. One must not only love the brethren but love the brotherhood itself (1 Peter 1:22, 2:17).

The basis of Christian brotherhood seems to be twofold. First and most obviously we are sons of God the Father. Paul told the Roman Christians, "Ye have received the Spirit of adoption, whereby we cry, Abba, Father" (Rom. 8:15).[4] Christ enjoined us to "call no man your father upon the earth: for one is your Father, which is in heaven" (Matt. 23:9). Christians, according to Paul, are "of the household of God," and the head of the household, it goes without saying, is the Father (Eph. 2:19). The prayer endorsed by Christ for regular use begins, "Our Father which art in heaven." Yet, although W. C. McWilliams can reasonably claim fraternity is unintelligible without the idea of a divine Father,[5] Blake does not take this ground. It is crucial to a grasp of Blake's essential thought, and not only of his idea of brotherhood, to understand that the notion of a transcendent father or creator seemed to Blake to be a profound error. From his earliest tracts through his last works he constantly repeats that God is "the Infinite in all things," that "All deities reside in the human breast," that God, as Jesus, is the same as Man (E 3, 38).

Several times Blake explicitly connects the idea of brotherhood with the immanence of God. In an annotation on Lavater's *Aphorisms* he writes:

> It is the God in *all* that is our companion & friend, for our God himself says, you are my brother my sister & my mother; & St. John. Whoso dwelleth in love dwelleth in God & God in him. . . . for our Lord is the word of God & every thing on earth is the word of God & in its essence is God[.]
>
> (E 599)

Blake is a Holy Ghost Christian, an "enthusiast," like Gerrard Winstanley; the only person of the Trinity that he cares much about is the third person, the spirit of Christ we bear in us, which he calls the Imagination. Ideas or metaphors associated with the Father or Son Blake appropriates for the Holy Spirit, with little regard for consistency. We should note, too, that even in orthodox doctrine the Holy Spirit is the basis of the Church, or brotherhood of believers. At the opening of *Jerusalem* Jesus speaks as the Holy Spirit to the declining Albion: "I am not a God afar off, I am a brother and a friend; / Within your bosoms I reside, and you reside in me" (4.18-19).

The other ground of brotherhood in the New Testament, as the *Jerusalem* passage manifests, is the one Blake prefers: the idea that we are "brethren in Christ" (Col. 1:2). This formula opens easily into the membership metaphor, and indeed one line later Blake has Jesus say, "Ye are my members O ye sleepers of Beulah." We should add that, while Blake rejects the orthodox transcendent father, his immanent brotherly Christ sometimes plays a paternal part: he "Gatherd Jerusalems Children in his arms & bore them like / A Shepherd in the night of Albion which overspread all the Earth" (J 60.8-9).

The unfallen state of Eden, of fully awakened Imagination, Blake also calls "the Universal Brotherhood of Eden / The Universal Man" (FZ 3.5-6). In that state our "Souls mingle & join thro all the Fibres of Brotherhood" in a joyous unity (J 88.14), "Cominglings," doubtless, "from the Head even to the Feet" (J 69.43). As the universal man begins his collapse at the opening of *Jerusalem*, he forgets he is a brother and grows deaf to the appeal of his brother and friend Jesus: "Thy brethren call thee, and thy fathers, and thy sons, / Thy nurses and thy mothers, thy sisters and thy daughters / Weep at thy souls disease" (J 4.18, 11-13). Albion, "Rending the fibres of Brotherhood," shrinks in pain and sinks into stony sleep (J 44.18).

People who live in the society symbolized by the fallen Albion are not only driven by fear and hatred of each other, as we would expect, but in no meaningful sense, Blake says, can we even say they are alive: "Rent from Eternal Brotherhood we die & are no more" (FZ 41.9). We may take this to mean that without brotherhood we leave the realm of tenfold life and enter Ulro or spiritual death, the basic poles of Blake's spiritual topography as they are, under various names, of the New Testament's. In fact, John 3:14-15 makes the same point:

> We know that we have passed from death unto life, because we love the brethren. He that loveth not his brother abideth in death.

Whoso hateth his brother is a murderer: and ye know that no murderer hath eternal life abiding in him.

Blake takes this idea further; he seems to say that man is in essence a brotherly being, and when he is alone, alive in some minimal sense though spiritually dead, he is not really an individual at all, not really a human. As one of the Eternals proclaims at the apocalyptic conclusion of *The Four Zoas*:

> we know
> That Man subsists by Brotherhood & Universal Love
> We fall on one anothers necks more closely we embrace
> Not for ourselves but for the Eternal family we live
> Man liveth not by Self alone but in his brothers face[.][6]

In a comparable speech to the reviving Albion at the end of *Jerusalem*, Jesus says, "This is Friendship & Brotherhood without it Man Is Not" (J 96.16). Blake's idea of the truly human is far from the noble savage or proud aristocrat who achieves his full potential only by isolating himself from the common herd. On the contrary, only by removing everything that separates him from his fellows can the Blakean man truly become an individual.

Blake's implicit definition of man as a brotherly being is an extreme Christian form of the classical view of man as naturally sociable. He would agree with Aristotle's definition of man as a *zōon politikon*, a social, or political, animal, and with Marx's extension of it: "man is . . . not only a *zōon politikon*, but an animal that can become an individual only in society."[7] "Freed" from society, man becomes not an integrated personality but a fragment, an atom, and the society, which in fact he cannot escape, becomes an aggregate of isolated units, united only in their similarity to each other. "The fully developed individual," Max Horkheimer writes, "is the consummation of a fully developed society. The emancipation of the individual is not an emancipation from society, but the deliverance of society from atomization."[8]

Two expressions appear beside "brotherhood" in the passages from Blake we have just quoted, "universal love" and "friendship," and it would be well to consider in what ways these terms are synonymous and where they diverge. Like "brotherhood," both "love" and "friendship" stand at times for the essential human quality, as in the New Testament they often refer to the highest Christian virtue. They appear together in Christ's speech to his disciples: "Greater love hath no man than this, that a man lay down his life for his friends" (John 15:13). In Blake, "brotherhood" remains the preferred or privileged term to which the others are assimilated. "Love" by itself will not do, for it is also Blake's normal term for eros, for the passional, sexual love between man and woman, which he identifies with the Zoa Luvah and which in its fallen form, as we shall see in the next chapter, he associates with woman's jealousy and external nature.[9] "Universal" more or less cancels these associations and reminds us that we must be "a Friend to the Human Race" (J 52)—though even this injunction Blake finds insufficient in "The Everlasting Gospel" (E 524)—but the resulting term ("universal love") is weaker, vaguer, and without certain connotations Blake finds in "brotherhood."

"Friendship" comes closer. It seems so often to be a free variant of "brotherhood," and Blake uses it in so many crucial formulations of his thought that in the rest of this chapter I will treat passages in which it occurs as equal in authority to those explicitly about brotherhood. It might seem, in fact, the better choice. In its literal sense "brother" is a limiting term: we can be brother to very few, and those few we cannot choose freely, whereas we elect our friends and may have as many as we wish.[10] For Aristotle, "friendship" (*philia*) includes brotherly and other familial relationships, such as parental love; it is the most general term for associations of all sorts (*Ethics* 8.6). Blake may have sensed the classical provenience of "friendship" and rejected it as he did nearly everything else from Plato, Aristotle, and Cicero, its most notable theorists. He scorns "The Friendship of these Roman Villains" praised by Bacon in his essay "Of Friendship" (E 628). As the term is also a Christian and inescapably everyday word, it probably bore no classical taint, but it is important to see how Blake very unclassically promotes the most narrow kinship term to the most universal range, very unreasonably demands we be brothers to everyone, and yet does not allow the connotations that distinguish "brother" from "friend" to dissipate. For whether we will or not, he insists, we are all brothers, and the only choice we have is whether to be true brother or false, to bind or rend the fraternal fibers. All hatred and warfare are fratricidal and suicidal; brotherly behavior is the only truly human behavior. We are all born, or reborn, into the eternal family; outside it we do not exist.

Whatever Blake thought of him, we can find in Aristotle's notion of citizenship (*politeia*) an analogue to Blake's idea, though Blake makes little explicit use of it. The obligations to the city or *polis* transcend, even though they are built upon, connections of kinship, religious gatherings, and communal pastimes. These connections are the stuff of friendship, but the political bond is higher than blood connections (family, phratry, tribe) or voluntary social groupings (see *Politics* 3.9). The city of which Blake would have us be citizens is "the spiritual Four-fold London eternal" (M 6.1), or Jerusalem, but we are no less innately *zōa politika* of that city than are Aristotle's citizens of Athens. In the King James Bible "citizenship" is once translated as "freedom" (Acts 22:28); when we act in true citizenly fashion we are given the freedom of the city, "and Jerusalem is called Liberty among the children of Albion" (J 54.5).[11]

A fourth term, "companion," usually appears in the company of "friend." Its etymology, "one who breaks bread with another," is rich in meanings Blake would have liked, but he does not exploit them.

Proper brotherly behavior, according to Scripture, includes hospitality and "ministering to the saints" in their need (Rom. 12:13, 15:25). Blake stresses two distinctly fraternal acts, one of which is perhaps derived from the Christian "ministry." If we are genuinely concerned for our brother's soul, we will honestly confront its unique individuality, its "Staminal Virtue" (E 601), and wrestle with it in love; "Opposition is true Friendship" (MHH 20). What too often passes for brotherhood, however, is mere benevolence or kindliness, well-meaning but blind to its object, the result being meddlesomeness or "officious brotherhood" (M 7.42). Blake was infuriated by this quality in his Felpham patron, William Hayley. Hayley must have seemed one of the "false brethren" of Galatians 2:4, "who

came in privily to spy out our liberty which we have in Christ
Jesus, that they might bring us into bondage." Blake calls him
Satan:

> . . . You know Satans mildness and his self-imposition,
> Seeming a brother, being a tyrant, even thinking himself a
>   brother
> While he is murdering the just; prophetic I behold
> His future course thro' darkness and despair to eternal death
> But we must not be tyrants also! he hath assum'd my place
> For one whole day, under pretence of pity and love to me[.]
>   (M 7.21-26)

Later Blake grants that the pity may have been genuine
enough, but by itself even heartfelt pity can only interfere,
weaken, and divide. It can lead to the hypocritical repression
of anger, fatal to friendship if not to the friend himself, that
Blake recounts in "A Poison Tree." Far better had Hayley lost
his temper and told Blake forthrightly what he thought of his
work, but "Satan not having the Science of Wrath, but only
of Pity," broke the fraternal bonds and brought about a ter-
rible separation (M 9.46, 49). "Half Friendship," says Los, "is
the bitterest Enmity" (J 1.8).

The true ministry of brothers is very different. It requires
the progressive strife of contraries from which truth will
emerge, the active challenge and response of companions
truly careful of each other's souls. "For the Soldier who fights
for Truth, calls his enemy his brother: / They fight & contend
for life, & not for eternal death!" (J 38.41-42). "Do be my
Enemy," Blake tells Hayley in his notebook, "for Friendships
sake" (E 506). In his "Public Address" Blake wonders whether
there is such a thing as "Generous Contention," for he has
not found it among his rival artists (E 577). Wherever one
finds it, it will not cease when all men awaken and recreate
Eternity. However peaceful the image of friends "meeting in
brotherhood around the table" may seem to us (J 18.15),
Blake does not think of them as just singing hymns or pouring
each other milk and honey. They are having a debate. Blake's
Eternity continues on a higher level the activity that is the

means to it; it is a permanent revolution. There the Imagination forms "the golden armour of science / For intellectual War" (FZ 139.8-9), for "Wars of mutual Benevolence" and "Wars of Love" (J 97.14). Eternal vigilance is the price of Christian liberty.[12]

To avoid the "self-imposition" of false fraternity we must carry out what Blake considers the most fundamental fraternal act, the annihilation of our Selfhood. That seems like death to us, but in Blake's terms we will lose our Self only to gain our soul and eternal life. The great exemplar of self-annihilation, of course, is Jesus, who voluntarily sacrificed himself for our salvation. We must each imitate Jesus or, better, activate the Jesus within us, as we willingly sacrifice our self for another. The Jesus within us, in other words, is the power to die and be reborn. The reciprocation of such acts generates brotherhood. To the awakening Albion Jesus says:

> . . . Fear not Albion unless I die thou canst not live
> But if I die I shall arise again & thou with me
> This is Friendship & Brotherhood without it Man is Not
>
> . . . .
> . . . Wouldest thou love one who never died
> For thee or ever die for one who had not died for thee
> And if God dieth not for Man & giveth not himself
> Eternally for Man Man could not exist! for Man is Love:
> As God is Love: every kindness to another is a little Death
> In the Divine Image nor can Man exist but by Brotherhood[.]
>
> (J 96.14-16, 23-28)

Rather than sacrifice our Selfhood, which is really only a crust of defensive reactions and myopic perceptions but which seems essential to our life and identity, we usually prefer to sacrifice someone else. Such sacrifice is what Blake calls "atonement." When Albion falls he passes "From willing sacrifice of self, to sacrifice of (miscall'd) Enemies / For Atonement" (J 28.20-21). The response of the miscalled enemies is not, as we might have hoped, to sacrifice themselves for Albion, wrongheaded though he is, but to flee to the mountains "to seek ransom," that is, to find someone else to atone for them. So the chain reaction goes on, and the "Divine Humanity and Mercy" of generous self-sacrifice are forgotten (J 28.25-26).

Blake's hatred of atonement rests in part on his critique of orthodox religion, with its transcendent external deity and its historical literalness. Blake admits of no salvation from outside, no imputation of grace (or sin, for that matter) from a unique historical deed; Jesus and Adam are states of our own soul, and there is no "outside" from which salvation might come. He associates atonement, too, with Calvinism and its detestable division of mankind into two immutable classes, the elect and the reprobate. In *Milton* he takes up this terminology and redefines it with mordant irony. The elect, he claims, "cannot be Redeemed, but Created continually / By Offering & Atonement in the cruelties of Moral Law" (M 5.11-12). This means, I think, not only that the so-called elect, contrary to their own confident expectations, cannot be saved by an atonement or involuntary sacrifice of another,[13] but that they are *created* by such an atonement. That is, they create themselves (their Selves) by their belief in the atonement; such a cruel doctrine can be the product only of a fallen and cruel mind. To the elect the atonement seems external and designed solely for themselves, but such an illusion is just the measure of their fallenness. "As the Eye—Such the Object" (E 645).

It is not a coincidence that election and man's utter abjectness before God (who alone can genuinely act) are cardinal tenets of Calvinism, and that the Calvinist God is inscrutable. "If we ask," Calvin wrote, "why God takes pity on some, and why he lets go of the others and leaves them, there is no other answer but that it pleased him to do so."[14] The three ideas cohere, and all three Blake vehemently attacks.

The arbitrary election of a few "before the foundation of the world," as Ephesians 1:4 and the Westminster Confession have it, seemed perverse and unchristian to many religious thinkers from Calvin's day to Blake's.[15] Milton was one of these, and in *Paradise Lost* he has God the Father explain that while "Some have I chosen of peculiar grace / Elect above the rest," none are strictly predestined to damnation, "for I will clear thir senses dark" and respond mercifully "To prayer, repentance, and obedience due" (3.183-93). Blake no doubt considered this an important step in the right direction, but his dislike of election had deeper reasons than that it is arbitrary and that all human action is unavailing. As I will argue in chapter eight, he shared the universalist belief that all humanity can and will be saved, and indeed that the salvation of none can occur without the salvation of all, a universal restoration. The affinity of even a liberal doctrine of the elect with the paternalist and elitist republicanism Milton espoused is easy to see, and it is equally evident that Blake is the spiritual heir of the sectarians to the left of Milton whose antinomianism and universalism suited their politics of radical democracy and even communism.

It is likely, at any rate, that Blake found the Miltonic God's insistence on "obedience due" to be a Urizenic residue in the great poet, and he must have disliked the same God's demand for a ransom for man's sins:

> He with his whole posterity must die,
> Die hee or Justice must; unless for him
> Some other able, and as willing, pay
> The rigid satisfaction, death for death.
>
> (PL 3.209-12)

This version of the Old Testament *lex talionis*, where "some other" renders satisfaction for our sins, is an expression of the fallen and alienated consciousness that the true Jesus, our inner divine light, annihilates.

Blake's seemingly unfair accusations against Swedenborg—that he is as much a predestinarian as Calvin, when in fact he pointedly rejected the doctrine—may lie in Blake's dismissal of an external agent of salvation (or damnation) and especially of an external creator who must have known as he created them that some of his creatures would go to hell. From Blake's point of view, the conservative reaction among the London Swedenborgians at the time he joined them, their protestations of loyalty, abhorrence of democracy and the French Revolution, and reverence for the Ten Commandments, would follow from their compromising on the predestination question.[16]

It might seem that the proper thing to do with the self-proclaimed elect is to condemn them, as they do all the rest of mankind. Blake certainly does not hesitate to denounce them; in fact, he names them Satan:

Satan is fall'n from his station & never can be redeem'd
But must be new Created continually moment by moment
And therefore the Class of Satan shall be calld the Elect[.]

(M 11.19-21)

It would be a mistake, however, to try to sacrifice them, for to fight with the enemy's weapons is to go over to the enemy's side and become a member of the elect oneself. The only way to deal with them, the only way to break the vicious cycle of injury and revenge, is voluntarily to sacrifice oneself for them. As *Milton* nears the apocalyptic harvest, Los, the creative and prophetic spirit, cries that "the Elect must be saved [from] fires of Eternal Death" (M 25.38; brackets are Erdman's). Blake seems to be advocating an act of mercy toward the elect, who in their own minds are indeed safe from Eternal Death or hell but who are completely in error as to where and what it is. What is in truth the consummation, where we join the wedding supper of the Lamb (M 25.59-61), the saintly elect call hell. Rather than condemn them to the real hell they now unknowingly inhabit, Blake wants us to forgive them and rescue them. They are not fit for the mental wars of Eternity, so they will be "formed into the Churches of Beulah" (M 25.39), the land of spiritual peace in the suburbs of the Heavenly City.

Toward the end of the poem the character Milton, who has voluntarily descended from a kind of static eternity or limbo where he has remained since his earthly death, confronts Satan and recognizes him as his own Spectre or Selfhood, which among other things is his own belief in election and atonement. He makes a speech that eloquently summarizes the differences between the Calvinist and Blakean versions of Christianity:

Satan! my Spectre! I know my power thee to annihilate
And be a greater in thy place, & be thy Tabernacle
A covering for thee to do thy will, till one greater comes
And smites me as I smote thee & becomes my covering.

Such are the Laws of thy false Heavns! but Laws of Eternity
Are not such: know thou: I come to Self Annihilation
Such are the Laws of Eternity that each shall mutually
Annihilate himself for others good, as I for thee[.]
                                    (M 38.29-36)

Blake does not explain very well the process by which self-annihilation saves another. One might think it is little different from sacrificing another for one's own benefit: both acts seem to entail intervention from outside. If you sacrifice another for your benefit, however, you have not annihilated his Selfhood—that he alone can do—and so you have not really got rid of an enemy. You have in fact given him an outpost in your own mind, for the fear and guilt that led you to crucify him remain, and they generate your own selfhood. To take the risk, on the other hand, of lowering your defenses and turning the other cheek will disarm your enemy and turn him into your brother. Perhaps not always. But only by such a risk can the cycle of injury and revenge be broken and the process of reciprocal forgiveness be started. The nonviolent resistance practiced by Gandhi and Martin Luther King required a refusal to retaliate in kind to violence from the authorities. Some of their people were hurt or killed (more would have been hurt or killed if they had taken up arms), but then that is what self-sacrifice demands. The authorities, for their part, wished the resistance would turn violent, so that they could then resume their ordinary defenses and solidify the moral support they were losing.

Blake, at any rate, is unequivocal in demanding that we follow Jesus' supreme act of mercy. Forgiveness of sins for Blake is a virtual equivalent to annihilation of Self, for the Self is the repository of memory, both in a moral sense, as the tablet of the law of revenge, and in an epistemological sense, as the accumulation of adventitious sensory impressions on the Lockean tabula. To forgive is to forget, to abrogate the moral law and to burn away the passive memory with an active inner flame. The experience of the falling away of the Selfhood is that of the lifting of the veil. On this side of the veil, we are solitary Selves; on that, we join our brothers around the table. We see, in Malraux's phrase, an "apocalypse of fraternity."[17]

His passionate hatred of oppression and tyranny sometimes leads Blake into accounts of human differences that seem to threaten the very possibility of human fraternity. Oothoon's long address to Urizen, who wants to recast everyone in his own image, begins with two remarkable lists of different kinds of persons:

> Does he who contemns poverty, and he who turns with
>   abhorrence
> From usury: feel the same passion or are they moved alike?
> How can the giver of gifts experience the delights of the
>   merchant?

and different species of animal:

> Does the whale worship at thy footsteps as the hungry dog?
> Or does he scent the moutain prey, because his nostrils wide
> Draw in the ocean? does his eye discern the flying cloud
> As the ravens eye?
>
> (VDA 5.10-12, 33-36)

If these people, playing different social roles, are as fundamentally distinct as different animal species, then what hope is there of healing the divisions of fallen mankind? Can one change a dog into a whale by forgiveness or by any other means? Oothoon's exuberant defense of unique individuality may have carried her too far. The man-beast analogy, after all, breaks down at another point, for Blake and Oothoon are passing judgment against usurers, merchants, and others but are not singling out dogs or ravens or whales as unworthy of their part in the animal kingdom.[18] Elsewhere in this poem, however, and in many other poems—it is indeed one of his main themes—Blake gives us accounts of the transformation of one species of human being into another, of one "world" into another. Generosity may grow into miserliness under the world's pressure; prudence changes a glowing virgin into a gray old maid. Under new pressures, with the help of imagination, forgiveness, and love, the fool may grow into a wise man and the virgin may "awaken her womb to enormous joys"

(VDA 7.3-4). Oothoon waits hopefully throughout the *Visions* for Theotormon to rouse himself and convert his world of resentment and jealousy into one of love and forgiveness. In so extreme a formulation of human difference and distance, then, Blake means to do justice to the real difficulties, but he does not relax his demand for forgiveness and self-sacrifice, even on behalf of Satan.

The New Testament makes clear that to join the Christian brotherhood requires breaking with one's community and kindred, abandoning familiar comforts and obligations for the new demands of the Christian way of life. One of the new demands, of course, is to refuse the obligation of blood-vengeance, the law of retaliation for injuries in one's natural clan. Membership in any fraternity, McWilliams argues, leads to conflicting loyalties with the larger society, in part because fraternities embrace goals they deem higher than those of ordinary life.[19] For the losses, the Christian is offered incomparable compensation, but the compensation is based on the fundamental split between this life and the next (wherever the next may be). "One thing thou lackest: go thy way, sell whatever thou hast, and give to the poor, and thou shalt have treasure in heaven." Leave house, brothers, sisters, and parents, and in the world to come receive eternal life (Mark 10:21, 29-30). "Follow me; and let the dead [of the ordinary life you have left] bury the dead" (Matt. 8:22).

The gap between this life and the next reflects the basic dualism between matter and spirit that governs this life as well. In entering the Christian brotherhood we leave behind the "world" and enter the realm of the spirit. The passage cited earlier that speaks of our heavenly Father also makes clear that we must have no father "on the earth" even as we dwell on it (Matt. 23:9). Our brotherly love is not an extension of our love for our blood brothers, for we are "taught of God to love one another," not of our earthly father (1 Thess. 4:9). We are also taught, especially by St. Paul, to abjure fleshly things. His epistles, filled with injunctions to avoid fornication and lust, have an almost gnostic strain of contempt for the natural world. We ourselves are split into two principles and must learn to overcome the lower one. "But the natural man receiveth not the things of the Spirit of God . . . because they are spiritually discerned. . . . But he that is spiritual judgeth all things. . . . There is a natural body, and there is a spiritual body" (1 Cor. 2:14-15, 15:14).

If he believed in it, Blake placed little stress on a literal afterlife, and everything he wrote about death and rebirth can be interpreted symbolically or phenomenologically. The compensations of the Christian life are abundant, but they are this-wordly: the joys of untrammeled love, imaginative creation, and great spiritual debates. Despite his rejection of the body-soul dichotomy in *The Marriage of Heaven and Hell*, however, he does use traditional dualistic language for some of his themes, and though he celebrates uninhibited sexuality he is consistently contemptuous of what he calls "nature." He shares, in other words, the general idea in the New Testament that the Christian fraternity is apart from the natural world. It is too simple a summary of Blake's complex views about nature, as we shall see in the next chapter, to say that he views it as the objectification and reification of inwardness, or as the illusion that there is an independent external world unaffected by our perceptions, but such formulas let us grasp Blake's consistent transformation of traditional terms to fit his radical Inner Light Christianity. Asceticism only widens the gap between our soul and the "outside." Love and exuberant sexuality close it by bringing "nature" back into us, as it were, and thus abolishing it as an external thing. Yet nature remains an attractive illusion, and once we allow our creativity to slacken and our products to appear self-sufficient, we tend to forget that we produced them and to set them up as fetishes. Nature appears as a continual threat to the spiritual brotherhood.

Blake expresses the essential break with the natural family in a remarkable passage of *Jerusalem* that seems to allude to Jesus' words about burying the dead:

> When those who disregard all Mortal Things, saw a Mighty-One
> Among the Flowers of Beulah still retain his awful strength
> They wonderd; checking their wild flames & Many gathering
> Together into an Assembly; they said, let us go down

And see these changes! Others said, If you do so prepare
For being driven from our fields, what have we to do with
      the Dead?
To be their inferiors or superiors we equally abhor;
Superior, none we know: inferior none: all equal share
Divine Benevolence & joy, for the Eternal Man
Walketh among us, calling us his Brothers and his Friends:
Forbidding us that Veil which Satan puts between Eve & Adam
By which the Princes of the Dead enslave their Votaries
Teaching them to form the Serpent of precious stones & gold
To sieze the Sons of Jerusalem & plant them in One Mans Loins
To make One Family of Contraries: that Joseph may be sold
Into Egypt: for Negation; a Veil the Saviour born & dying rends.

                                        (J 55.1-16)

Just who the Mighty-One is (probably Los) and what he is
doing in Beulah (building Golgonooza) are not important for
our purposes. What is central here is the distinction between
spiritual brotherhood and natural or generative brotherhood.
Spiritual brotherhood is a state where none are inferior or
superior and all equally share in benevolence and joy, a state
of unity founded on, and symbolized by, the Eternal Man who
walks among us, Jesus the Imagination or Albion the collective
man himself. Spritual brothers wear no veil of modesty or
deceit but reveal themselves to one another in innocence and
candor. Like Milton's angels, they find no obstacle of mem-
brane when they make love, mixing totally without restraint
(PL 8.624-29), in head-to-toe comminglings. Natural broth-
erhood, to which Blake never actually gives the name of broth-
erhood, is not so much the fact of blood kinship as the spiritual
error of so narrowing one's perceptions as to define one's
brothers as those who have passed through common loins.
That error arises through sexual pudency and shame, a state
of mind that according to Blake preceded the division of Eve
from Adam: "The Sexes sprung from Shame and Pride."[20]
The loins of Adam and Eve might seem common enough for
universal brotherhood, but here they are the prototypes of
sexual shame and division, those who first shrank their orig-
inal joy down to a veil (both figleaf and hymen) and a serpent
(one of whose meanings is the phallus). The world of brothers

also shrinks through the funnel of "One Mans Loins" with Noah and then again with Abraham; the Chosen People are the original self-proclaimed "superiors" or elect, and like Calvin's elect they treat everyone else as inferior and of no account. Even within the family crimes are committed, as Jacob's sons sell their brother Joseph into slavery. The "Divine Benevolence" of the spiritual brotherhood is the mutual ministry of "Contraries"; now made into "One Family" (I take "of" to mean "out of") the Contraries become Negations, the Sons of Jerusalem or liberty become sons of Jacob and slaves in Egypt, the land of nature and death. As a sacrificial victim who redeems the brothers who sacrificed him, Joseph is the type of Jesus, and the veil of sex and shame that began the long slide down to Egypt is also the hymeneal veil of Mary (still intact from *her* modesty) that Jesus rends at his birth as well as the veil of mystery and exclusion in the temple that Jesus rends at his death (Matt. 27:51). The serpent of precious stones and gold is connected later in *Jerusalem* (96.12) with Albion's Selfhood, which like a veil separates him from his brothers (as Joseph's coat separated him from *his* brothers) and wraps him up in his own fears and hatreds. When Albion recognizes the serpent for what it is, he has come much closer to waking up. It is then that Jesus offers to die for Albion in the lines we quoted earlier. His dying is our revelation, the rending of the veil of our natural Self.[21]

Wordsworth tells how he owed to nature the high thoughts and love of man that the loathsome sights of London threatened:

> 'Twas thy power
> That rais'd the first complacency in me,
> And noticeable kindliness of heart,
> Love human to the Creature in himself
> As he appear'd, a stranger in my path,
> Before my eyes a Brother of this world[.]

Blake could not have seen this passage, but if he had, it would have filled him with pity and disgust. The very title of Book 8 of the 1805 *Prelude*, from which this quotation is taken (ll.74-79), would have seemed a succinct formulation of a basic error: "Love of Nature Leading to Love of Mankind." Love of nature can lead to nothing of the sort. However unfairly, Blake would have found damning Wordsworth's admission that it was his appreciation of solitary shepherds, who seemed so like nature herself, and of other men "purified, / Remov'd, and at a distance that was fit" (ll.439-40), that led him to brotherly feelings. "I see in Wordsworth," Blake wrote, using terms drawn from the Corinthians verses quoted earlier, "the Natural Man rising up against the Spiritual Man Continually. . . . Imagination is the Divine Vision not of The World nor of Man as. he is a Natural Man but only as he is a Spiritual Man" (E 666).

When the fallen Albion, then, convinced that brotherhood is a deceit, denounces "unnatural consanguinities and friendships" (J 28.7), he is speaking more accurately than he knows. Natural attachments are the real threat. Personified as the beautiful Vala, nature arouses a "love of Nature" that displaces true "love of Mankind." She cheerfully admits to Albion that "the Divine appearance is Brotherhood, but I am Love / Elevate into the Region of Brotherhood," and he succumbs to her, even though he knows she has usurped his inner realm: "Why have thou elevate inward: O dweller of outward chambers[?]" (J 29.52-30.1; 30.10). When Albion rends the fibers of brotherhood he tries to distract Los with "Feminine Allegories" (J 94.18), but Los stands firm. Los has already lamented the dominion over man by woman—"To have power over Man from Cradle to corruptible Grave" (J 30.26)—but to pursue Blake's seeming antifeminism, here and elsewhere, we should turn once again to the New Testament.

St. Paul's misogyny goes beyond his asceticism, though he was doubtless at one with the customs of patriarchal Judaism and the Mediterranean gentile communities. The Christian fraternity is a fraternity in the literal sense: the only full participants are male. "Doubtless," Simone de Beauvoir ironically concedes, "there is in the Gospel a breath of charity that extends to women as to lepers; . . . women were to be treated with relative honor when they submitted themselves to the yoke of the church; they bore witness as martyrs side by side with men,"²² but according to Paul women were to be absolutely subordinate:

> Let the woman learn in silence with all subjection.
> But I suffer not a woman to teach, nor to usurp authority over the man, but to be in silence. (1 Tim. 2:11-12)

Paul even extends the membership analogy for the Church to relations within the family: "For the husband is the head of the wife, even as Christ is the head of the church" (Eph. 5:24). Similarly, "he is the image and glory of God: but the woman is the glory of the man" (2 Cor. 11:7).

Blake's fraternity does not seem to exclude women, at least if we can judge from passages like the one cited earlier in which Jesus appeals to Albion on behalf of "Thy nurses and thy mothers, thy sisters and thy daughters," as well as of his brethren (J 4.12). Among his more symbolic women, too, Blake created the courageous spirit of free love, Oothoon, as well as the sinister figures Vala and Rahab. It is also true that most of Blake's female figures are symbols of mental states or their projections that can be found in any mind, male or female. There are nonetheless passages hard to square with this stance, like those that bemoan the necessity to be born of women. Even though he changed their references, Blake was content to deploy the traditional symbols and analogies, which bore indelibly the stamp of the patriarchal society where they were established. We shall return to this conflict in the next chapter, after taking a closer look at "nature."

Though Blake could find most of his terms and ideas for brotherhood in the New Testament, he probably owed something to the small Protestant sects he knew in London. Some of them, such as the Quakers and Muggletonians, were descendents of the radical explosion of the 1650s; in many of these sects, "brother" and "sister" were regular terms of address. From the craft guilds and friendly societies, too, he may have drawn ideas and expressions, though he seems not to have been a member of any of them. It would be interesting to know how much the sects and guilds, including the Freemasons, nurtured the rhetoric of brotherhood in eighteenth-century England. Blake's chief inspirations, in any case, were the revolutions of America and France. In *America*, as Erdman points out, the equivalent of fraternity is the "rushing of th' inhabitants together" (14.12) from the separate colonies to repel the plagues sent by George III.[23] In *The French Revolution* the decisive event, which spells the end of the *ancien régime*, is the convening of the people:

> For the Commons convene in the Hall of the Nation; like spirits of fire in the beautiful
> Porches of the Sun, to plant beauty in the desart craving abyss, they gleam
> On the anxious city; all children new-born first behold them; tears are fled,
> And they nestle in earth-breathing bosoms. So the city of Paris, their wives and children,
> Look up to the morning Senate, and visions of sorrow leave pensive streets.   (54-58)

We have already discussed the example of the sans-culottes of 1793 and their militant fraternizing. In 1776, 1789, 1793, and perhaps again in 1800 (when peace with France seemed possible), Blake may have believed universal brotherhood to be imminent.[24] If he did, he did not despair, or despair long, when it failed to appear, but returned to his labor on its behalf. It may be naive ever to expect universal brotherhood, but it is not naive to expect smaller and briefer but still potent fraternities periodically to shatter the social customs that keep us alienated from each other. No one, to invoke only recent events, who joined SNCC in Mississippi, or the draft-resistance movement, or the early consciousness-raising sisterhoods, no one who took part in the spontaneous mass movements in Paris or Prague in 1968 or took part in Solidarnošč in Gdansk in 1980, will doubt the possibility of an apocalypse of fraternity. Of such a possibility, though expressed in terms not easily available to us today, Blake remains our chief poet and prophet.

4

Nature and the Female

It is sometimes argued that Blake was a "revolutionary naturalist" for a few years following the French Revolution in 1789,[1] the chief exhibit in this case being "The voice of the Devil" in *The Marriage of Heaven and Hell* (4). It is not nature that the Blakean devil endorses, however, but "Energy" and "the Body." The Body, furthermore, is "a portion of Soul" as perceived by our five senses. These five senses being "in this age" only the remnant of the "enlarged & numerous senses" of a former age (11), the Body is presumably a temporary but necessary illusion. When we regain all our perceptual powers the Body will either vanish or be subsumed as a bounding form or "outward circumference" of the Soul. If this is the right way to read the devil, then it is somewhat of a surprise to learn that Energy, which is "the only life," is nonetheless "from the Body," as if what is primary can be derived from what is secondary and even illusory. Perhaps this is a devilish overstatement that Blake does not fully endorse; it must be "married" to the angelic viewpoint for it to progress through contraries to the truth. Or perhaps in this age, though we see it wrongly as a Body, our circumference and the circumferences of others generate energy through mutual interpenetration, like brothers waging an intellectual war. There may be a hint of the necessary fall described in many ancient cosmologies, whereby Soul feels listless and incomplete until it dallies dangerously with its material shadow, gets lost in Body, finds its way home somehow, and feels the more energetic for having exercised itself in shadowboxing. There is more than a hint that Blake wanted to endorse uninhibited erotic love, and he may have stretched the diabolic principles to accommodate it.

The target of these assertions is less an antinatural asceticism than it is the sharp division of body and soul stated by St. Paul and deeply inscribed in western thought, the doctrine that there are "two real existing principles" that are independently created and mutually hostile. Blake and his devil are monists, and Soul is the primary power. To repress and deny the Body in the name of the Soul is an error because the Soul created the Body out of itself in the first place, both as the portion of Soul seen and the portion of Soul (the five senses) seeing. You cannot push the Body out of sight. The way to overcome it is to accept it, enjoy it, "take it up" energetically into your consciousness until it no longer seems a separate thing. Dualism is a state of mind. It seems true only when our mind is dual, our Soul divided against itself.[2]

If by distinguishing Body from nature in this way we can remove a supposed inconsistency in Blake's developing thought, it remains true that the tone of most of what Blake says about nature, throughout his career, is out of harmony with the devil's pronouncement. The language is sometimes sharply dualistic and the attitude toward nature and the "Vegetable Earth" is almost always hostile.

Babylon the City of Vala, the Goddess Virgin-Mother.
She is our Mother! Nature! (J 18.29-30)

the Deus
Of the Heathen, The God of This World, & the Goddess Nature
Mystery Babylon the Great, The Druid Dragon & hidden
Harlot . . . (J 93.23-25)

Nature is a Vision of the Science of the Elohim.
(M 29.65)

And the vast form of Nature like a serpent playd before them . . .
. . . .
And the vast form of Nature like a serpent rolld between . . .
(J 43.76, 80)

Even the occasional neutral uses of "nature," as in "human nature," release a negative meaning in certain contexts. One artful example is a line Blake writes twice: we live in "A World in which Man is by his Nature the Enemy of Man" (J 38.52; 49.69). We may wonder if this world is the "natural" world before the arts of civilization, in which case Blake is following Hobbes. Or perhaps this world is the artificial social world, which invokes a nastier state of nature to vindicate the nasty state of society, in which case Blake is following Rousseau, who criticizes Hobbes in just this way. This world, according to the *Jerusalem* context, is made by man, "accumulated" by the errant sons of Albion through pretense and hypocrisy, false religion and false patriotism, luring and cajoling youths into warfare with their French brothers. We are not "born" enemies, but we are born into a world in which it seems *second nature* to hate and fear other people. By something other than this nature, presumably, we are friends, but for Blake, as opposed to Rousseau, we find friendship when we are reborn in another "world" beyond our "natural" state. Blake dismisses "the Selfish Virtues of the Natural Heart" and praises the spiritual or "intellectual" intervention of forgiveness, an unnatural force. "Rousseau thought Men Good by Nature; he found them Evil & found no friend. Friendship cannot exist without Forgiveness of Sins continually" (J 52).

Though we may find ways to reconcile them with his more attractive ideas of brotherhood and imagination, Blake's extreme statements about nature remain confusing and troubling. He treats nature as a demonic force whose power must be broken and trampled under foot. It gets in the way of everything he honors: forgiveness, brotherhood, imagination, art. It fosters war, tyranny, and slavery, it perverts religion, it degrades art. It is a snare and a delusion. And it is female.

Even after showing the extent of his internal consistency it is not surprising that critics often feel the need to rescue Blake from himself. Though Blake is not a Romantic, they may say, he is almost a Romantic (which is why he is usually first in a college course on the Romantics), and we have learned in recent years to read Wordsworth himself as much more uneasy over the power of nature to obliterate his imagination than our older view of the "simple" Wordsworth had allowed. Blake has, besides, some lovely passages about nightingales and larks, wild thyme and meadow-sweet (plate 31 of *Milton* is usually cited), and he certainly liked lambs. What he despised was not nature but an abstract concept of nature found in Bacon and Locke, equally despised at times by Wordsworth and Coleridge. The rest is vivid personification. Things may go wrong sometimes because of the internal momentum of a complex and cumbersome mythology; vehicles may now and then run over their tenors. And it is unfortunate that Blake made nature female, another vehicle somewhat out of control, but he was not exactly a male-supremacist, just the child of his time making use of traditional symbolism.

I largely agree with this effort at rehabilitation, though it is difficult to present it succinctly without a little irony. It is too pat, too selective, and the Blake that results is too modern and sanitized to be quite the ornery eccentric we also know him to be.

My own attempt to explain Blake's more malodorous opinions relies in part on translating metaphysics into phenomenology, a method implicit in much recent criticism of the Romantics and found throughout Northrop Frye's, as when he remarks that "the material world is in a way feminine to the perceiver."[3] Blake himself demythologized orthodox Christian metaphysics and the secular empiricism that succeeded it, though there remain a few passages in his works recalcitrant to his own "infernal" method, and he seems, to judge by a few of his letters and reports of friends, to have held some Christian tenets in a literal, "angelic" sense. Frye's "in a way" leaves a few things out, however close his demythologizing and analogizing come (and it is the best we are likely to get) to a complete and unified inner elaboration of Blake.

It is superior, certainly, to the various reductions of Blake into better understood paradigms of anti-naturalism, such as gnosticism, Neoplatonism, cabalism, and the "perennial philosophy" according to Jung. Blake's contempt for "nature" being as scandalous as it is, to resort to these models for precedents or parallels is understandable. They do give some help. But even where they do, their own doctrines are often left unexplored and the reasons Blake was drawn to them or to ones like them are left unexplained. They are removed from history and their social or political edge goes unacknowledged. It has been shown, for example, that one source of gnostic ideas in Blake is the Hermetic work *Poimandres*, translated as *The Divine Pymander of Hermes Trismegistus* by John Everard. Kathleen Raine and others cite several plausible influences and an allusion or two. What I find interesting, granted its presence in Blake, is that John Everard, who lived until about 1650, was a radical Protestant troublemaker, frequently in jail for heresy (King James said his name should be "Never-out"), who preached to the lowest classes that God was immanent in man and nature, though preeminently in man, and that heaven and hell were in our hearts. The social implications of his teachings, not very different from Gerrard Winstanley's, were clear to the bishops, who continually prosecuted him. Today, it may be, gnosticism is a resort of those who claim to be beyond politics but who really fear change; Everard's *Pymander* is still to be found in occult bookstores. In 1650, and perhaps again in 1790, the thrust of gnostic speculation seems to have been subversive, radical, and democratic.[4]

For another example, consider Blake's notoriously negative use of stars. Here and there he draws from lore about specific stars, as with Arcturus and King Arthur in *A Descriptive Catalogue* (E 542), but stars as stars he presents as warlike, hierarchical, and tyrannical; they represent nature at its most distant and cold, the Inner Light externalized and reduced to the minimum, visible only in the night of our imaginative slumber. "Starry Jealousy" imprisons earth. Phrases like "starry wheels" and "starry mills" denote, in Hazard Adams's words, "the movement of a delusory scientific time and the concave, inner surface of the mundane egg, which is the fallen world."[5] Most metaphysically minded commentators ignore the political allegory here, but Blake makes it clear enough, and he has good biblical precedent for it in Isaiah and Revelation: "And all the host of heaven shall be dissolved, and the heavens shall be rolled together as a scroll: and all their host shall fall down, as the leaf falleth off from the vine, and as a falling fig from the fig tree" (Isa. 34:4). The young Coleridge turned to the same passages in his "Religious Musings" (1794) to refer to the French Revolution:

> The hour is nigh
> And lo! the Great, the Rich, the Mighty Men,
> The Kings and the Chief Captains of the World,
> With all that fixed on high like stars of Heaven
> Shot baleful influence, shall be cast to earth,
> Vile and down-trodden, as the untimely fruit
> Shook from the fig-tree by a sudden storm.[6]

But there is more to it than political allegory, something more literal and cosmic. Stars represent law and fate. Under the system of astrology perfected by the Babylonians all stars have "influences" on our lives, and all influences are baleful because they deny our freedom. The gnostics, according to Hans Jonas, understood this very well, and they despised astrology and Greek "sidereal piety" as a capitulation to the order of the world, which included the political order sanctified by the state gods. The authors of the Christian ur-gospels may have felt the same way; in making the star of Bethlehem a nova, they are maneuvering ideologically against the astrology of the Magi and perhaps Roman-Persian political hegemony.[7] The alternating rejection and accommodation of astrology within a Christian worldview is an index of how worldly and conservative the Church has been. A strict Christian might think there are too many stars in the *Divine Comedy*. Milton, who admired Galileo, expresses his uneasiness in his similes: twice in *Paradise Lost* Galileo's telescope is trained on the sun or the moon to make them similes for Satan and his shield, and once Raphael sees better than Galileo could. If paradise is within us and hell is within Satan, the point seems to be, we are looking in the wrong direction when we peer through a telescope.

In his writing on enthusiasm that we discussed in the second chapter, Locke argues that direct revelation from God cannot conflict with "natural revelation" or reason, and sums up: "So that he that takes away reason, to make way for revelation, puts out the light of both, and does much-what the same, as if he would persuade a man to put out his eye, the better to receive the remote light of an invisible star by a telescope" (*Essay* IV.19.4). Blake would have been struck with this telescope simile. To suggest that divine revelation is like "the remote light of an invisible star" is not only to reinforce the notion of the distant father-god Locke believes in but to denigrate the Inner Light and Christian liberty. There is nothing out there to see except the artifacts of our telescoped consciousness.

Then there is Isaac Newton, with his stars and "particles of light" and gravitational influences, all of which from Blake's point of view consolidate the error of star-worship and reverence for the changeless order of things. To consolidate error, of course, is to prepare it for discard, but that is another Blakean theme.

To come back to earth: the approach to Blake's "nature" I will take in this chapter rests on the phenomenological translation of Frye and others but brings out the social thrust more explicitly. I would suggest, in fact, that Blake's animus against "nature" arises in large part from his understanding of its ideological function: "nature" sanctifies the existing social order by placing it beyond human control. Although it is true that reformers and revolutionaries also appealed to natural law and natural rights against custom, charters, positive law, and arbitrary rights, Blake (no doubt unfairly) saw their appeal as ultimately submissive to an inhuman force. Thus "nature" is unreliable as a standpoint for a human social renovation.

I take it for granted that no cosmology or philosophy of nature, especially before the relatively more insulated and independent procedures of science in very recent times, is politically neutral or innocent; all cosmologies have at least covert social meanings. These are hard to miss in the now quaint notions of the Chain of Being, the "primates" of animal kingdoms, "noble" gases, and so on, but they are no less present in modern scientific theories such as Darwin's natural selection. The extension of "the struggle for existence" from the natural world to the human world (Social Darwinism) is made easy, as Marx and Engels argued, by the prior extension of the economic theories of the English bourgeoisie to the realm of plants and animals (natural Malthusianism).[8] Blake's own eye for ideological messages smuggled into supposedly "objective" science was as eager as Marx's or Engels's, if not always as discriminating, and indeed he goes beyond them into terrain defined by the Frankfurt School in his suspicion of science itself.

The fundamental maneuver in any ideology is the "naturalization" of something social. William Godwin observes in *Political Justice* (1793) that "persons of narrow views and observations regard everything as natural and right that happens, however capriciously or for however short a time, to prevail in the society in which they live."[9] Godwin generalizes a common and indispensable argument. So Rousseau:

> In reasoning on the principles he lays down, [Hobbes] ought to have said that the state of nature, being that in which the care for our own preservation is the least prejudicial to that of others, was consequently the best calculated to promote peace, and the most suitable for mankind. He does say the exact opposite, in consequence of having improperly admitted, as a part of savage man's care for self-preservation, the gratification of a multitude of passions which are the work of society, and have made laws necessary.[10]

"Nature," to a young radical like Blake, was the sign of an ideological ruse, the stitch-marks on the seamy side of the apparently seamless web of Church and state orthodoxy. Taken a few distinctly Blakean steps further, this critical suspicion grows into the notion that nature itself is a veil of illusion.

The ideological function of "nature" in silencing further inquiry into the way things really are Blake sees as the same function as that of the traditional mysteries of Babylon and the other ancient empires. The rationalist critics of traditional Christianity may cry "écrasez l'infâme!" but they only breed new religions, and worse ones, based on nature. This relation seemed so important to Blake that he made the recognition of it the climax of both *Milton* and *Jerusalem*. Ololon's penultimate speech acknowledges her role as Milton's and everyman's feminine portion in generating the new natural religions:

> Are those who contemn Religion & seek to annihilate it
> Become in their Femin[in]e portions the causes & promoters
> Of these Religions, how is this thing? this Newtonian Phantasm
> This Voltaire & Rousseau: this Hume & Gibbon & Bolingbroke
> This Natural Religion! this impossible absurdity[.]
>
> (M 40.9-13)

She no sooner speaks than Babylon appears as a consolidation or crystalization of mystery that need only be looked upon directly to be defeated. In *Jerusalem*, the last of Los's climactic speeches, part of which is quoted near the beginning of this chapter, serves as a similar crystalization and catalyst of the apocalyptic dawn:

> if Bacon, Newton, Locke,
> Deny a Conscience in Man & the Communion of Saints & Angels
> Contemning the Divine Vision & Fruition, Worshipping the Deus
> Of the Heathen, The God of This World, & the Goddess Nature
> Mystery Babylon the Great, The Druid Dragon & hidden Harlot[.]
> Is it not that Signal of the Morning which was told us in the
> Beginning [?] (J 93.21-26)

Another way to put this is that "nature" is the Other, the "not-human," which must be reclaimed or reabsorbed into the human. It is congruent with Hegel's doctrine that nature is Spirit estranged from itself, a doctrine derived through Schelling from Boehme and his "exhalations" or "emanations" of Soul and God (these ideas coming in turn from the Kabbalah and more ancient sources).

As with other central Blakean ideas, this one can be recast into something unexceptionable, and it is useful to do so, not just so as to swallow it more easily but to reveal something of the historical and social truths inscribed in it. Thus one can argue that what Blake is "really" talking about is our *feeling* of estrangement from the world. In our unfallen condition we lack the notion of nature entirely, since it is continuous with ourselves; indeed, we have no notion of self since we are not self-conscious. We are conscious only in unreflective spontaneous openness to our brothers and sisters who share our garden. Fallen from this consciousness, because of selfishness, possessiveness, shame, and a desire to fix the flux of inter-relatedness into permanent boundaries, everything grows apart, alien, other, and the garden turns into a wilderness, a desert, or "nature." On a social scale, we may contrast the seemingly unselfconscious interaction with the environment visible among primitive tribes to the modern "conquest" and "exploitation" of nature as conceptualized by "objective" science. Lukács reminds us that "nature is a social category"[11] and that the rise of a concept of nature as something out there, subject to objective laws, is due to the emergence of an urban class in society that feels both separate from the traditional agrarian order and called upon to rationalize and manipulate both society and material goods. This essentially bourgeois development had ancient precedents—indeed, Alfred Sohn-Rethel and others have connected the invention of geometry and the rise of speculative natural philosophy with the invention of coins in the seventh century B.C., and the Frankfurt School theorists have written back the idea of the "bourgeois" to the same period.[12]

Despite these assimilations into social phenomenology and the history of ideology, something scandalous still remains of Blake's idea of nature. We can attribute it to metaphoric excess, of the sort even a rational materialist like Marx yields to when he makes Blakean prophecies of a time when man will "conceive of nature . . . as his own real body."[13] We can see the distorting effects of the larger syntax of Blake's mythology on his discrete idea about nature—the pressure, in other words, to unify all his ideas into one story with human characters and an independent momentum. Blake's ambition to absorb into one literary and graphic work of art the epic, the psychological allegory, and a philosophical system, has its own ideological interest, as do the strangely fractured and multifarious results. We need only grant for now that Blake's general ambition may have etched odd features onto his notion of nature. We may also be dealing with a kind of "mystical phenomenology." There is no methodological reason to confine phenomenology to reports of "normal" consciousness, and indeed Aldous Huxley and Milton Klonsky, among others, have found entries into Blake through the experience of mescaline and LSD.[14]

I would add one other reason, before returning to the idea of nature itself. Blake wishes to distinguish his "thinking" from normal discourse lest it become contaminated and subverted. His hero Los is constantly struggling in this fallen world with the constraints of his art and with his own Spectre, the spirit, perhaps, of his concessions to the normal and worldly. The system he claims he must create or be enslaved by another man's (J 10.20) can be taken itself as a concession to the world, a compromising choice to use the enemy's weapons, but we may also take it as a vow to create a way of thinking and imagining in a mode altogether different from the prevalent ones. A "system" of this sort would preserve a kind of "negative moment" in Hegel's and Marcuse's terms—unassimilable, because inconceivable, to the one-dimensional "single vision" of Lockean reasonableness, natural philosophy, and utilitarian ethics. It is almost of no importance, for this purpose, what the idea or image is: the madder the better, to shock and disarm the right-thinking readers. We come back then to the matter of Blake's difficulty: a certain irreducible weirdness might be deliberately placed.

Before we turn to the most troublesome feature of Blake's "nature," that it is female and secondary to the male, two or three other features deserve discussion. "Nature" is one of the most abstract concepts there is, and abstraction, to Blake, is one of the prime mental sins, in fact the first sin, according to *The Book of Urizen*. Blake felt the horror of it almost viscerally. As we discussed in chapter two, Urizen's first act, from which all the other events cascade down to the withered, deafened, and cold condition at the book's end, is to withdraw: "unknown, abstracted / Brooding secret, the dark power hid" (3.6-7). As soon as his withdrawal is established he imposes his abstraction—"One command, one joy, one desire"—upon the "chaos" his withdrawal has engendered. What abstract concepts and laws do, clearly enough, is conceal or obliterate the unique character of each individual, making them uniform bricks in the geometric mausoleum of the state. When liberals in the spirit of Locke derive new social laws from what they deem the individual social atom they merely compound the error by camouflaging it in pseudo-individualism. They may believe they have released individuals from arbitrary social (feudal) bonds and shown them the way to undertake contracts freely with other individuals, but in rending all the fibers of a unique social whole the liberals have reduced people to the most abstract (both conceptually general and socially withdrawn) condition. Working up to "laws" by association and comparison, liberals make derisory progress in knowledge but all too much progress in social domination.

> You accumulate Particulars, & murder by analyzing, that you
> May take the aggregate; & you call the aggregate Moral Law:
> And you call that Swelld & bloated Form; a Minute Particular.
> (J 91.26-28)

But "Minute Particular," we know, is Blake's phrase for the irreducibly unique individual whose real social bonds live in love and mutual benevolence and forgiveness, in the body of Jesus:

> But General Forms have their vitality in Particulars: & every
> Particular is a Man: a Divine Member of the Divine Jesus.
> (J 91.29-30)

We noticed in the second chapter the conflict between the content and form of Blake's argument, the conflict between the assertion of minute particularity and the abstract terms (like "Minute Particular") by which the assertion is made. Blake fights with his enemy's weapons here as elsewhere. Has he a choice? Modern deconstructionist critics will point to this as an obvious example of the general impossibility of escaping the assumptions one attacks, but that case is too general, in my opinion, to be very interesting, and of course it no more escapes its own attack than its targets do. Blake may have gone further rhetorically than he had to go logically—he may have become what he beheld, as he often puts it—and his recognition of his contamination may lie behind his extensive pictures of the seductions of Vala and Tirzah and the other representatives of "natural" forces. Jonathan Swift's remark to Alexander Pope that "I hate and detest that animal called man; although I heartily love John, Peter, Thomas, and so forth" (Letter of 29 September 1725) welds form to content better, though a short meditation on proper names will draw us back from pronouncing this an undeconstructable success.

Edmund Burke offers a relevant comparison. Throughout his famous *Reflections* he rails against abstract social theorists who leave their object "stripped of every relation, in all the nakedness and solitude of metaphysical abstraction." These "speculatists" erect "mazes of metaphysical sophistry," a "theoretic experimental edifice" that can offer only the "arithmetic" of majority rule or the geometry that replaces our beloved ancestral neighborhoods with districts like "Checquer, No. 71." So far, in spirit, Burke is not far from Blake, alert as they both are to the destructive effects of the capitalist system now emerging into near-dominance. Blake, of course, remains loosely in the camp of the Dissenters Burke attacks, and he scorns Burke's resort to nature and ancient custom, as when Burke says, "This sort of people are so taken up with their theories about the rights of man, that they have totally forgot his nature." "Nature" works hard in Burke, dictating this and forbidding that until it seems to act as Burke's factotum. Nature demands that we accept the ancient laws as an entailed inheritance, that we revere age itself, that we celebrate the wisdom of the Act of Settlement of 1689. Our laws are "the happy effect of following nature, which is wisdom without reflection, and above it." "Our political system is placed in a just correspondence and symmetry with the order of the world." Burke's is a classic exhibit of the ideological function of nature, and he displays its contradiction in a set of *Reflections* that prefer wisdom without reflections, in a sustained argument against abstractions that must resort as an argument to the sign of abstractness itself, nature.[15]

Burke seems uneasily to have sensed this problem, but his way out of it is less honest than Blake's. Retreating further into mystery, into decent draperies and ceremonies, Burke appeals to "the disposition of a stupendous wisdom" in flights of intimidating prophetic rhetoric that Paine rightly castigated as empty dramatic posturing. Blake is not above wishful and

even intimidating prophesying (which Paine might have con-
sidered empty), but he does not halt before nature or anything
outside and above human comprehension or labor. He keeps
lifting and rending the curtains Burke would let fall over
everything, and he is very much the spiritual ally of the Paine
who would inquire a little closer into all the pedigrees and
charters Burke holds up, at a distance, for our admiration. It
is precisely the obscurity or opacity of abstractions and the
quintessential abstraction of "nature" that Blake believes must
be broken open and washed with light if we are to achieve
genuine liberty and brotherhood.

It may have been with Burke's seemingly unideological trea-
tise *Sublime and Beautiful*, published the year Blake was born,
that Blake the artist was more crucially engaged than with the
Reflections; it is interesting to see, in any case, that Blake carried
the fight against nature into aesthetic theory with the same
anger and stubbornness he showed in his campaigns for peace
and justice. Other scholars have treated well his quarrel with
neoclassic aesthetic standards.[16] I will touch only on his rescue
of the concept of the sublime from the clutches of the natural
obscurantists; it will also give us bearings on Blake's differ-
ences with the great Romantic poets.

Blake did not find the sublime on mountains, and indeed
he probably never saw anything higher than the hills of Sur-
rey. The many mountains in Blake are parts of a symbolic
geography and topology, and are often only names.[17] His few
extended descriptions of natural things and his watercolors
of the natural environment—both mainly products of his
three years' stay in rural Felpham—belong more to the realm
of the "beautiful" or the "picturesque," though these are not
distinctions Blake had any use for. He dismissed Burke's trea-
tise as derivative of Locke and Newton, that is, of the view
that nature or the environment is the source of all that we
know or see. The sublime in literature or painting is based
on the feeling of the sublime in nature, and that feeling, at
its highest, is astonishment. "In this case," says Burke, "the
mind is so entirely filled with its object, that it cannot entertain
any other, nor by consequence reason on that object which
employs it."[18] Blake's reply is easy to imagine: any mind en-

tirely filled with a natural object must have been very small to begin with, and it is the mind's business to employ objects, not the other way round. Such objects get command of us, Burke goes on to say, by their obscurity, and Blake might well agree, but then it is for the mind to clear up obscurity, not relish it. Burke himself tells how obscurity has been used by despots and heathens to enthrall the mind: "Those despotic governments, which are founded on the passions of men, and principally upon the passion of fear, keep their chief as much as may be from the public eye. . . . Almost all the heathen temples were dark."[19] Burke does not mention, of course, the crepuscular light of Catholic or Anglican churches, or the mysteries of drapery that cajole us into accepting the Act of Settlement.

Blake makes clear in his comments on Reynolds's *Discourses on Art*, which he associates with Burke and Locke, that he wants sublimity without obscurity. "Obscurity is Neither the Source of the Sublime nor of any Thing Else"; "Singular & Particular Detail is the Foundation of the Sublime" (E 658, 647). He knew very well how obscurity can work in a poem or painting to generate a terrible grandeur. His own poem "The Tyger," as Morton Paley has shown in detail, draws on the tradition of the sublime in which Burke shares.[20] Whether or not a contemporary reader "would have recognized 'The Tyger' as an apostrophe to the Wrath of God as a sublime phenomenon," there is no question that the power of the poem lies far less in the tyger itself—barely described except for its fiery eyes—than in the immeasurable cosmic events hinted at in the speaker's obscure fragmentary questions. Sublimity is in the mind of the beholder, the poem seems to say, and not in the object which, removed from its obscure habitat, is shown in normal light at the bottom of the plate to be a rather unprepossessing tomcat. Elsewhere, however, Blake says, "The roaring of lions, the howling of wolves, the raging of the stormy sea, and the destructive sword, are portions of eternity too great for the eye of man" (E 36), and I am not sure how to square this more or less Burkean sentiment with Blake's usual confidence in human powers as against those of nature. Perhaps we are to take the eye here as only a "natural organ subject to Sense" (E 1), an organ we are meant to see through, not with, to the eternity that greets our eternal spirit, but which "in this age" sees only through a glass, darkly.

Burke praises Milton's use of "a judicious obscurity" in describing Death at the Gate of Hell—"The other shape, / If shape it might be called that shape had none / Distinguishable, in member, joint, or limb; / Or substance might be called that shadow seemed, / For each seemed either" (PL 2.666-70)—and adds, "it is astonishing with what a gloomy pomp, with what a significant and expressive uncertainty of strokes and colouring he has finished the portrait of the king of terrors."[21] This may or may not be a fair description of Milton's verse, but it represents everything Blake despised in painting. "Broken Colours & Broken Lines & Broken Masses are Equally Subversive of the Sublime" (E 641). His own pen-and-watercolor versions of Satan, Sin, and Death at the Gate of Hell (1807) show Death transparent but definite in shape, with a clear outline. Some would say he has sacrificed the sublimity that his friend Fuseli achieved in his oil painting of the same subject (1802) or his earlier *Sin, Pursued by Death* (1794-1796), in both of which Death is murky and frightening.[22] But then Blake might reply that Death is not mysterious at all; seen aright he is transparent and clear in outline, a state to be seen through and passed through, like nature.

Opaque, impenetrable, wholly other, indeed a form of death itself—if nature seems to be these things to us we must be either its victim or its victor. As long as it is "nature," domination of one by the other is the only possible outcome. Blake even suggests that it is the attitude of domination itself, directed at no object but the fluid interpenetration of subjects, that brings about nature as something to dominate in the first place. So Urizen fights against fire, air, and water, the three fluid elements, out of some primordial discontent with the vital exchanges of eternity, until he defeats them and all that remains is the "wide world of solid obstruction" (U 4.10-23). But out of that world emerge new forms of obstreperous energy, and Urizen can only renew his efforts to impose iron laws. If you have a mind bent on controlling things, you will find things always out of control; law generates sin; domination breeds nature.

We noted in chapter two the political connotations of the language of epistemology. If you make yourself a subject over against an object, you may become "subject to" your object; even in conquest over it you will have joined it in a dance of death, as the master defines himself, according to Hegel, in relation to his slave. One of the wise young women of William Morris's *News from Nowhere* asks about the people of the nineteenth century: "Was not their mistake once more bred of the life of slavery that they had been living?—a life which was always looking upon everything, except mankind, animate and inanimate—'nature,' as people used to call it—as one thing, and mankind as another. It was natural to people thinking in this way, that they should try to make 'nature' their slave, since they thought 'nature' was something outside them."[23] It was "natural" to people who had enslaved one another, who had turned other people into things, that they should extend that process into the world they lived in, turning it into a nature to be struggled with.

Though he sees through the errors of reason on this score, Blake's frequently dualistic language leads him sometimes into figures of domination, and even rape, when he discusses nature. In contrast to, say, William Morris, who combines the Romantic theme of imaginative participation in the natural world with the socialist theme of joyful "unalienated" labor (we are part of nature, and during labor of the right kind we cooperate with nature), Blake's images of harmony and balanced interaction embrace different people or different mental faculties, but never nature.

Blake draws from the Pauline tradition, of course, and it is in his use of that older language that we can most neatly trace his divergence from Wordsworth and the Romantics. When Wordsworth emerges from the city at the opening of *The Prelude*, what is shaken off is "That burthen of my own unnatural self." It is his natural portion that rejoices in liberty, that breathes again, that receives creative trances of thought and mountings of the mind. In evoking the imagery of Exodus Wordsworth is in effect rewriting the New Testament, which may itself be considered a grand commentary on the liberation theme of Exodus, and he specifically revalues the Pauline dualism of the natural man and the spiritual man (as in 1 Cor. 2:14). Blake holds to the traditional uses; he even inscribes on one of his designs ("To Tirzah," e 30) the second half of a prime Pauline text: "It is sown a natural body, it is raised a spiritual body" (1 Cor. 15:44). Having read other poems by him, Blake saw in Wordsworth precisely the "raising" of the natural man; to return to the annotation we excerpted in the last chapter, "I see in Wordsworth the Natural Man rising up against the Spiritual Man Continually & then he is No Poet but a Heathen Philosopher at Enmity against all true Poetry or Inspiration" (e 666).

Blake, who wrote this comment sometime after 1815, may have grown too settled in his opinions to discern how much he and Wordsworth had in common. Blake's radically Protestant transformation of the false and falsely projected creator God is formally similar to Wordsworth's relocation of the divine into a "Being" or "Under-Presence" in nature, and in this both poets are heirs of the Enlightenment. The Enlightenment critique of religion had restored to man most of what the priests had confiscated from him, but it left an abstract Creator or Prime Mover as a logically necessary entity. Blake and the young Wordsworth were more revolutionary. Where the deists and *philosophes* had made God into a constitutional or even titular monarch, stripping him of all attributes but the power to found the state and reign in name over it, Blake and Wordsworth exposed God as a legal formality, "a mere fiction of what never was," in Wordsworth's phrase, and dethroned him. New wine burst old deist bottles.

Romanticism, in Northrop Frye's definition, is "a profound change, not primarily in belief, but in the spatial projection of reality." "What corresponds to heaven and hell is still there, the worlds of identity and alienation, but the imagery associated with them, being based on the opposition of 'within' and 'without' rather than of 'up' and 'down,' is almost reversed."[24] The metaphors of depth and surface are everywhere in Wordsworth and in Blake. One way to take the confusing spatial movements in *America* and *Europe*, for example, is as the outburst of a horizontal and democratic immanence from within and beneath the traditional vertical structures of a hierarchical social order. In Blake's most succinct version of the Enlightenment critique of religion, plate 11 of *The Marriage of Heaven and Hell*, he restores "All deities," implicitly including the abstract "Pantocrator" of Newton, to "the human breast." Wordsworth similarly passes unalarmed by God, "Jehovah—with his thunder, and the choir / Of shouting Angels, and the empyreal thrones," to take his stand reverently by "the Mind of Man."[25]

Formally similar their arguments may be, but for Blake Wordsworth overcomes one error only to fall into another, indeed, a version of the same one. External nature is no better a lodging for the human imagination or creativity than the traditional heaven. It may even be worse, for as Wordsworth, no less than Locke and Newton, conceives it nature has nothing human in it, or has at most an occasional solitary in his "animal tranquillity": "Where man is not nature is barren" (E 38). Wordworth's unalarmed passage by Jehovah rankled Blake, for he saw that Wordsworth was heading not just toward the mind of man, where Blake himself considered paradise to be planted (M 2.7-8), but toward a mind "fitted" to nature. Had that mind remained alarmed or responsive to the imaginative power of thunderous Jehovah and the choiring angels it would have been a region better suited to Wordsworth's song. Blake's comment on Wordsworth's passage is interesting:

> Solomon when he Married Pharohs daughter & became a Convert to the Heathen Mythology Talked exactly in this way of Jehovah as a Very inferior object of Mans Contemplations he also passed him by unalarmd & was permitted. Jehovah dropped a tear & follwd him by his Spirit into the Abstract Void it is called the Divine Mercy Satan dwells in it but Mercy does not dwell in him he knows not to Forgive[.]
>
> (E 666)

It may have been the imagery of Wordsworth's own poetry that prompted Blake to think of Solomon's marriage to Pharaoh's daughter (1 Kings 3:1), for Wordsworth chants "the spousal verse / Of this great consummation" of the intellect of man "When wedded to this goodly universe / In love and holy passion." Pharaoh's daughter is nature, the external world, which, as befits a representative of Egypt, enslaves the mind by the tasks she teaches it. Jehovah (seldom a pejorative term in Blake, unlike "Elohim") follows Wordsworth into the region of nature, the Abstract Void where Satan dwells. This seems a rather witty way of saying that Jehovah, if he was once a transcendent orthodox God, has come to agree with Wordsworth that in that transcendent state he was only a fiction and so descends with him as the Holy Spirit, "God himself / the divine Body / Jesus." The question of mercy or forgiveness may seem extraneous here (we shall take it up in chapter seven), but we know that the spirit of mercy is also the imagination for Blake, the power to liberate us from the burden of past sins and present submission to another's will. Wandering "at liberty" in the English countryside, Wordsworth will be haunted by the ghost of his abandoned imagination, to which he was right and truly wedded before he went whoring after false goddesses.

Wordsworth's marriage to the whore of nature, Blake probably sensed, was arranged by the despised triumvirate of Bacon, Newton, and Locke, all of whom Wordsworth praises. It is especially interesting to recall that Bacon himself combined the imagery of marriage with that of the torture chamber in his reflections on scientific research. Nature is a slave-woman who must be put on the rack until she yields her secrets by "experiment"; she is to be "under constraint and vexed" until "she is forced out of her natural state, and squeezed and moulded." If she escapes this "inquisition of nature," "you have but to follow and as it were hound nature in her wanderings." Under proper control, obediently yielding her secrets to her inquisitive husband, we see "a chaste and lawful marriage between Mind and Nature, with the divine mercy as brideswoman."[26] It is easy to imagine Blake's rage and scorn over passages like these—as if the Divine Mercy (who is Jesus, not some maiden) would consent to hallow this infernal "chaste" marriage to external nature! The mind has bound itself to a lesser thing, submitting to an inferior, even a creature of itself. Science is not the utterance of an independently existing nature brought to speech by the artifice of the inquirer; the supposed existence of an independent nature is an artifact of the inquisition itself.

This is Blake's crucial reversal of perspective, and it finds many forms, of which the simplest is "As the Eye—Such the Object" (E 645). With Bacon's tortures in mind, we may wonder why it is usually the females who torture the males in Blake's poems. The answer has something to do with Blake's understanding, in which he anticipates the Frankfurt School, that man's domination of nature by rational and technical means is inseparable, and may even arise from, his domination over himself—not only over woman, the first social conquest, but over all people, a portion of all minds. To pursue "enlightenment" technology in this broad sense entails the repression of an imaginative or mythical dimension of the psyche of everyone in the society, as well as the regimentation or enslavement of one class by another. Domination over external nature entails domination over human nature; Blake's domination *by* nature is a return of the repressed. When our minds lapse into passivity, as they necessarily must do under such social conditions, nature will return to haunt and torture us. In historical terms, the social division of labor and the technology invented to extract wealth from nature will seem themselves natural, inescapable, and tyrannical. The imagery of the hunt, of unveiling, and of violating nature's virgin depths is what Jean-Paul Sartre calls "the Actaeon complex."[27] It is a good name, for it reminds us that Actaeon's fate was to be hunted and torn apart by his dogs, that is, by nature unleashed, the return of the repressed. In Blakean terms, "nature" is an emanation of our spirit which our spirit has forgotten it emanated; it appears outside of us and autonomous (Blake's "female will") until it is summoned home and sheds its "natural" identity. This reciprocity of subject and object in Blake is well expressed by his reassignment of a speech in *The Four Zoas* from a male speaker to a female when he put it in *Jerusalem*:

Why wilt thou number every little fibre of my Soul
Spreading them out before the Sun like stalks of flax to dry?
The Infant Joy is beautiful, but its anatomy
Horrible ghast & deadly! nought shalt thou find in it
But dark despair & everlasting brooding melancholy!

(J 22.20-24; cf. FZ 4.29-33)

In *The Four Zoas* it is Tharmas who is thus complaining to
Enion, but in *Jerusalem*, as if Blake remembered that it is the
male (the spirit) who is ultimately responsible for whatever
happens, these lines are spoken by Jerusalem herself to the
rapidly declining Albion. His first words in reply are a com-
mand—he is responsible after all—"Hide thou Jerusalem in
impalpable voidness." "Impalpable voidness" is precisely what
Blake thinks nature really amounts to, when it is not given
illusory substantiality by the void in our minds. Scrutiny and
mystery are twins.

For all Blake's insight into the reciprocity of domination,
analysis, externality, and so on, it remains true that, being
female, nature even in resurrection never quite achieves
equality with the creative and procreative male spirit. The
same is true of the other female figures who represent the
passive and created forms of the human faculties. Ahania can
recall the former days of fertile bliss with Urizen, he with his
lap full of seed and she with her bosom filled with milk, and
though that time was infinitely better than her condition now,
alone, cast out by Urizen's cruel jealousy, even then it was he
who took the initiative, planted the "seed of eternal science,"
and gave form to their offspring, while she only received,
housed, and nourished them, like a garden (*The Book of Ahania*
5).

The state of Beulah, on the outskirts of the strenuous city
of Eden where male spirits conduct "the great Wars of Eter-
nity, in fury of Poetic Inspiration," is a female garden, shady
and restful, where the emanations retreat trembling from the
center. They know they are "but for a time, & . . . pass away
in winter," but hope that if they keep their distance from the
poetic furor they will survive. Are they ideas, or thoughts,
seeking a home in language or in art? Are we to imagine
artistic ideas fearful lest the latest creative afflatus blow them

away? Something like this allegorical equation is invited, yet the vehicle of femaleness is not fully absorbed into the tenor of intellectual or artistic production, and even less into that of "nature." They remain women, and distinctly secondary, however necessary to the totality of spiritual life. Men are inspired, they inhale the creative "breath of the Almighty"; women are "emanated," exhaled—as if gently banished upstairs from the library where men discuss serious things (see m 30-31).

Feminist scholarship in the last twenty years has made us aware of the prevalent transcultural assumption that the natural realm is distinctively female and the cultural realm, invariably higher, is distinctively male. (The etymologies of "nature" and "culture" provide a rich anthropological lesson in themselves.) It has also been suggested that, though biological differences are "given" and may even engender "natural" psychological differences, most of what passes for proper social roles has no natural sanction at all. In the protracted war against the naturalization of social facts characteristic of all ideology, probably the most sharply contested terrain in America today is not the natural acquisitiveness of *homo economicus* celebrated by apologists for capitalism, though they have felt a new burst of confidence recently, but the ideal of woman's natural place as wife, mother, and housekeeper. Taught by the new struggles on this old ground, feminist scholars have written well on the male-supremacist assumptions Blake shared with nearly everyone else in his day, and I will defer to them.[28]

The usual defense, as I mentioned in the last chapter, is that the dominant males and passive females are not, for the most part, real men and women, but forces or faculties or phenomenological categories. Each real man and woman contains both aspects. There is something like an androgynous ideal occasionally visible in Blake; once or twice we see male emanations, as if the Human is the primary force and both male and female are garments for it, or its "Temporal Habitations" (m 30.29). There are a few strong female characters who seem almost real people, such as Oothoon, though she is still bound, rather unaccountably, to her hopelessly jealous lover. In *America* and elsewhere "the female spirits of the dead," who seem to be real young Englishwomen, are released briefly from the fetters of religion—of false naturalization of their traditional subordinate roles. All this and more may be said, but it remains the case that a residue of traditional assumptions about men and women is traceable throughout Blake's work.

I would add two clauses in Blake's apology. One of them is obvious enough but requires some careful study before it can be properly argued. Against the background of prevalent assumptions in 1790, with respect even to the few feminist thinkers of the time, how advanced or liberatory can Blake's world of argument and imagery be said to be? One thing needed is a closer comparison of Blake with Mary Wollstonecraft, whom he knew at least slightly and whose *Original Stories from Real Life* (1788) he illustrated. It is interesting that Blake and Wollstonecraft, in her *Vindication of the Rights of Woman* (1792), each disparage "love" and praise "friendship." For Wollstonecraft, however, what commends friendship is its compatibility with reason; her ideal is a marriage based on friendship, not passion, where the partners are equal in dignity but rationally assigned distinctive duties—hers, of course, having to do with the home, children, education, and so on. The point of departure for a Blakean reading of the *Vindication* might well be Wollstonecraft's standard of reason, well within the Dissenting tradition she had absorbed. What one would bring away from a close comparison, I would guess, is the feeling that Wollstonecraft was the braver soul and her work the more useful, for a century or more, in the long struggle for women's rights, while Blake was the more profound and revolutionary thinker whatever his unsound tendencies.

And that is my second point. Blake's great usefulness today, in large part, is as a phenomenologist of liberation. He catches by a great variety of verbal and pictorial means the way it feels to suffer at least spiritual enslavement and to enjoy release from it. A sense of Blake's historical moment ought to lead feminists to forgive the disturbing connotations of imagery, the contamination of tenor by vehicle, and find Blake's total vision an inspiration in our struggle against the tyranny of patriarchy—a tyranny strong enough in 1790 to infect the most liberated souls of the time, and still strong enough today to forbid the luxury of dispensing with imperfect spiritual allies.

Blake's phenomenology of liberation, because it is sufficiently metaphorical and abstract, can be brought into fruitful dialogue with recent socio-ecological theories that are mindful of the limits to economic growth, the revenge of exploited nature, and the lessons to be learned from stable primitive and archaic societies. Blake's nature-metaphysics can be translated into states of mind: confronted as a menacing or alluring alien, whether a female or the forests of the night, nature will lead us astray, trap us, or destroy us, but the confrontational stance is not the only one we can take. There is, however, no getting around nature's secondariness in Blake. The fundamental division of "nature" from "culture," which Max Weber posited as a precondition for the culture of modernity, is inscribed as deeply in Blake as it is in his more rationalist Dissenting contemporaries, many of whom were promoters of the industrial revolution. Going back at least as far as the Hebrews' hatred of the fertility cults of their powerful agricultural neighbors, through the Pauline dualism of spirit and flesh, to a resurgence in the Protestant Reformation (as against Christianity's long accommodation of astrology and pagan nature cults) of spiritual alienation from the world, this separation made possible the rise of scientific and instrumental (or operational) reason. Blake may have deplored the latter, but he is at one with the Protestant separation that prepared the way for it.

Everywhere in his work we find barren wildernesses transformed into gardens when man asserts himself, and gardens transformed into wildernesses when he falls or weakens spiritually. The opening of *America* begins with something very like a rape (though it is welcomed by the female), as the spirit of revolution claims the fertile American plains, and later the spirit of Boston indignantly demands to know why "the ungenerous" or idle (absentee landowners?) are allowed to "perform" the energies of nature while the strong and "generous"

Americans are given a sandy desert (A 11.4-15). Like virtually every American colonist and their English supporters (such as Price and Priestley), Blake celebrates the exploitation of America's abundant natural resources; it would be surprising if he did not. What he fears is the accommodation *to* nature that he sees among the philosophers *of* it. In order to attain mastery over it they first admit nature into themselves; really its creatures, their victory is illusory.

Despite its dualist moments, Blake's view of the world seems ultimately monist, a one-term system whose opposites are only illusions. There is no genuine dialectic with regard to nature or externality itself. The danger is that the system may have no outside, no check or reality principle. As we saw in the last chapter, however, Blake posits internal checks to keep his system from justifying anything the individual ego may desire: there are other people, and the individual ego is not even fully individual until it acknowledges the totality of other souls. The single term that generates all the others is not the self but the total Man or Human, informed by the Holy Spirit, which is the basis of the universal Church. What informs Blake's own system, in the terms we quoted from *Jerusalem* earlier, is the "Conscience in Man & the Communion of Saints & Angels" (J 93.22).

As with his residual male-supremacism, we would want to reconstruct Blake's spirit-supremacism in order to acknowledge the limits and informing structures given by nature. Even Karl Marx, who shared the assumption of his age that nature is to be conquered and transformed into a human world, has recently undergone revision by socialists mindful of ecology and the increasingly dangerous local breakdowns of energy and transportation systems. From within Blake there are episodes one could tease out and redefine somewhat to build up a sounder, more genuinely interactive view of nature and culture, though the general drift of Blake is in the other direction. As ecology has become a popular cause, we now find versions of nature-monism everywhere, one-term systems that endorse "natural" this and "organic" that, despise chemicals, idealize the Native Americans, and so on, as if these systems are not themselves cultural artifacts that generate concepts of nature as tendentious as Locke's or Burke's. For advocates of these theories, Blake may be an antidote more palatable than the prevalent notions of scientific progress, manifest destiny, new frontier, and similarly suspect ideologies. A child of his time no less than anyone else, Blake was also an adoptive child of times before his own—before the hegemony of western instrumental rationalism—and for that reason he can speak in many different registers to ours.

5

Liberty

We have had several occasions to compare Blake to Milton, Winstanley, and other seventeenth-century writers and to consider the relation of his historical moment to theirs. In this chapter I want to dwell on the central theme of Blake's ideological affiliation to the radicals of the Commonwealth period—liberty—and especially on the tradition of Christian antinomianism. As this affiliation has not been fully discussed before, I will give it more space than his relations with contemporaries or the details of his own elaboration of the theme, both of which Erdman and others have treated at length. The resulting imbalance seems preferable to another restatement of all his ideas and systematic symbolism, a vice that still swells so many new Blake books. Blake himself is the problem, to be sure, for there seems to be no way of presenting him both adequately and elegantly. I think it reveals more about Blake to confess the presentational difficulty than to emulate him in producing a rounded and complete system, about which Blake himself confessed difficulty more than once.

In his notebook Coleridge drew a distinction between two basic kinds of religion. What he called the "Pagan-plotinic Religion" proceeds "from the Intellect as from the apex, downward to the *moral* Being—from the speculative to the practical Reason." Christianity, on the other hand, with the exception of Socinianism, "begins with the moral will, and ends with it, and regards the intellect altogether as *means*."[1] It is quite clear to which camp Blake belonged, for though he was a Christian the main terms of his system were intellectual or epistemological, and if they generated a morality it is only in the most general sense of the word:[2] "I care not whether a Man is Good or Evil; all that I care / Is whether he is a Wise Man or a Fool" (J 91.55-56). To say that is to raise the flag of antinomianism, a tradition that may well have begun in a "Pagan-plotinic" context but which has been an embarrassing camp follower of Christianity from its earliest days. Coleridge was right to except Socinianism from his rather narrow and Judaic definition of Christianity; he should have excluded much besides. If Blake, as A. L. Morton claims, "was the greatest English Antinomian, but also the last," he had a long and rich tradition behind him, a tradition that produced one of its most dramatic displays just a century before Blake's birth in Blake's country and city.[3] As we turn to that tradition we should remember that there is no evidence of direct influence between, say, the Ranters and Blake. "In the study of Blake," however, as Northrop Frye says, "it is the analogue that is important, not the source."[4] Seventeenth-century antinomianism provides a horizon against which to view Blake's ideas on liberty and forgiveness of sins. We shall also look more closely at Gerrard Winstanley, not strictly an antinomian but a radical Protestant with antinomian leanings and one of the most interesting radicals of the Commonwealth. Winstanley was freer than Blake to express his thoughts and act on them, and may therefore help us see the social and political tendencies in Blake's beliefs.

Antinomianism in the strict sense is the doctrine that, for Christians, Christ's crucifixion has abolished the Mosaic law. As Milton's Michael explains it to Adam:

> But to the Cross he nails thy Enemies,
> The Law that is against thee, and the sins
> Of all mankind, with him there crucifi'd,
> Never to hurt them more who rightly trust
> In this his satisfaction. . . .
>   (PL 12.415-19)

Its scriptural warrant lies in several Pauline epistles, notably that to the Galatians: "Christ hath redeemed us from the curse of the law"; "Stand fast therefore in the liberty wherewith Christ hath made us free, and be not entangled again with the yoke of bondage"; "For Christ is the end of the law for righteousness to every one that believeth" (Gal. 3:13, 5:1; Rom. 4:10). Paul even claims that it was not God who gave the law at Sinai, but that "it was ordained by angels in the hand of a mediator," Moses (Gal. 3:19). As Christians we are children of the promise, the second covenant of the free Jerusalem above, mother of us all, and so we are the legitimate heirs of Abraham, not the children of his concubine, the bondswoman Agar (Gal. 4:22-31). Thus one need not be circumcised (that is, Jewish) to be Christian; it may, in fact, hinder salvation (Gal. 5:2-6). By the law no righteousness is possible, for we are sinners all, but through faith in Christ we may be justified by his grace (Gal. 2:15-21).

Near the heart of Christian doctrine, then, is a belief of great subversive potential. If all the laws of Deuteronomy are null for believers, why shall we not do whatever we wish? Are not all our sins forgiven? Paul is nothing if not equivocal, however, and he seems to have feared the consequences of his doctrine for moral and even political behavior. "For, brethren, ye have been called into liberty; only we use not liberty for an occasion to the flesh" (Gal. 5:13). He brings to bear his strict dualism of spirit and flesh to limit the scope of liberty. "For the flesh lusteth against the Spirit, and the Spirit against the flesh" (Gal. 5:17). Elsewhere, he praises the law unstintingly: "the law is holy, and the commandment holy, and just, and good" (Rom. 7:12). Moreover, Christ himself seems not to have countenanced the libertarian view, for in the Sermon on the Mount he said, "Think not that I am come to destroy the law, or the prophets: I am not come to destroy, but to fulfill. . . . Whosoever therefore shall break one of these least commandments, and shall teach men so, he shall be called the least in the kingdom of heaven" (Matt. 5:17-20). At a time of great restiveness among Jewish sects under harsh Roman rule, Paul (and perhaps Christ) was cautious. He sheared his doctrine of its subversive if logical outgrowths and confined it to spirit—one might almost say to theory—alone. "Let every man abide in the same calling wherein he was called" (1 Cor. 7:20). We are to play no active part in ushering in the kingdom but are to leave it all to Christ:

At his *Parousia*, which was imminent, Christ would do away with the Old World-order completely and finally. Until then the believer should not anticipate events by revolutionary action, but conform himself outwardly still to that old scheme of things, marked out though it was for complete obliteration, in which he found himself on his entry into the Christian community.[5]

As Christ's Second Coming was postponed and matters of Church organization gained importance, the tensions in the account of Christian liberty had to be resolved. It had to be defended against Jewish veneration for the law on one side and gnostic contempt for the law on the other. Against the latter Paul's dualism was probably of little use, for the equally dualistic gnostics could despise the flesh so thoroughly as to care not at all what it was doing. They could also seize on Paul's "angels" of Sinai as consonant with their own view that the Yahweh of the Old Testament was an evil demiurge who imprisoned our spirits in carnal laws. Various stratagems in this two-front controversy led to compromises in the formulae, in which, for example, only some of the law, the cultic or ceremonial part, was abolished or the whole law remained in force only in the spirit, not in the letter.[6] A set of exegeses, firmly based on Paul's dualism if not on his angels, became orthodox; they restricted antinomianism to a safe other-worldly realm. This orthodox view we might call "right antinomianism" and distinguish it from "left antinomianism" or antinomianism in the usual sense, with its usual implications of libertine or revolutionary behavior.

Luther and Calvin were both right antinomians. Luther, it is true, granted that the whole Mosaic code was abrogated, not just the rituals, but he confined the resulting liberty to the conscience only and enjoined his fellows to obey temporal authority. He even admitted that the law may be useful as a measure or test of our consciences.[7] Calvin did not go as far as Luther. He agreed that the law is not a factor in our justification, which is by faith alone, yet "Christian freedom . . . inclines the conscience to observe the Law, but that, being delivered from the Law, they are freely obedient [*ultro obediant*] to the will of God." Though their obedience is free, Calvin made it clear that Christians are still subject to the law;

far from abolishing it Christ made it all the more potent for believers.[8] Both Luther and Calvin, moreover, sometimes applied the law to the "ungodly," who "seek only a carnal freedom," and the Gospel of liberty to the elect, whose consciences had already been properly terrified by the law.[9]

Milton, like Luther and Calvin, insisted that the entire Mosaic law was abolished: according to his *Christian Doctrine*, we are "absolved from subjection to the decalogue as fully as to the rest of the law." "It is to be observed, however," Milton adds, citing Matthew 5:17, "that the sum and essence of the law is not hereby abrogated." The spirit if not the letter remains, and its injunctions are written not on tablets but on the hearts of believers, who if anything are more perfect than those under the law. Their obedience is entirely willing.[10]

Left antinomianism was a problem for the early Church and remained one, at least intermittently, until modern times. The primitive community at Corinth may have followed the implications of their freedom into libertine behavior. "It is reported commonly that there is fornication among you," Paul wrote, and other sins that he had to denounce (1 Cor. 5:1).[11] Gnostic sects may well have had an antinomian influence on early Christianity. Even among pre-Christian Jews there may have been antinomian "Ophite" sects that revered Cain, Seth, and Melchizedek as liberators from the law,[12] and there were certainly similar sects to plague the orthodox during the first two Christian centuries. Gnosticism, it is true, need not engender a libertine or amoral practice. Marcion, a leading Christian gnostic, preached asceticism: the enlightened soul should minimize contact with the filthy world and thus obstruct the plans of its evil creator.[13] But, if the hostile Irenaeus is to be believed, some gnostic pneumatics "serve intemperately the lusts of the flesh and say you must render the flesh to the flesh and the spirit to the spirit."[14] No one at this time seems to have taken Blake's stand that the body is an aspect of the soul and the source of the soul's energy and delight.

We have little from this early period on which to reconstruct the doctrinal elaboration of antinomianism, and it may be misleading to attribute the seventeenth-century English expression of it, as we find it in the writings of the "Ranters" and other groups, to its historical beginnings. It seems likely, however, that most of the following tenets were implicitly or explicitly held by early antinomians: God or Christ dwells in all human beings (and perhaps only in human beings), so whatever we do God does, and God cannot sin; sin is a state of mind, derived from false social or moral codes; there is an Eternal Gospel or Word that supersedes not only the Old Testament but perhaps the New, or at least there is an inner sense or "mystery" of the Scriptures available to the enlightened; history falls in periods of progressive illumination, and we are now in or near the last. By the seventeenth century there seems to have been a tendency toward monism as well, denying the separation of mind and body, as if to say we should not scorn our animal nature or "natural man"—God will save that too. Finally, we can isolate another tendency, by no means universal, that we might call "ultraleft antinomianism," the argument that only through sin can we be saved.

This last corollary is probably more than a rhetorical exaggeration *pour épater les bourgeois*. Irenaeus ascribes to Carpocrates and the Cainite sects a program of systematic sinning, either in this life or in future incarnations, to exhaust the world's possible deeds and thereby gain salvation. "At every sinful and infamous deed an angel is present, and he who commits it . . . addresses him by his name and says, 'O thou angel, I use thy work!' "[15] The antinomian Lawrence Clarkson (1615-1667) at one time believed "that there was no man could be free'd from sin, till he had acted that so-called sin, as no sin."[16] The Ranter Abiezer Coppe (1619-1672) put it eloquently:

> And then (behold I shew you a mystery, and put forth a riddle to you) by base things, base things so called have been confounded also; and thereby have I been confounded into eternall Majesty, unspeakable glory, my life, my self. . . . And then again, by wanton kisses, kissing hath been confounded; and externall kisses, have been made the fiery chariots, to mount me swiftly into the bosom of him whom my soul loves, (his excellent Majesty, the King of glory.)[17]

In 1650 Parliament made it a crime to avow most antinomian doctrines, including the belief "that such men or women are most perfect, or like to God or Eternity, which do commit the

greatest Sins with the least remorse or sense."[18] The belief in
the sacramental character or sinful acts appears a few years
later on the Continent in the doctrines of the self-proclaimed
Jewish Messiah Sabbatai Zevi. He seems to have taught that
we must commit sins in order to release the sparks of spirit
from their prisons, the *kelipoth* or "shells," in this world. Just
as a grain of wheat must rot in the earth before it can sprout,
so the deeds of the believers must be truly "rotten" before
they can germinate the redemption.[19]

In dwelling on this extreme antinomianism I do not mean
to imply a close parallel with Blake. A doctrine like this would
seem to have more affinities with some of his contemporaries
in England and on the Continent. M. H. Abrams invokes this
tradition, from gnosticism to the Sabbatians, as precedent for,
and perhaps influence on, Arthur Rimbaud's systematic "dis-
ordering of all the senses" and calculated debaucheries;[20] I
think it also lies behind a broader literary archetype, one that
includes Faust and the Byronic hero, the Satanic or outlaw
nobleman, whose charisma (an equivalent of grace) derives
from his thorough immersion in the forbidden. When Blake
praises the delights of energy and sensuality he speaks in the
persona of the devil. "Hell" tells Blake that the apocalyptic
consummation "will come to pass by an improvement of sen-
sual enjoyment" (MHH 14). His revolutionary figure Orc,
whose name probably derives from *Orcus*, "hell," is a devilish
figure, red and hairy like his prototype Esau, whom Blake
also defends (MHH 3). To be a reprobate, in Blake's termi-
nology, is to be saved. This is more than satire; he is in earnest.
If he meant to shock, he could have found no better way than
to invoke the ultraleft antinomianism which a smug eight-
eenth century had half forgotten but which the orthodox of
a century before had denounced as the work of the devil.

The systematic and exhaustive character of ultraleft anti-
nomianism is analogous to the general pattern of ancient cos-
mologies, gnostic, Zoroastrian, and Plotinian, as well as Chris-
tian and Nordic, wherein the cycle of development cannot be
reversed or short-circuited but must run on to its furthest
extent before it returns. One engenders two, and two engen-
ders seven, and so on through increasing degrees of multi-

plicity and distance from the source of light and goodness to the utmost degree of alienation, materialism, darkness, and evil; only then, as if the greatest expansion of evil causes it to burn out, does the cycle of return begin. It must get worse before it gets better. It is evident that this cosmic *politique de pire* lies behind the Book of Revelation, where the powers of darkness muster their forces for the final contest and the Beast is even allowed one last fling *after* the millennium. It is also evident that it lies behind Blake's mythology and his recurrent motif of the consolidation and clarification of error.

The coherence of the set of tenets we have identified as antinomianism (of at least the English Protestant variety) allows us to begin at any convenient point in discussing them. Let us begin with Blake's critique of orthodox religion. By returning all the gods to the human breast he has basically psychologized religion, as he has also done by calling religious categories "states": "Death / And Hell & the Grave: States that are not, but ah! Seem to be" (M 32.28-29). The Ranter Lawrence Clarkson declared in 1660 and no doubt earlier that "in the grave there is no remembrance of either joy or sorrow after."[21] Heaven and hell are mental states, or conditions of our life in this world. To Jacob Bauthumley (1650) hell was "an accusing Conscience."[22] Such a view was widespread among Ranters, early Quakers, Muggletonians, and other sects.[23] The more narrowly antinomian aspect emerges with the similar pronouncements about the subjective basis of sin. "The very title Sin," Clarkson wrote (1650), "it is only a name without substance, hath no being in God, nor in the Creature, but only by imagination . . . sin admitting of no form in itself, is created a form in the estimation of the Creature."[24]

The psychologizing and allegorizing tendency seems to be a natural development of Holy Ghost Christianity, from a stress on the indwelling Christ at the expense of the external aspects of the godhead to the complete exclusion of the latter. The logical next step is to deny the possibility of sin, for anything we do God or Christ does in us, and He cannot sin. "I must tell you," Clarkson wrote, "that as all Powers are of God, so all acts, of what nature soever are produced by this Power, yea this Power of God: so that all those acts arising from the Power, are as Pure as the Power, and the Power as Pure as God. So from hence it comes, there is no act whatsoever, that is impure in God, or sinful with or before God."[25] This is close to Blake's claim that "all Act is Virtue," that a vigorous expression of our "staminal virtue" or "leading propensity" is not only right but the working of Jesus within us (E 601).[26]

The state of mind that frees one from sin is simply faith in that freedom. "The Spirit of Christ sets a believer as *free* from *Hell*, the *Law*, and *Bondage*, as if he was in Heaven, nor wants he anything to make him *so*, but to make him *believe* that he is so."[27]

It is another small step to the universalist doctrine that everyone, in the long run or the short, is saved. For the most radical and secular thinkers it was clear that all men may, by their own efforts, attain grace and happiness in this world. Universalism, however, had a broader appeal, and many embraced it who stopped short of full antinomianism. It was a flat repudiation of the Calvinist doctrines of predestination and the division of men into reprobate and elect. Richard Coppin (1653) argued that election and reprobation applied not to persons but to qualities in men, to "states" in Blake's sense.[28] Christ dies for all men; a portion of Christ is in each of us; his resurrection is the resurrection of all mankind, a universal restoration. The hostile witness Thomas Edwards wrote in 1646 that antinomianism included the belief "that there shall be a generall restauration, wherein all men shall be reconciled to God and saved."[29] Whether we expect the restoration to occur in this world or the next depends on other beliefs, but the revolutionary and egalitarian thrust of the expectation is obvious. (We shall turn to some less obvious aspects of Blake's universalism in the final chapter.)

It is probably true, as A. L. Morton claims, that the Ranters were "a main link in the chain that runs from Joachim of Fiore to William Blake,"[30] but it is also true that the links between the Ranters and Blake have disappeared from history. No doubt many radical ideas continued among the surviving sects—Muggletonians, Traskites, and the like—in Blake's London. Another possible link lies in the antinomian

ferment among Methodists from about 1750 to at least the
1770s. "Antinomian principles have spread like wildfire
among our societies," the Methodist preacher John Fletcher
reported. "Many persons, speaking in the most glorious man-
ner of Christ, and of their interest in his complete salvation,
have been found living in the grossest immoralities."[31] Blake
wrote with respect of John Wesley and George Whitefield—
"Men who devote / Their lifes whole comfort to intire scorn
& injury & death" (M 23.1-2)—but, if he had known about
them, Blake's sympathies would probably have been with the
heresies Wesley and his hierarchy opposed.

No doubt there are other links, some of which may have
left no traces in the written record.[32] But it should also be
kept in mind that heresies may regenerate themselves not just
linearly from the remnants of the last heresy but dialectically,
as it were, from the continuous orthodox tradition. Christian
doctrine, if complex, is finite, and a mutation in one tenet will
entail a train of changes in others. Blake may have thought
first of one transformation (that of the Holy Ghost, for in-
stance, into the supreme power) and then, steeped as he was
in the Bible, generated a system that, for all its unique fea-
tures, resembles overall and in many details several of the
systems that preceded it. Probably Blake's ideas are a result
both of "influence" in the usual sense and of the logic of
opposition to orthodoxy. The combination of his ability to
pick up scraps from others—mystics, antiquarians, mythog-
raphers, as well as poets—and his sense of the pervading logic
that must govern their use, may be precisely what gives Blake
the power we sense in him.

Blake is one of the great poets of liberty in all its forms. All
his rulers are tyrants, all his subjects slaves. The chimney
sweeper, the African, Orc in America, all are chained by both
real and mind-forged manacles. Much of Blake's most elo-
quent and moving poetry either protests oppression or cele-
brates liberation.

Let the slave grinding at the mill, run out into the field:
Let him look up into the heavens & laugh in the bright air;
Let the inchained soul shut up in darkness and in sighing,

Whose face has never seen a smile in thirty weary years;
Rise and look out, his chains are loose, his dungeon doors
     are open.
(America 6.6-10)

But we need not multiply examples. Blake places a value
on freedom so nearly absolute that the word "law" is invariably
pejorative. In this partly secularized version of Christian an-
tinomianism we find no compromising in the manner of Paul,
Luther, Calvin, or Milton: Christ simply abolished the law and
forgave our sins.

> He laid His hand on Moses Law
> The Ancient Heavens in Silent Awe
> Writ with Curses from Pole to Pole
> All away began to roll
> . . . .
> Good & Evil are no more
> Sinais trumpets cease to roar[.]
> > (*Everlasting Gospel*,
> > [f] 11-15, 21-22)

Liberty and forgiveness of sins are identical states and
values. The forgiveness that brings freedom must itself come
freely or it is not forgiveness. "We behold it is of Divine /
Mercy alone! of Free Gift and Election that we live"—so the
"Elect" will say when they finally recognize Jesus. And in an-
tinomian irony Blake has them add, "Our Virtues & Cruel
Goodnesses, have deserv'd Eternal Death" (M 13.32-34; see
Rom. 5:15-16). The quality of mercy is not strained.

Blake declares forgiveness and freedom each to be the es-
sence of Christianity: "The Religion of Jesus, Forgiveness of
Sin . . . The Glory of Christianity is, To Conquer by Forgive-
ness" (J 52); "I know of no other Christianity, and no other
Gospel than the liberty both of body & mind to exercise the
Divine Arts of Imagination" (J 77). In this second passage we
meet more than the claim of liberty of conscience, which at
first glance it resembles, the goal of religious toleration that
the Dissenting interest struggled for in the late seventeenth
century. We also see more than an artist's claim to freedom
from censorship. Christianity teaches liberty of the body as

well as of the mind, and the body will do other things than carry the mind to chapel or shop. Imagination must do more than exercise the arts of the cloister or "create an amorous image / In the shadows of his curtains and in the folds of his silent pillow" (VDA 7.6-7). Imagination demands action to rid society of tyranny and warfare and usher in the city of brotherly love.

It should be clear by now that Blake uses "liberty" in a very broad sense, one that includes both the "negative" or liberal use (freedom from) and the "positive" use (freedom to). Indeed, the ebbing of the Dissenting interest from its high-water mark in 1650 is neatly reflected in the shift in the kind of liberty it demanded, from Christian liberty in defiance of worldly law to the right to be left alone to worship quietly in peace; from the demand to be one's own master to the plea to the masters to tolerate one's private eccentricities. I have taken the terms "negative" and "positive" freedom from Isaiah Berlin's essay, "Two Concepts of Liberty."[33] Negative freedom is the comparatively modern concept developed by the classical English political theorists (Hobbes, Locke, Mill et al.); it is an area, large or small, where the individual may not be interfered with by other individuals or the state. Positive freedom, with classical and religious sources, is self-mastery, a broad concept that may range from participation in the government of one's country to the control of one's unruly self or passions. The latter image, quite frequent in Greek and Christian authors, can lead to Rousseau's paradox that one can be "forced to be free." Rousseau, indeed, made the same distinction between kinds of liberty as Berlin makes: civil liberty is the right to do what the laws do not forbid, and moral liberty is obedience to the law one prescribes for oneself, or self-mastery.[34] Joseph Priestley also drew that distinction, though for him the positive variety emphasized collective rather than personal self-government:

> POLITICAL LIBERTY, I would say, consists in the power which the members of the state reserve to themselves, of arriving at the public offices, or, at least, of having votes in the nomination of those who fill them: and I would choose to call CIVIL LIBERTY, that power

over their own actions, which the members of the state reserve to themselves, and which their officers must not infringe.[35]

That Dissenters like Priestley should have written in such a vein may indicate that the Dissenting tide was turning. It was certainly a distinction the American colonists could use.

It is interesting that the English language has not clearly distinguished the meanings of "freedom" and "liberty," though there have been attempts to do so.[36] "Freedom" does have a slightly greater "positive" connotation than "liberty," as we see in "freeman" and in the contrast between the "freedom of a city" (which is a kind of ownership or power) and the "liberty of a city" (which is an area), and even the "liberty of a prison"! As we have noted, "freedom" has occasionally meant "citizenship," as in the Authorized Version of Acts 22:28—"with a great sum obtained I this freedom [of being a Roman]"—where it translates *politeia*.[37] There is thus some linguistic as well as doctrinal warrant for interpreting "Christ hath made us free" (Gal. 5:1) as containing the idea that Christ has conferred citizenship on us in the heavenly city. It is an idea Blake would have liked. In general, however, the two words cover a largely overlapping range of meanings, both for Blake and in the English language as a whole.

Most of Blake's eloquent passages about tyranny and slavery are in the first instance a defense of liberty in the negative sense. He was perfectly willing to side with liberal reformers of the reasonable Lockean tradition in their campaigns to abolish the slave trade and alleviate the sufferings of chimney sweepers. Such freedom, however, is a precondition for a higher (positive) freedom. This freedom we would not ordinarily call freedom at all, but rather reconciliation, community, or citizenship. In large letters on plate 26 of *Jerusalem* Blake writes his most astonishing statement about liberty: "Jerusalem is named Liberty among the sons of Albion." Later he says more exactly what he means:

> In Great Eternity, every particular Form gives forth or Emanates
> Its own peculiar Light, & the Form is the Divine Vision
> And the Light is his Garment. This is Jerusalem in every Man

A Tent & Tabernacle of Mutual Forgiveness Male & Female
  Clothings.
And Jerusalem is called Liberty among the Children of Albion[.]

(J 54.1-5)

Blake's main source for his Jerusalem, of course, is Revelation
21:2: "And I John saw the holy city, new Jerusalem, coming
down from God out of heaven, prepared as a bride adorned
for her husband." His character Jerusalem is the emanation
of the collective man Albion, and the story of her exile and
return is the main plot of *Jerusalem*. But she is also a city, a
city of peace and brotherly love, in which we shall all dwell
when we gather in our alienated emanations, remove the bar-
ricades of our Selfhoods, and forgive our enemies—all finally
the same act.

That this positive and Christian liberty should be given the
name of a city, and especially a city we may build in this life
and this land, already takes Blake some distance from the
quietist and individualist tradition defined by Luther. Blake's
Jerusalem may be "in every Man," but the weight falls more
on "every" than on "in," and it depends on "Mutual Forgive-
ness" for its building. For an interesting contrast we may take
William Cowper's *The Task* (1785), which, after praising Eng-
lish (negative) liberty as a release from the "constraint" that
"hurts the faculties, impedes / Their progress in the road of
science," and so on, and alluding in proper Dissenting style
to "our Hampdens and our Sidneys," goes on to sing "a liberty,
unsung / By poets, and by senators unprais'd, / Which mon-
archs cannot grant," namely, "liberty of heart, deriv'd from
heav'n; / Bought with HIS blood who gave it to mankind." This
higher liberty is an individual state of mind, an inward power
which, having quelled all inner vices, is superior to all outward
chains. Between the laissez faire of negative liberty and the
private transcendence of the world, Cowper offers nothing—
no public positive liberty (political participation), no negative
private liberty (release of appetites), and nothing like Blake's
spiritual community in this world. Once, suggestively, Cowper
approaches the idea of citizenship—"He is indeed a freeman.
Free by birth / Of no mean city"—but this city is pointedly the

opposite of the worldly city he alludes to (Acts 21:39). It is the transcendent realm of God, "plann'd or ere the hills /Were built."[38]

A dozen years later, despite the colossal events in France, Coleridge's thinking falls into the same dichotomy, notably in *France: An Ode* (1798). The negative liberty of a "disenchanted nation" at war with tyrants has been lost because the French are "sensual" and "dark," "Slaves by their own compulsion," with no inward self-mastery. For one who, like Coleridge, carried its torch, liberty is to be found now only in nature, by a solitary man, among such "transcendent" natural phenomena as clouds, ocean waves, and the "imperious branches" of woods.[39]

Blake's female character Jerusalem, lost and restored to Albion, may have another lineage besides the Book of Revelation, and that is the largely poetic tradition of the goddess Liberty and her once lost and now restored English shrine. We see it in William Collins's *Ode to Liberty* (1746): her shrine, once a "hoary pile" in a "religious wood," has grown into a majestic temple in mixed Gothic and Grecian style. Now returned to England, she has won the love of England's youths, who "Play with the tangles of her hair" and then join the chorus of her coronation: "Thou, lady, thou shalt rule the West!"[40] Though it is likely that Blake took an interest in this imagery, as he did in the "westering" of liberty and poetry as he found it here and in James Thomson and Thomas Gray, his Liberty can ultimately be neither coquette nor queen, like Collins's, two of the roles the fallen Vala assumes as Tirzah and Rahab. We are to marry her; there is no temple for her worship. She is a city, and like the new Jerusalem of Revelation she holds no temple (21:22). We are to enter her, and walk there in conversation with our brothers and sisters.

6

Labor

The opposite of liberty, Christian or civil, is slavery, but slavery is also the antithesis of creative labor. When we allow a tyrant to get control of our spirits or our cities, the first thing he will do is put us to work at backbreaking and stultifying tasks. Blake felt the tyranny of the English Church and state not only in its censorship and prosecution of radical writers but also in the way it governed public taste, driving radical artists to drudgery for the market. The Hebrew slaves built pyramids for the Egyptians; Blake engraved other people's designs for other people's books. In its worst mutation, tyranny mobilizes and regiments its population for war, turning the whole of society, including writers and artists, into a machine of destruction, a "military-industrial complex," which devours its own workers.

We shall begin this chapter by laboring through two important passages about labor in *Jerusalem*. Reworking slightly a passage in Night the Seventh [b] of *The Four Zoas*, Blake included in *Jerusalem* an account of "alienated labor" that has quite a modern ring but is nevertheless rich in distinctively Blakean symbolism:

> Then left the Sons of Urizen the plow & harrow, the loom
> The hammer & the chisel, & the rule & compasses; from
>   London fleeing
> They forg'd the sword on Cheviot, the chariot of war & the
>   battle-ax,
> The trumpet fitted to mortal battle, & the flute of summer in
>   Annandale
> And all the Arts of Life. they changd into the Arts of Death
>   in Albion.

The hour-glass contemnd because its simple workmanship.
Was like the workmanship of the plowman, & the water wheel,
That raises water into cisterns: broken & burnd with fire:
Because its workmanship. was like the workmanship of the
     shepherd.
And in their stead, intricate wheels invented, wheel
     without wheel:
To perplex youth in their outgoings, & to bind to labours in
     Albion
Of day & night the myriads of eternity that they may grind
And polish brass & iron hour after hour laborious task!
Kept ignorant of its use, that they might spend the days
     of wisdom
In sorrowful drudgery, to obtain a scanty pittance of bread:
In ignorance to view a small portion & think that All,
And call it Demonstration: blind to all the simple rules of life.

(J 65.12-28)

The Sons of Urizen frequently appear in *The Four Zoas*—they seem to be the powers (they are called "lions") or ideas ("constellations") of Urizen—but they are named only here in *Jerusalem*. In the first instance they are English youths forced into working for the highly rationalized (Urizenized) war machine, but in carrying over "Sons" from its quite different original context Blake suggests that Urizen has gotten hold of them even more intimately than does a foreman of factory workers, as if they are not just "hands" but "heads." In a gruesome earlier passage (J 58.6-20), Blake tells how Urizen has adopted the Sons of Albion as his own through a kind of circumcision of their minds: they "Feel their Brain cut round beneath the temples shrieking / Bonifying into a skull," as if the skull were a scab hardening over a wounded or lobotomized brain, "Once open to the heavens," as *Europe* states it, and "Now overgrown with hair and coverd with a stony roof" like a tomb (Eur 10.28-29). There may be a pun in "beneath the temples," as Urizen is acting like a high priest; in any case he puts youths to work on "a Mighty Temple" that embraces the entire known world within its "stupendous Works" of "dark Rocks" (J 58.21-51). "Stupendous" is also well chosen, for the temple strikes its viewers stupid because those already struck stupid have built it. This very impressive structure of

abstract reason, it seems, is now erected in the mind of each
Son of Albion. Once they were the Sons of Jerusalem, as the
phrase "myriads of eternity" (J 65.23) suggests, but now all
of Albion is cut off from the liberty of spirit Jerusalem rep-
resents.

The newly regimented youth of England, our passage says,
leave a realm of simplicity and peace to enter one of per-
plexing intricacy and war. The flute and the shepherd evoke
the pastoral tradition and its contrast to the turmoil of the
city, but Blake is also recording, as Wordsworth does, the real
devastation of the English countryside during the Napoleonic
Wars. By heading his list of peaceful implements with the
plow and his list of weapons with the sword he is also making
sure we do not miss the reversal of Isaiah's vision.[1] There is
another odd reversal, however. We would expect a line about
the desertion of the villages and the migration to the cities,
but instead we have the phrase "from London fleeing." Blake
seems to propose a symbolic meaning of "London" that con-
flicts with the geographical one. "London" must mean the
spiritual center of Albion, and spiritual centers have no par-
ticular location in space. Thus to flee London is to lose the
sense of the center or the whole, the "All" that now perplexes
the youth. We remember how the counties of Great Britain
fled out from Jerusalem much earlier in the poem (16.28f);
these perplexed "outgoings" of the youth reenact the original
spiritual diaspora.

All the place names in the latter passage are absent in the
Four Zoas version, and it is possible that the next two names,
Cheviot and Annandale, were added for the same reason
London was. If London is the center, Cheviot and Annandale
are the circumference or apogee, the border of England far-
thest from London. The Cheviot Hills and the Solway Firth,
into which the River Annan flows, more or less make up the
boundary between England and Scotland. The Cheviots were
known for their sheep, and Annandale, I presume, for its
farmland; together, as hills and valley, they are the sites of
the two kinds of "workmanship" Blake names in this passage.
But both places have also been named in plate 63 as the
settings for a Druidic sacrifice of Jehovah, who is here virtually

identical with Jesus: "And Jehovah stood in the Gates of the Victim, & he appeared / A weeping Infant in the Gates of Birth in the midst of Heaven / . . . Such the Appearance in Cheviot" (63.16-17, 23). Such the *parousia* in Cheviot, we might say: the redemptive possibility in the midst of the slaughter of the English innocents.[2]

Innocence, under this kind of compulsion, becomes ignorance, and it is striking how the emphasis slides from the destruction of youth through warfare, which reappears in the passage following this one, to the destruction of youth through meaningless mechanized labor in large factories. The first kills their bodies in "mortal battle," the second kills their souls in the leveling negations of Satan's mills. The two deaths recombine in a brief shiver of meaning at "Kept ignorant of its use," for the use to which this brass and iron will be put is warfare. The cannons and other weaponry on which they labor will be turned on their equally sorrowful and ignorant French counterparts, and even on themselves if they shrink from battle: "Chaind hand & foot," in chains they may have literally forged themselves in the ironworks, the next passage says, "compelld to fight under the iron whips / Of our captains; fearing our officers more than the enemy" (65.35-36). The rest of our passage, however, dwells on the two kinds of work, and after reading it we see that "the Arts of Death" are deadly not only in their ends but in their means of manufacture.

The hour-glass and the water wheel are not randomly chosen, because the complex machine that binds youth to labors absorbs and replaces both of them. It multiplies the simple wheel of the shepherd into a series of gears and drive shafts, harnessed to a different kind of water wheel in a millrace, or perhaps to a steam engine, whose original function, Blake must have known, was to pump water out of mines. In Blake's day the Newcomen and Watt engines pumped water into London. The intricate structure of "wheel without wheel" suggests a clock, which had replaced the hour-glass throughout England in the seventeenth and eighteenth centuries and thereby had made possible the industrial revolution itself. As E. P. Thompson and others have shown, the precision of clock time, essential to the competitive functioning of factories, relentlessly eroded the older, more variably paced time of work and play, which was tied to season, weather, and social need while softened by communal traditions.[3] Machines run all night and all year; those who labor at them—and the young were often thought most malleable to their demands—must become parts of the machine themselves, laboring "day & night," "hour after hour."

Blake brings out another resonance in "Arts of Life" and "Arts of Death" by picturing his "water wheel, / That raises water into cisterns," as not only contemned but "broken & burnd with fire." This picture summons up one of the images of death in Ecclesiastes 12:6: "Or ever . . . the wheel [be] broken at the cistern." When the body dies, in other words, then shall the dust return to the earth.[4] The breaking of this product of simple workmanship implies the death of the simple workman. By adding "burnd with fire" Blake adds murder to what from Ecclesiastes we might take to mean a natural death; the devastation of the countryside is not a "natural" and willing abandonment of old ways for new and better ways but a deliberate policy of state, Church, and munition-makers, a policy of forcible conscription and scorched earth. Ecclesiastes may also have suggested "the days of wisdom" the youth have lost, for the tyranny of time and chance, to which the author of Ecclesiastes submits, finds almost literal embodiment in the machinery that binds them. Under such conditions, "the days of thy youth" are vanity and waste. Wisdom, for Blake, is a gift of eternity; ignorance is a product of counted and mechanized time. "The hours of folly are measur'd by the clock, but of wisdom: no clock can measure" (Prov. 12, E 35).

This machine breeds ignorance by so confining its servants' functions that they "view a small portion & think that All." In saying this Blake is restating the observations of the very theorists whose doctrines he in general despised. Adam Smith put it bluntly in *The Wealth of Nations*:

> The man whose whole life is spent in performing a few simple operations, of which the effects too are, perhaps, always the same,

or very nearly the same, has no occasion to exert his understand-
ing, or to exercise his invention in finding out expedients for
removing difficulties which never occur. He naturally loses, there-
fore, the habit of such exertion, and generally becomes as stupid
and ignorant as it is possible for a human creature to become.[5]

Before Adam Smith, his fellow Scotsman Adam Ferguson
noted a similar degradation induced by the division of labor:
"Manufactures . . . prosper most, where the mind is least con-
sulted, and where the workshop may . . . be considered as an
engine, the parts of which are men."[6] For Blake, however,
the machines are products of a myopic general theory of the
mind, a theory that turns the mind itself into a machine. As
usual with Blake, the material and social structures that re-
produce ignorance (or tyranny or war) are themselves repro-
ductions of ignorant (or tyrannical or bellicose) minds; his
social materialism, often imagined in vivid detail, is a dialec-
tical phase of a larger idealism. So it is that the machine whose
chief byproduct is ignorance is a literal version of the machine
of ignorance itself, the schools and universities of Europe:

I turn my eyes to the Schools & Universities of Europe
And there behold the Loom of Locke whose Woof rages dire
Washd by the Water-wheels of Newton. black the cloth
In heavy wreathes folds over every Nation; cruel Works
Of many Wheels I view, wheel without wheel, with cogs tyrannic
Moving by compulsion each other[.]

(J 15.14-19)

We should note, incidentally, that the youths are at work
not in a textile mill with power looms but in a munitions
foundry: they "grind / And polish brass & iron." There were
plenty of them in operation during the wars. One well-known
factory, a Scottish one at that, the Carron ironworks near the
Firth of Forth, replaced wooden cogwheels (of "simple work-
manship") with cast-iron gearwheels and produced huge guns
known as "carronades." As a French visitor described the
workshop in 1784,

Amongst these warlike machines, these terrible death-dealing in-
struments, huge cranes, every kind of windlass, lever and tackle
for moving heavy loads, were fixed in suitable places. Their creak-

ing, the piercing noise of the pulleys, the continuous sound of hammering, the ceaseless energy of the men keeping all this machinery in motion, presented a sight as interesting as it was new.[7]

Whether loom or foundry, the vision contrary to both of them, as Blake goes on to say, is a form of social organization where we are all somehow concentric to one another and there are no big wheels to tyrannize little cogs. Newton's wheels, "wheel without wheel," are "not as those in Eden: which / Wheel within Wheel in freedom revolve in harmony & peace" (15.19-20). This, of course, invokes Ezekiel's vision of the chariot with "a wheel in the middle of a wheel" beside each creature (1:16), a passage of great importance for Blake. This chariot, unlike "the chariot of war" forged on Cheviot, is a chariot of life, powered by the four "living creatures" (Blake's Zoas) who will draw it to freedom.[8]

In *Jerusalem* this is the only appearance of the Sons of Urizen. Urizen himself slips out of view until his redemption is announced briefly at the conclusion; to tie up a loose end, we may assume that his Sons return to freedom (freedom, in effect, from Sonship) when Urizen returns to his proper task at the plow (95:16). In *The Four Zoas*, however, Blake had elaborated a continuous role for the Sons, and something was lost when he left them out of *Jerusalem*. We see them at various jobs set by their father, though they occasionally rebel.[9] In Night the Second they are given their chance to remake "the infinite Earth" into a "Non Entity" of geometric ratios when "many" humans turn away from visions and indeed from visionary labor and busy themselves with their families and money-making instead (FZ 28.11-21; E 312). So licensed, the Sons, or "Lions of Urizen," beat out pyramids and cubes, divide the deep with compasses, and weigh masses in scales. The Newtonian and Lockian universe they create, of course, is the ideological precondition for the real labor in the munitions factory that Night the Seventh (b) presents.

Yet, the idealism that sets mental states as causes of material conditions, as I have said, remains dialectical, at least metaphorically. Marxists, and many others, argue the priority, "in the last instance," of material conditions to social structures and the priority of both to intellectual or cultural activity and "consciousness," though they may, and should, go on to examine how consciousness in turn is partly independent and often a decisive force in the organization of labor itself. Blake, it could be argued, comes as close to this view as his opposing framework permits when he presents the scientific worldview not as the result of contemplation or cognition, as this worldview would itself declare, but as the product of laborious activity. Metaphorical it may be at this stage, but Blake preserves the creative activity of the subject, the human laborer who remakes the human world, as against what Marx called "contemplative materialism." In German philosophy, Marx argued, "the *active* side was developed abstractly by idealism—which, of course, does not know real, sensuous activity as such."[10] Blake, who certainly knew real sensuous activity as such quite intimately, goes beyond Hegel in presenting intellectual activity as labor, and not only as the Hegelian "labor of the negative." Such labor is portrayed, concretely if metaphorically, as pounding on anvils and weighing on scales, and finally perhaps more than metaphorically—as if Newton's system grew not only from his habit of contemplating under trees (until gravity struck him) but also from his habit of hard work among inclined planes, scales, compasses, and cannons.

The damage done by the Sons of Urizen in Night the Seventh (b) they undo in Night the Ninth. Urizen, reconciled with his emanation Ahania and contrite over his errors, brings about a sudden transformation of the universe. The law of gravity, which kept the dead in their graves, is repealed, and "the bursting Universe explodes / All things reversd flew from their centers" (FZ 122.26-27). The oppressed of all the ages arise to accuse their oppressors and the Last Judgment begins. Urizen assists the now nearly regenerate Man, Albion or (among other meanings) the English people, to arise and meet Jesus, but "flames repelld them." As Stevenson tersely states it, "The thought [Urizen] of repentance is not enough; a change of activity is needed."[11] That change the Sons of Urizen now undertake, as they beat their swords into plowshares.

Then siezd the Sons of Urizen the Plow they polishd it
From rust of ages all its ornaments of Gold & silver & ivory

Reshone across the field immense where all the nations
Darkend like Mould in the divided fallows where the weed
Triumphs in its own destruction they took down the harness
From the blue walls of heaven starry jingling ornamented
With beautiful art the study of angels the workmanship
    of Demons
When Heaven & Hell in Emulation strove in sports of Glory

The noise of rural work resounded thro the heavens of heavens
The horse[s] neigh from the battle the wild bulls from the
    sultry waste
The tygers from the forests & the lions from the sandy desarts
They sing they sieze the instruments of harmony they throw away
The spear the bow the gun the mortar they level the fortifications
They beat the iron engines of destruction into wedges
They give them to Urthonas Sons ringing the hammers sound
In dens of death to forge the spade the mattock & the ax
The heavy roller to break the clods to pass over the nations
                        (FZ 124.6-22)

The archetypal plow in this passage[12] has lain idle since the days before the Fall of the rebellious angels (or their Rise, if we keep the terms of *The Marriage of Heaven and Hell*), days when Angels and Demons competed like two teams for the glory of superior art. The power of unity amid division is transferred to the plow itself, rather as the two themes of war and peace are transferred onto the shield of Achilles in the *Iliad*, for the plow must first cut furrows before we can gather in the harvest. "Divided fallows" may doubly characterize the fallen human condition, for if the division is by furrow within one field then we have been insufficiently plowed and will never put forth life until we have been plowed properly; if the division is between fields, like "the nations" of Europe at war, then we need to be plowed *together*, as one people, before regeneration can begin. As one people again, the corporeal war that strides like a grim reaper among the European nations will be retooled into spiritual emulation, or "wars of love." Meanwhile there is work to be done, "rural work," and the four powers of the former wildernesses transform their realms first by singing and playing musical "instruments" (Blake brings out the etymological richness of that word) and then by turning weaponry into agricultural tools. The plow itself is handed to Urizen, who uses it to prepare the ground for the "Seed of Men," the souls who must die in order to be reborn, for "Except a corn of wheat fall into the ground and die, it abideth alone: but if it die, it bringeth forth much fruit" (John 12:24). As Urizen then casts the seed they are rather surprisingly winnowed by a wind so that the souls are sorted in advance for the final harvest. And as Blake reverses the order of events he also reverses vehicle and tenor of the Parable of the Sower (Matt. 13:3-8). Where Jesus likens souls to kinds of ground in their varying receptivity to the word he disseminates, so that sometimes the sown word falls upon "stony places" and takes no root in those who do not truly hear it, Blake has the "Kings & Princes of the Earth," who while they reigned were deaf to the cries of the miserable, fall "on the unproducing sands & on the hardend rocks" (125.10-11).[13] "Unproducing" reminds us that kings and princes only consume like parasites the products of their subjects. Blake's punishment is a Dantean *contrappasso* like that of the sterile abusers of God's gifts who are flung onto a sandy plain that rejects every plant from its bed (*Inferno* 14.11). In the midst of all this metaphorical or archetypal labor, Blake does not forget labor's literal enemies, the idlers who confiscate the wealth produced by those he calls "the generous" in *America*.

Though it is at Albion's command that Urizen repents, it is Los who emerges, after an unpromising start, as the hero faithful at his post and at his task. By the time he began the last reorganization of his material for *Jerusalem*, Blake had settled on Los as his epic hero, an unlikely choice in many respects, certainly less "heroic" in traditional terms than Orc, or even Milton.

* * *

Looking at the changing demographic profiles of western epics from Homer to Blake, we get the impression that the descendants of Hephaestus-Vulcan the smith-god, Eumaeus the swineherd, and the bards Phemius and Demodocus have pulled off a *coup d'état*. The aristocratic warriors, though there are still plenty of them in Blake's epics (in fact, they are still resisting the upstarts), are no longer the main actors; all the important characters, even the negative ones, work for a living. The bow-shot that brings *Jerusalem* to its climax is one of the few redemptive upper-class deeds, and this comes from a special "Bow of Mercy & Loving-kindness: laying / Open the hidden Heart in Wars of Mutual Benevolence Wars of Love" (J 97.13-14). Such wars, as I have said, require retooling, and there are fitter wielders of the new epic machinery than "the silly Greek & Latin slaves of the Sword" (M 1). Having stood in the wings with his sleeves rolled up, Blake's Los, heir to Homer's *demioergoi* who worked for the people, now a demiurge who builds the world people believe they inhabit, walks out onto center stage, hammer in hand.

Blake, of course, had several precedents and premonitions before him, and they give us ways to assess the central importance he gives to labor. There has been a kind of emigration of people from the lesser classical genres to the greater, a revolt arising in the pastoral and georgic suburbs to which shepherds and farmers had been confined and spilling into the public world of heroic action reserved to the nobility. Irruptions of plebeian and provincial Dionysus-worshippers with their "sweet labor" and especially of Christians with their "work of faith and labour of love" left explosive cultural deposits that the dominant hierarchies of ancient and feudal Europe then tried to layer over and hedge about with allegories and apologies.[14] With the Protestant reprise of the Christian revolution came a new rejection of the world and its violent politics, a new internalization of Christian doctrine, and a new insistence on the redemptive power of labor. Blake could see Spenser and Milton as having "refunctioned" the heroic epic (to use Brecht's term) from its relapse, after early radical Christian impulses had spent their strength, into the "long and tedious havoc" of its Rolands and Arthurs. Milton's theme, "the better fortitude / Of Patience and Heroic Martyrdom," left unsung by previous poets, fits well enough the character of Blake's hero, but Blake might reply that in singing of patience Milton left unsung a hero's action, his creative work. Whether out of a Puritan denial of justification by works, or out of his sense of futility after the dissipation and defeat of a great revolution, Milton seems to have found little room in his Christian economy for human agency and social change.[15] Blake, no Puritan but imaginatively engaged in the revolutions of his own day, which were thwarted only a little less decisively than that of Milton's, wavered between Milton's injunction patiently to serve and an indignant venturing into the workshop of the world. Los in *Jerusalem* combines active undertakings with passive undergoings—after every bout of despair he rouses his fires—and yet his activity, as we shall see, is a kind of holding action, a demonstration of faith that what he is ostensibly working toward must eventually come about. Much of the heroic labor in Blake's poems is a figure for his own preservation of artistic and spiritual integrity, but to be true to one's vision is in Blake's universe a social act; it is to rescue one's brothers and sisters from dissolution and death.

The distance in social vision between Homer's epics and Blake's is nicely marked by an interesting reversal of vehicle and tenor. Many of the similes of the *Iliad* compare the deeds of the battlefield with agricultural or artisanal labor, with reaping, winnowing, shearing, tanning, carpentering, weaving, and the like. Warfare is in the foreground and literal; work is elsewhere, far away and figural, almost allegorical. In Blake's poems labor is in the foreground and primary, though to call it literal would be misleading, and it is often made to represent the warfare of a Christian soldier. So in *Jerusalem* Los at his anvil beats a "spiritual sword" out of sighs and tears (9.18) and then forges an ax to cut apart the woof of Locke that vegetates over Albion (15.22), and then his hammer itself becomes a mace (8.3, 78.3). His work at his forge, even while it is a figure for another kind of labor—building a city of art— also becomes struggle or combat:

> Yet ceasd he not from labouring at the roarings of his Forge
> With iron & brass Building Golgonooza in great contendings[.]
> (10.62-63)

With these contendings Blake may be invoking not only the epic tradition but the Epistle of Jude, which enjoins us to "contend for the faith" while reminding us of Michael "contending for the devil": we are to "fight the good fight of faith"

(Jude 3, 9). Blake notes in his "Public Address" that Homer speaks of "Generous Contention," a sort of contention Blake has not encountered among his rivals in the graphic arts (E 577); we may think of the games of the *Iliad*, the "sports of Glory" which Blake would redefine as emulation among artists. Another great contention, the climactic confrontation of Milton, the hero of *Milton*, with his great enemy Urizen, is not a battle at all but, as David Punter has noted, a labor. Milton takes clay and builds or sculpts new flesh on the rational skeleton.[16] As for "the roarings of his Forge," it later howls loud in fury and despair like a contending warrior itself, and in so doing it neatly reverses the simile in the *Iliad* (17.88) where Hector's shout flames up like Hephaestus' fire. In Pope's version:

Sheath'd in bright Arms, thro' cleaving Ranks he flies,
And sends his Voice in Thunder to the Skies:
Fierce as a Flood of Flame by *Vulcan* sent,
It flew, and fir'd the Nations as it went.

We are now in a position to enjoy the pungent ironies of Blake's phrase "the silly Greek & Latin slaves of the Sword." To say of such warriors as Achilles and Aeneas, who in their own eyes are masters of the sword and masters over many slaves, that they are themselves slaves of the sword, is to add a fine impudence to a fine insight into the imperious demands of the warrior code. To call them "silly" is a splendid finishing touch, for the word meant more than "foolish": it could mean "weak" or "feeble," it carried the condescending social connotation of "rustic" or "lowly," and here, I feel sure, it is meant to evoke a special usage in the poetry Blake grew up reading, "silly" as a standard epithet of sheep. With such a word, which Blake uses only here, we have crossed the immense social distance from the wrath of Achilles, which opens the *Iliad*, to "the wrath of the Lamb," which closes the New Testament.

Both the Old and New Testaments place a much higher value on labor than classical literature does. Of the twelve "labors" of Hercules only one, the cleaning of the Augean stables, sounds like real work; the rest are deeds of hunting, theft, or battle, the usual heroic displays of force or fraud. The comparable Hebraic champion, Samson, suffers the full bitterness of brute drudgery in the mill at Gaza. The hard labor fate imposes on Aeneas is the not un-Blakean task of founding a city, but he mainly slaughters his enemies while nameless others build the walls. It was no doubt in the crucible of the Egyptian bondage that Hebrew culture took its distinctive shape, and the idea of the Exodus, of liberation from slavery, governs most of the crucial biblical events from Genesis to Revelation. Only briefly an independent nation, at no time an empire large enough to support much of an aristocracy, Israel never grew away from its plebeian and pastoral origins so far as to scorn labor itself. Its god was a laborer, at least on the sixth day when he worked with clay to make man (he was more of an overseer the first five), and the firmament is later said to show his "handiwork." Although Genesis is silent about it, tradition has it that Adam and Eve worked in the Garden; it was only after the Fall that work became toilsome and brought sweat to the brow. Jesus was a carpenter who spoke in parables about sowers and laborers in the vineyard. "My father worketh hitherto," he said, "and I work," even on the Sabbath.

In the face of Greek and Latin contempt for labor, among other cultural pressures, some early Christian thinkers stressed the contemplative or worshipful character of work. Some gnostic sects decided that the creator-god of the Hebrews was a demon who made an evil mess, and the true god was a pure spirit or mind who could lead us up out of it unsoiled. It is tempting to see in Blake a blending of these two contrary ancient attitudes: the gnostic demiurge who makes the fallen material world is Urizen, the humble worker who saves us from it is Los. Such cosmological contendings derive readily enough from the slavery theme of the Old Testament, no doubt, and Blake had other promptings for them, as we have seen, in the world around him. It is always interesting nonetheless to find precedents for his distinctive ideas, even if he is unlikely to have known of them, not least because they make salient the latent points of growth or tension in the tradition he worked with. It is pleasant to think about the venturesome speculations of St. Maximus, a seventh-century Greek theologian, who saw the universe as a workshop, and man, the microcosm, as a builder like God and a "living workshop" himself.[17]

* * *

If we came to *Jerusalem* without much prior experience of Blake and tried to place it somehow in the epic tradition, expecting perhaps a Protestant version of Tasso's *Gerusalemme Liberata*, it would take us a good deal of time to recognize familiar paths through the strange thicket at our feet. Not the least strange of the epic revisions is the declaration of the conflict between Los and the twelve Sons of Albion (5.24-33); it immediately follows the Saviour's theme song, Albion's rejection of it, and Blake's invocation of the Saviour's spirit as his muse. If the division of Albion from Jesus corresponds to the divisions in heaven that Homer and Virgil name in their opening lines, the conflict between Los and the Sons reflects the mortal disputes consequent on the heavenly ones, such as Achilles' quarrel with Agamemnon. So far Blake preserves the epic *topoi*. But what is at issue here below is a kind of contest among masons and architects. Albion having threatened to "build my Laws of Moral Virtue," what Los must do is undertake "the building of Golgonooza," the first of Blake's announced themes (5.24), and outbuild Albion. As if Blake is conflating an *Iliad* where a city is destroyed and an *Aeneid* where one is built, we next learn that the twelve Sons go to war against the city of Los, but what they "revolve most mightily upon" are Los's furnaces. Los is "Lord of the furnaces." Soon enough they "labour mightily" in their own furnaces (8.41f), in a war of production.

And so it goes throughout the poem. Hammers, anvils, tongs, bellows, and chains howl and pound and clank incessantly, except during a period or two when the work in interrupted by the counsels of despair (the Spectre of Los) or grief over Albion's sleep of death. Sometimes the labor modulates to another form, as when Los becomes a guard or watchman who explores and "proves" Babylon with his globe of fire; eventually (83.79f) it is said that Los labors by day at the furnaces and moonlights as a watchman. Once, when they are in the spirit of Los, the "living creatures" plow life out of death, reminding us of the agricultural provenance of the word "labor" when they chant, "Labour well the Minute Particulars . . . labour well the teeming Earth" (55.51, 53).[18] Los's companion Enitharmon, of course, weaves at the loom. Through all this we sometimes glimpse William and Catherine Blake at work together in the studio.

It is important to see that the kind of building and laboring Los does and the kind the Sons of Albion do are very different. The Son named Hand, who absorbs all his brothers at this point, condenses his emanations (thoughts and desires) into hard opaque substances and forges them into the sword of war and other weaponry. Los takes the sighs, tears, and groans of Hand's suffering emanations, puts them in his own furnaces, and forms the spiritual sword that lays open the hidden heart (which Hand has buried alive); at the same time, and perhaps as the same act, Los condenses the sighs and tears into "forms of cruelty," the twelve Daughters of Albion, who correspond to the twelve Sons. This may not seem to undo the war preparations of the Sons, but such a direct contention is not possible for Los, as of course it was not possible for an obscure engraver in London to intervene in the wars with France. Los's indirect method is educational: to hold up to the bellicose Sons the emanations they have repressed in a form they recognize, that is, images of themselves, now doing the work of cruelty. By drawing forth the implications of their own acts Los hopes "That he who will not defend Truth, may be compelld to defend / A Lie: that he may be snared and caught and snared and taken." This eduction of buried premises is a reduction to absurdity, but the argument is conducted by means of art.[19] The task is to give "a body to Falshood that it may be cast off for ever" (12.12) and to "demand explicit words" (17.60); the ultimate goal is to get those who produced the falsehoods to acknowledge them as their own and repent.

The Sons of Albion, like Los, are active throughout the poem. In a more subtle, though confusing, development, Albion himself, who vows, "here will I build my Laws of Moral Virtue" in his opening speech, falls passive if not altogether asleep while the "building" goes on. Whether this is the labor of his Sons is not quite clear, but we are soon told that Albion "Was built in from Eternity, in the Cliffs of Albion" (11.15), presumably by someone else. A little later Albion's bosom hardens "as he builded onwards / On the Gulph of Death in self-righteousness" (19.30-31). This is an interestingly ambiguous use of the verb. If "builded" is a kind of absolute transitive then we must supply the object, perhaps the cliffs he has been "built in" (and in which Los is "roofd in from Eternity" in the following lines). If it is an intransitive verb, on the pattern of "harden," it suggests a similar uncertainty as to agency, an active passivity or passive activity, or a dream of labor while sleepwalking. By extension, the labor of the Sons, though less ambiguous grammatically (Albion, too, eventually simply "builds"), is not really labor: it does not create, preserve, or redeem as Los's does.

The act of building that turns into a state of being built reflects the frequent Blakean theme of alienation, the loss of one's own products and even one's surrender to them as "given" facts. Sartre's term "practico-inert" is suggestive of Albion's plight; it refers to the alienated and congealed form of a group's past praxis (labor or political action), whether as material goods, buildings, institutions, structures of behavior, or habits of thought. The gravest error is to forget that human beings, with varying degrees of lucidity and collaboration, built these things, and that they can change and rebuild them if they want to and can organize themselves to do it. Most of us are "forgetful," however, and stumble through the human landscape as if it were an eternal datum. One who, like Blake, spent his life in meticulous labor producing nearly everything in his art from scratch, and whose art explicitly produced an alternative world, would be well placed not to "forget" that human labor is the origin of everything we see, and even how we see it.[20] The constant efforts of Los at his furnaces and anvils are certainly autobiographical, but it is also the case that Blake's life of labor placed him at a vantage from which to grasp a universal social process.

The reader of *Jerusalem* will be well paid for the labor of building up an infrastructure of meanings around such words as "labour" and "build," and I will insult my reader no further by holding up blueprints. The laboriousness of reading Blake, as I have suggested in chapter two, seems to have been a deliberate feature of the total aesthetic or spiritual effect. Intentional or not, something of the continual struggle to make things out, put things together, and march onward is inscribed in the implicit theme of process itself, of being in the midst of things. In the midst of things is where epics traditionally begin, and it is also true that, like traditional epics, *Milton* and *Jerusalem* end somewhere else, in an apocalypse. Surely, however, no other epics make us feel so deeply immersed in the endless ongoingness and perplexities of life: waiting and watching, with small advances and retreats, turning things around in a hundred different lights, groping and pressing for possibility, raging and hoping and losing hope again. As many critics have complained, Blake's narrative sense is very weak (though that may have to do with his beliefs about time); negotiating the plot of *Jerusalem* is like watching the slow crawl of a prickly caterpillar along a branch, only to have it burst into a butterfly and soar away. "Works-in-progress" they could be called, despite the supremely "finished" effect of the engraved and colored plates, as if they are a series of bulletins from Blake's workshop.

The theme of process finds frequent expression in Blake's use of participles and participial adjectives, and especially in their sometimes awkward sequence and subordination to finite verbs.

> While Los arose upon his Watch, and down from Golgonooza
> Putting on his golden sandals to walk from mountain to
>   mountain,
> He takes his way, girding himself with gold & in his hand
> Holding his iron mace[.]   (J 83.75-78)

Does the clause beginning with "Putting" amplify the clause, governed by "takes," that it splits—this is how he takes his way? Or is Los down from Golgonooza before he puts the sandals on, leaving "takes" to be modified by "girding" and "Holding," themselves quite different in meaning though parallel in syntax? However we parse it, the effect of these lines is a blurred overlapping of the phases of an action, of constant puttings on and girdings up.

Participles often become gerunds, as mine just did, giving "roarings of his Forge" and "great contendings" in a passage we quoted earlier, and continual "shudderings" and "howlings" and "provings." The words "continual" and "continually" continually appear. Los is continually laboring, continually building, continually creating, continually destroying falsehoods, continually going into eternal death, and continually forgiving—or at least continually wrestling with the great message of Jesus that salvation lies "in the Continual Forgiveness of Sins / In the Perpetual Mutual Sacrifice in Great Eternity" (61.22-23). *La lutte continue.* The struggle is eternal, and Eternity is a struggle. At the visionary close of *Jerusalem,* though the scattered faculties have reassembled as spiritual warriors armed with bow and arrow and riding in chariots, what they seem to do when together is to take on a form of labor—"living going forth & returning wearied"—not a form of amusement. War, conversation, and labor have all been transfigured and identified with one another, but the predominant paradigm remains the most mundane and essentially human of all activity, labor.

To so privilege the artisan Los and to suggest that labor will be found even in Eternity, labor much more energetic than it was in Milton's unfallen Paradise, is to break not only with bourgeois thought but with nearly all of western tradition, including the Hebraic. In bourgeois theory, labor is a means to an end. Once past the classic phase of Calvinist theology, as studied by Weber, early bourgeois Protestantism tended to the easy assumption that industry on earth would be rewarded in heaven. It would also be rewarded on earth, of course, as material prosperity, eventual retirement for oneself, and leisure for one's children. This still prevalent scheme says little about the redemptive quality of labor itself, or of certain imaginable forms of it. Whatever may have been the case before the Fall, the Bible stresses the harshness and frustration of postlapsarian toil. The Greek philosophers disparaged it, praising leisure and contemplation as the highest goods. Not until the time of the industrial revolution, which threatened with extinction many of the immemorial patterns of labor, patterns of technology and social organization so old they seemed the order of nature itself, do we find sustained discussion of what "good" labor might be, whether simply the least degrading to mind and body or, in the most radical speculations, redemptive, intrinsically satisfying, unalienating, and expressive of the whole soul. Karl Marx's early manuscript on alienated labor is part of this discussion, but it has not been Marxism, by and large, that has preserved a notion of "good" work. Most Marxists, including such innovators as Herbert Marcuse, concentrate on ways to shorten the working day and make work less onerous (as well, of course, as socializing decisions concerning the economy as a whole). Some Marxists, to their shame, have endorsed the draconian labor measures of the USSR in its rapid industrialization, as if such a forced march, whatever its justification, has anything to do with socialism.[21]

The vision of redeemed labor is found sometimes on the fringes of orthodox socialism but especially among the utopian socialists and the anarchists. In England one of the greatest of those who kept this vision was William Morris. Granting, to be sure, that "hope of rest" and "hope of product" are two of the chief informing features of work worth doing, he also laid weight on a third:

> The hope of pleasure in the work itself: how strange that hope must seem to some of my readers—to most of them! Yet I think that to all living things there is a pleasure in the exercise of their energies, and that even beasts rejoice in being lithe and swift and strong. But a man at work, making something which he feels will exist because he is working at it and wills it, is exercising the energies of his mind and soul as well as of his body. Memory and imagination help him as he works. Not only his own thoughts, but the thoughts of the men of past ages guide his hands; and, as a part of the human race, he creates. If we work thus we shall be men, and our days will be happy and eventful.[22]

I do not mean to suggest that Los's dire struggles at his forge against recalcitrant material and menacing spiritual forces, including his own treacherous alter ego the Spectre, represent Morris's vision of pleasure. Yet the motto of *The*

Four Zoas is "Rest before Labour," as if the end of rest is labor and not the seemingly self-evident contrary. Eternity, as we have said, is not restful. Moments of grace as well as moments of terror descend on Los at his furnaces as they must have come to Blake in his workshop, but those moments arrive in a world prepared for them by constant creative effort.

> Every Time less than a pulsation of the artery
> Is equal in its period to Six Thousand Years.
> For in this Period the Poets Work is Done[.]
>   (M 28.62-29.1)

"Done" does not mean "finished" here. It is never done in that sense, only raised to a higher level. The equivalent in the experience of Blake's reader is the continual growth of comprehension and imaginative reach by dint of hard work. Northrop Frye has the happy idea that *Jerusalem* is itself a kind of machine, elaborate and squeaky and cumbersome, designed to fight the machine age.[23] We who are set at work on it are meant to find in our diligent toil and growing mastery a paradigm of what all labor ought to be.

7

Time, Eternity, and History

For the realm we enter when our imagination is fully awake, Blake at first preferred the term "infinite." "He who sees the Infinite in all things sees God." Ezekiel wanted to raise men "into a perception of the infinite." The Atlantic Ocean has already barred out the "infinite mountains of light" (of Atlantis) and now threatens to overwhelm America, "another portion of the infinite." Oothoon tells how her "infinite brain" was inclosed in a circle by those who instructed her in Lockean philosophy (E 3, 39, 56, 47). By the time of the Lambeth prophecies, however, "infinite" is giving way to "eternity" or "eternal life"; a term in the mode of space giving way to a term or terms in the mode of time. As early as *Thel*, it is true, the realm of the infinite is called the "eternal vales," but of course the issue of *Thel* is precisely time, how to face time's passing and one's own death. So it is with Oothoon's phrase, "A palace of eternity in the jaws of the hungry grave." "Joys," we also note, belong to the highest realm of both time and space; they are "Holy, eternal, infinite!" (E 49, 48). The great opening quatrain of "Auguries of Innocence" (E 490) puts infinity and eternity together in parallel, neither subsuming the other: "Infinity in the palm of your hand / And Eternity in an hour." Yet, "Eternity" (and sometimes "Immortality") largely takes over in Blake's work, absorbing not only the abstract sense of "infinity" (limitlessness) but also sometimes even its spatial connotation. Milton and Ololon for example, are "in" Eternity, and Eternity shudders when Milton descends.

The apocalyptic finale of *Jerusalem* seems to recur to a balance like that of "Auguries of Innocence" in its account of the visionary transformation of both modes. Albion stretches his hand "into Infinitude" to take up his bow for the final annihilating shot. The four cardinal points and the four rivers of Paradise make an appearance, and we are told that the four Living Creatures are creating space and creating time. Still, it is the emanations who are named Jerusalem, a place name, whereas the Living Creatures who emanate them ultimately dwell in a mode of time. As we last hear of the Creatures (J 99) they are "living going forth & returning wearied / Into the Planetary lives of Years Months Days & Hours reposing / And then Awaking into his Bosom in the Life of Immortality," almost as if they are the essence of temporal rhythm itself.

The priority of time over space is one of the abstract assertions whose implications we shall explore in this chapter, especially as they merge into social and political issues. I am particularly concerned with history and historical change. It seems obvious that any radical or revolutionary view of the world ought to have at least a tacit theory of history to account for how the world has come to its present pass and how it might change, or how we might change it, for the better. The theory need not posit a linear or progressive view of history, which nearly all modern liberal and Marxist models assume, but it must at least be cyclical, as indeed the very word "revolution" implies. Blake lived at a time when history as a subject had begun to attract a recognizably modern critical method and when history as a common idea was abandoning biblical and classical patterns (God's plan, exemplary stories) for modern notions of the spread of enlightenment or the evolution of a people or culture. He seems untouched by any of these ideas, so important in various ways for Burke, Price, and Paine, or Wordsworth, Coleridge, and Shelley. Blake is not interested in autobiography or the growth of the soul. His ideas about time and history, and the importance we should grant them, are entirely traditional and "quaint." I hope to show, however, that they are not for that reason incapable of supporting Blake's otherwise critical and radical social philosophy.

* * *

The fallen world, the world bereft of our imaginative appre-
hension, is chaos, mere indefinite immensity and duration. It
exists in the two modes of space and time, but Blake's imagery
sometimes conflates even this minimal division, as when he
names this world "the Sea of Time and Space" (m 15.39). The
sea is mainly a spatial image, of course, though we may think
of its repetitive tides, and so are most of the images Blake
uses for chaos: the forest, the desert, the cloud spreading in
all directions. Sometimes an image apposite for time, like the
wheel, is still as much a spatial image as a temporal one, for
Blake could hardly evade what he called the "stubborn struc-
ture" of the English language, which, like perhaps all western
languages, is pervasively optical in its vocabulary. But if a
fallen language tempts us to describe our fallen condition in
spatial terms, that only reflects Blake's point that a transfig-
ured temporal realm is our unfallen home.

As our position in space is a function of our perception, so
is our standpoint in, or above, time. The lowest form of time
is mere succession, the irreversible, unvarying, linear move-
ment of clock time. Such time is the time of the fool. "The
hours of folly are measur'd by the clock, but of wisdom: no
clock can measure" (mhh 7). Caught on such a track we rely
on our memory of the past or anticipations of the future to
define ourselves (that is, our Selves), for the present moment
seems to vanish into nonexistence as we try to fix it. To rely
on the past or the future, however, is to rely on something
that is either already dead or not yet alive, and it is to make
ourselves into an adventitious construct of whatever has hap-
pened to us or will happen. Alan Watts makes a similar ar-
gument in his book on the intuitive or phenomenological basis
of Christian myth:

> To the extent that the human mind identifies itself with the
> individual ego, it is confusing its life with its past since the ego is
> an abstraction from memory. Hence history and facts become
> more valuable than reality. Because the ego and its values have
> no real life, the real present becomes empty, and existence a per-

petual disappointment, so that man lives on hope and prizes nothing more than continuity.[1]

The past being the safer and more familiar of the two spectral dimensions of linear time, we tend to use only our memories to get hold of ourselves as we are hurled along. Indeed, our reasoning power, separate from the imagination, can only be "a Ratio / Of the Things of Memory" (J 74.11-12), of whatever happened to make an impression on our blank slates. As Albion turns his back on the Divine Vision, "his Spectrous / Chaos before his face appeard: an Unformd Memory" (J 29.1-2). The rational Spectre, in defining our Self, also defines our social relations as functions of memory:

> But Albion fell down a Rocky fragment from Eternity hurld
> By his own Spectre, who is the Reasoning Power in every Man
> Into his own Chaos which is the Memory between Man & Man[.]
> (J 54.6-8)

When people depend on their memory they are also vulnerable to the manipulations of priests, who as we see in plate 11 of *The Marriage of Heaven and Hell* create systems to enslave us. They are as skilled in controlling memory as they are in inducing oblivion, and what they want us to "remember" is original sin, a notion that obscures our real spiritual history. So the Druids build "Rocky Circles" like Stonehenge "to make permanent Remembrance / Of Sin" (J 92.24-25).

In most traditional cosmologies the fallen condition is oblivion rather than remembrance. The God of the Old Testament, anxious that his people remember his name and deeds, gives them books and memorials of stone lest they slide into the chaos of their neighbors' vegetation cults. The fallen realm of Platonic and Neoplatonic speculation is called the "Plain of Oblivion (*Lethe*)" or a similar name (see *Republic* 621a); incarnate souls can escape from it only by "recollection" (*anamnesis*) of forgotten spiritual truth or power. Sometimes Blake takes this traditional stance. About the only thing Enitharmon remembers of her fall, for example, is that "forgetfulness quite wrapt me up" (FZ 83.28). When Los is about to surrender to despair over the state of things, "He recollected an old Prophecy" that Milton would begin the process of redemption (M 20.56-61).[2] Usually, however, in a typically Blakean reversal of tradition, it is "the perishing Vegetable Memory" that dominates our fallen minds (M 26.46), or the "deluge of forgotten remembrances" that drowns us (J 29.16). Salvation is deliverance *from* memory, the power "To cast off the rotten rags of Memory by Inspiration" (M 41.4). If Blake seems to contradict himself, one answer might be simply that what matters is the content of memory rather than memory per se, but a better way to resolve the conflict is to take "recollection" (though Blake does not invariably use this term) as a different kind of mental act from "memory." The latter fixes on one of the vanishing points along a line; "recollection" causes the line itself to vanish and the point to open into Eternity. "Recollection," as its etymology suggests, is a gathering in of the dispersed fragments of imaginative life, an active re-membering of the dismembered whole.[3]

Though less fixed and defined than the past, and seemingly the repository of all the hopes of mankind, the future is no less a source of delusion. Urizen is particularly tormented over it in both *The Book of Urizen* and *The Four Zoas*. In the latter he is so obsessed with "futurity" that it darkens all his present joy (37.10); he sets about making instruments "to measure out the immense" so that "all futurity be bound in his vast chain" (73.16-20); but when he finally sees the light he repents of his obsession in words worth quoting in full:

> . . . O that I had never drank the wine nor eat the bread
> Of dark mortality nor cast my view into futurity nor turnd
> My back darkning the present . . .
> .   .   .   .
> Then Go O dark futurity I will cast thee forth from these
> Heavens of my brain nor will I look upon futurity more
> I cast futurity away & turn my back upon that void
> Which I have made for lo futurity is in this moment[.]
>   (121.3-5, 19-22)

It is fascinating to note that in this recognition scene all five instances of "futurity" are substitutions for earlier readings, "the past" in line 4 and "remembrance" in lines 19 through 22. At some point in his reworking of this manuscript it came to Blake that to fix one's gaze on a point in the future, whether on an afterlife or, perhaps, on any stage of "success" or "progress" that demands present sacrifice, is no better than to lock oneself into the past. One could see a political despair here as well, but it is another question whether Blake had lost hope in social change or whether "futurity" has a meaning too narrow to include all that might betide.

The important thing, as Urizen realizes, is the moment. It is to "hold" eternity in an hour, but not to grasp at hours to make them eternal. There seems to be something of Wordsworth's wise passiveness in Blake's imaginative activity. The "industrious" alone can find the crucial renovative moment of each day and multiply it during creative labor, yet such a moment seems to be given for us to find—we cannot arbitrarily seize a moment and wring eternity out of it (M 35.42-45). The one to be found, perhaps, is the one that happens to be there when we are ready to find one, and that readiness entails the sort of unpossessive opportunism Blake urges in his notebook poem "Eternity":

> He who binds to himself a joy
> Does the winged life destroy
> But he who kisses the joy as it flies
> Lives in eternity's sun rise[.]
>
> (E 470)

M. H. Abrams traces the emergence of the "moment" of revelation from its Christian context into the secular and psychological world of Rousseau and the German and English Romantics.[4] It would be interesting to discover why these seeming admonishments from another world, in Wordsworth's phrase, assumed such importance in Romantic literature. They are obviously bound up in the oppositional stance of intuition, imagination, and art against reason, "fancy," and science, a reaction against the Enlightenment that more or less defines what we usually mean by Romanticism. The interiorization of spatial categories that goes with this reaction almost compels the privileging of time over space, and of sacred moments over sacred places. In this, as scholars have noted, Romanticism is heir to the Protestant redefinition (or rehabilitation) of Christian doctrine and practice. We shall return briefly to the Protestant legacy later in this chapter. What deserves a little more consideration here is the connection of the privileged moment with the redemptive power of memory and with Blake's personal and professional situation, and all of these with the tensions of an early phase of rapid historical change.

Is it an accident, for instance, that the moment or spot of time in Wordsworth is often bound up with surges of memory, and that one of his main themes is the obliteration of the traditional forms of life by "progress" or "improvement"? The "other world" that seems to speak to Wordsworth in moments of revelation is both the world of his boyhood and the world of the English countryside, both irretrievably "other " to the mature man and the England of 1800 (or soon thereafter: Wordsworth's grief is premonitory). The leech-gatherer, who seemed "a man from some far region sent, / To give me human strength, by apt admonishment," has such numinous powers himself, we suspect, largely because he is nearly the last of his kind. The "far region" is the recent past.[5]

Blake, though he sometimes laments the passing of the craftsmanship of an earlier technology, as we have seen, never lingers nostalgically over the historical past. He shows a much more modern-seeming and certainly un-English impatience with it, an eagerness to be done with history and open a new world on a new day. He has something of the spirit of the *novus ordo saeclorum* which he met among radical Americans (and which suffuses his *America: A Prophecy*) and the spirit of radical destruction and rebirth which he absorbed from the Book of Revelation. But of course Blake's expansive sense of universal opportunity, as an epitome of which we might take the great drawing (in several versions) of an Orc-like Albion standing or dancing triumphantly ("Albion Rose" or "Glad Day"), eventually gives way to an anxious scanning of buried possibilities, for which a good emblem would be the frontispiece to *Jerusalem*, a traveler entering a door and carrying a globe of light.

Blake's own career declined in approximate parallel to the failure of revolution in England and France, and one sign of his difficult situation, more eloquent than the complaints about neglected geniuses and fashionable bootlickers that fill his notebook, is the straitened, bipolar world that his character Los inhabits in *Jerusalem*. There he seems to do only two things, labor at his forge and walk through the city. We might say, indeed, that his workshop and the city, the latter seen as a foreign observer might see it, as a one-dimensional panorama of nearly unrelieved misery, are the only two "real" places or spaces in *Jerusalem*; all the rest, like the thoughts Richard II hammers out to people his prison, are imaginary: Golgonooza, Ulro, Beulah, Jerusalem. Having never traveled outside England as he had once hoped, his one stay away from London having ended in danger and frustration, his early circles of Dissenting intellectuals and possible patrons having dwindled or excluded him, only briefly associated with a church (the Swedenborgian Society) and never, it seems, a member of a political club or benevolent society, and with no children—Blake's sense of belonging to a habitable public space must have grown very weak. A Byronic posture of contempt for the herd, escape to exotic places, and so on, was ruled out by his poverty and by his absolute convictions about human solidarity and brotherhood. He also kept free of "Romantic" nostalgia. But he created times as he created imaginary spaces where the work of redemption could go on, and this meant some sort of coming to terms with history.

* * *

Before we turn to Blake's historical ideas a look at recent developments within Marxist or post-Marxist thinking will suggest how complicated the question of memory and respect for the past can be. Marxism speaks not of an end to history but of an end to prehistory and the inauguration of a truly human history after the overthrow of capitalism. The notion of a radical break remains. We can find in the practice of professed communists all the examples we wish of the sweeping extirpation of past social structures, even of "obsolete classes," and equally wholesale installations of new ones, from communes to "socialist man." But we can also find a contrary thread as early as the opening chapter of Engels's *Condition of the Working Class in England* (1844), which somewhat ambiguously describes the "idyllic" preindustrial world, through the late letters of Marx to Vera Zasulich, which entertain the possibility that the village commune or *mir* could serve as the basis for a socialist Russia without going through the agonies of capitalism. It is bourgeois capitalism that has destroyed the past. As the *Communist Manifesto* proclaims, the bourgeoisie must constantly revolutionize its means of production and therefore the relations of society, and that means stripping the halo from "every occupation hitherto honoured and looked up to with awe." Everyone is reduced to a wage relationship.

As industrial capitalism triumphed in Europe, many socialists saw their role as its heirs rather than its enemies; they pronounced as "progressive" the most violent cases of capitalist rapacity if it brought the "consolidation" of capitalism closer. (There is a parallel here to Blake's satisfaction in the consolidation of error as a prelude to the apocalypse.) But in the twentieth century, when both capitalism and a self-proclaimed socialism aping its methods have paved half the world in asphalt, the better to sell us plastic food and electronic games, serious socialists still loyal to the Marxist project are looking with new eyes at history and memory. The romantic socialist William Morris has grown in stature. Another emblem of this new concern is Walter Benjamin—indeed, his posthumous rediscovery is an example of his own project—the collector of old books and bric-a-brac, student of the ancient art of storytelling, expositor of Freud and Proust on the subject of memory and recollection, and a Marxist.[6] Had Benjamin been English, he might have chosen Wordsworth instead of Proust as the vehicle for reintroducing the recollection of the past as a measure of the redemptive power of a future revolution, and he might have measured his own ideas of *apocatastasis* against Blake's.

It is clear enough in Blake that the only thing that matters in the passing flow of time is the possibility of an "opening" to eternity in one of the passing moments. The relationship between the two modes of time Blake does not make very clear, but he seems to have had some momentary illuminations on the subject. "Eternity is in love with the productions of time," for example, has the air of a long-sought-for summary suddenly achieved, but it remains one of the most cryptic of the Proverbs of Hell. It seems to imply that eternity initiates the relationship, in parallel to the idea that the Self, which sees only finite and time-bound things, is a secondary and reactive formation on the spirit or soul, which sees the eternal. Beyond that it brings to mind instances from Greek mythology where Zeus, Hades, Aphrodite, or another god falls in love with a mortal. Blake, however, treated such stories rather as Milton does in *Paradise Lost*, as fallen caricatures of the truth (though the truth is not, as it is for Milton, the biblical version). For a Christian it is the truth that God does love mortal man and, as Christ, came to be with him. Jesus may be the hidden term in the aphorism, and Jesus, as Blake tirelessly reminds us, is the Divine Imagination, the faculty that gives us to see eternity in the productions of time.[7]

It is probably with Jesus in mind that we should read another difficult passage:

Time is the mercy of Eternity; without Times swiftness
Which is the swiftest of all things: all were eternal torment[.]
(M 24.72-73)

This seems to say there is a worse temporal mode than the mercifully swift stream of time, something like absolute stasis. It is not unlike T. S. Eliot's thought in "Burnt Norton":

Yet the enchainment of past and future
Woven in the weakness of the changing body,
Protects mankind from heaven and damnation
Which flesh cannot endure.

There are other suggestions in Blake of intermediate notions of time which we shall take up shortly, but this one seems to refer to his idea that Jesus put a bottom on the Fall by constructing the "limit of Contraction" (Adam) and the "limit of Opakeness" (Satan) (cf. J 42.29-36). It is clear at any rate that the way out of the contraction and opacity of our fallen condition is through the Imagination or Jesus, for "Jesus breaking thro' the Central Zones of Death & Hell / Opens Eternity in Time & Space; triumphant in Mercy" (J 75.21-22).

When we have achieved our spiritual potential and inhabit the City of Imagination, our four powers or Zoas will create

> . . . Visions
> In new Expanses, creating exemplars of Memory and of
>   Intellect
> Creating Space, Creating Time according to the wonders Divine
> Of Human Imagination[.]   (J 98.30-32)

These lines confirm the idea that Jesus creates time. When *we* are Jesus we too will create time (and space) as artists create works of art. We will make the new expanses, it seems, simply by expanding: "if we raise ourselves / Upon the chariots of the morning. Contracting or Expanding Time!" (J 55.44-45). To do so is to open up a center in the "Central Zones" of this world and see another world expanding without limit. To do so is to raise the pitch or temperature of our perceptive powers until all barriers peel off like a husk. When we relax and withdraw from such a peak, ordinary time and space emerge again. It is the inhaling and exhaling, the diastole and systole, of the Divine Man. It may be that the phase of relaxation is meant to suggest the way Milton's God created the world: the "deep," boundless when filled with God, acquires bounds when "I uncircumscrib'd myself retire" (PL 7.165-73).[8] It is true, in any case, that man, who dwells in time, is capable of the creative feats traditionally attributed to God, who dwells outside it.

*   *   *

Though we have left quite a few questions unanswered, we shall turn now to Blake's treatment of historical time, which we have artificially separated from personal time only for the sake of exposition. The two modes of time, fallen time and eternity, obtain on the historical scale as well. History, in fact, is often shown as entirely fallen, as the nightmare from which Albion, like Joyce's Stephen Dedalus, is trying to awaken. In *Europe* the dream is Enitharmon's, for in that poem she represents among other things the dominance of a fallen view of time:

> Enitharmon slept,
> Eighteen hundred years: Man was a Dream!
> The night of Nature and their harps unstrung:
> She slept in middle of her nightly song,
> Eighteen hundred years, a female dream!
>
> Shadows of men in fleeting bands upon the winds:
> Divide the heavens of Europe:
> Till Albions Angel smitten with his own plagues fled with
>   his bands[.]
>
> (9.1-8)

The last three lines are remarkable in the way they summarize all of European history up to the time of imperial England as a brief insubstantial pageant.

Eternal reality, the state of wakefulness, has been obliterated by the oppressive institutions of this world, until it seems only a dream itself, as Blake explains elsewhere:

> These were the Churches: Hospitals: Castles: Palaces:
> Like nets & gins & traps to catch the joys of Eternity
>   And all the rest a desart;
> Till like a dream Eternity was obliterated & erased.
>
> (*Song of Los* 4.1-4)

Blake has the traditional Christian worldview behind him here, according to which time, created by the Fall and brought to an end at the Last Judgment, is in its essence a fallen mode of being. Nothing in human history is of significance except as a "shadow" of Providence, which alone acts. Men are vehicles or vessels of the Lord, or of his adversary Satan, and can "do" nothing of eternal consequence. The only event in the flat stretch of mortal history is the Incarnation, and while that may have been decisive in the spiritual realm, here in this world nothing seems to have changed.

In some respects Blake takes over this tradition intact. In his apocalypse, as in the traditional one, time is brought to an end. "The times are ended," Orc proclaims in *America* (8.2), "shadows pass the morning gins to break." At the point of

Albion's redemption, "Time was Finished! The Breath Divine Breathed over Albion" (J 94.18). But for Blake, as we know, Jesus was not confined to a unique historical appearance: he is the ever-present possibility of the full visionary life. To the extent that Blakes's stance can be comprehended in orthodox terms, we may say that he is as little impressed with Christ the second Person of the Trinity as he is with the Father, and prefers instead the Christ assimilated into the Holy Ghost, which remains in us who have faith no matter what happened to the historical Jesus of Nazareth.[9] The moment of revelation is available to each of us through Christ within us, and it is available to society as a whole through Christ "in the midst" of us. Collective man, Albion, has the power to transcend history, and if he has not done so he has no one to blame but himself. We get the governments we deserve, and the worst ones—Egypt, Babylon, Pitt's England—arise when our imaginative powers droop the lowest.

We have seen Blake's Jesus in several aspects as we have taken up different facets of Blake's philosophy: Jesus as vision, Jesus as brother, and Jesus as self-sacrificer. The aspect Blake most emphatically stresses, however, is the one most relevant to human history and its transcendence, Jesus as forgiver of sins. "The Spirit of Jesus is continual forgiveness of Sin" (J 3). "And this is the Covenant / Of Jehovah: If you Forgive one-another, so shall Jehovah Forgive You: / That He Himself may Dwell among you" (J 61.24-26). Forgiveness underlies all his other facets, for when we forgive an enemy we sacrifice or purge off the Selfhood that he injured, making him a brother while removing a barrier to true vision. How forgiveness is directly relevant to human history may seem obscure, but it will become clear when we consider just what, according to Blake, this history consists of. It is little more than an interminable cycle of injury and revenge, each avenger becoming a copy or "covering" of his predecessor (as in M 38.29-36). This process is admirably summed up in the final stanza of "The Grey Monk" (E 490):

> The hand of Vengeance found the Bed
> To which the Purple Tyrant fled

The iron hand crushd the Tyrants head
And became a Tyrant in his stead[.]

Revenge, we said, is a function of memory, itself a function
of the fallen mind that seeks security in fixed events of the
past. When Jesus preaches and practices forgiveness he
teaches us to cease remembering the wrongs we have suffered:
"When I appear before thee in forgiveness of ancient injuries /
Why shouldst thou remember & be afraid" (FZ 87.48-49). To
forgive is to forget. To overcome the Druidic priests who
chisel laws and chronicles in rocky monuments "to make per-
manent Remembrance / Of Sin," we must invoke the Lamb
of God:

Come O thou Lamb of God and take away the remembrance
    of Sin
To Sin & to hide the Sin in sweet deceit. is lovely!!
To Sin in the open face of day is cruel & pitiless! But
To record the Sin for a reproach: to let the Sun go down
In a remembrance of the Sin: is a Woe & a Horror!
A brooder of an Evil Day, and a Sun rising in blood
Come then O Lamb of God and take away the remembrance
    of Sin[.]

(J 50.24-30)

Blake invites us to identify time itself with this long cycle of
cruelties and to identify eternity with the new society that will
replace the old when we forgive and forget our mutual in-
juries. Forgiveness is the only way to end the chain of con-
sequences comprising our past. To brood on our injuries is
to breed more of them.

It may seem that forgiveness is unpolitical or antipolitical.
But a case can be made that forgiveness is necessary to a
healthy political process. Hannah Arendt argues that for-
giveness is a guarantor of the freedom essential to genuine
political life:

In this respect, forgiveness is the exact opposite of vengeance,
which acts in the form of re-acting against an original trespassing,
whereby far from putting an end to the consequences of the first
misdeed, everybody remains bound to the process, permitting the
chain reaction contained in every action to take its unhindered

course. In contrast to revenge, which is the natural, automatic reaction to transgression and which because of the irreversibility of the action process can be expected and even calculated, the act of forgiving can never be predicted; it is the only reaction that acts in an unexpected way and thus retains, though being a re-action, something of the original character of action. Forgiving, in other words, is the only reaction which does not merely re-act but acts anew and unexpectedly, unconditioned by the act which provoked it and therefore freeing from its consequences both the one who forgives and the one who is forgiven. The freedom con-tained in Jesus' teachings of forgiveness is the freedom from vengeance, which encloses both doer and sufferer in the relentless automatism of the action process, which by itself need never come to an end.[10]

Arendt involves forgiveness in a subject we have only touched on: action. We mentioned the orthodox belief, stressed particularly in Calvinism, that mortal men cannot genuinely act in history. They cannot freely choose a course of action and carry it out, but are instead the unwitting vessels or instruments of the one Actor who disposes of them ac-cording to His plan. Blake accepts the traditional assignment of activity solely to God, as he gives the initiative in love to eternity, but he redefines and relocates that God as the true Human, the inner potential of man. "Some will say, Is not God alone the Prolific? I answer, God only Acts & Is, in ex-isting beings or Men" (MHH 16). Genuine action, for Blake, is a self-caused or self-initiating process that issues from the "Staminal Virtues of Humanity":

> Each thing is its own cause & its own effect[.] Accident is the omission of act in self & the hindering of act in another, This is Vice but all Act is Virtue. To hinder another is not an Act it is the contrary it is a restraint on action both in ourselves & in the person hinderd.
>
> (Annotations to Lavater, E 601)

Such hindrance is not action but reaction. It is entirely a prod-uct of our envious and frightened Selfhood, the Selfhood Blake frequently identifies as Satan. That is why Satan is once called the "Reactor": "The Reactor hath hid himself thro envy" in the forests of Albion; that is, he is invisible because his opacity serves as camouflage in the opaque environment he created, and he "hath founded his Reaction into a Law / Of Action," compelling us into what Arendt calls the "relentless automatism" of reflex and revenge (J 43.9-15). But "Jesus was all virtue, and acted from impulse. not from rules" (MHH 23-24). When he acts in us, when the human potential that is Jesus-within-us actualizes, we break the chain of history and begin a new age and world. Implicit in genuine action, though Blake does not quite say this, is the possibility that we may make a new and higher history, no longer a dreary chronicle of slavery and slaughter etched in stone but a body of exemplary acts, a set of "exemplars of Memory and of Intellect," preserved perhaps in works of art, to make us recollect our collective spirit and remind us of our human possibility.

* * *

There is a side to the process of renewal that does not sound as gentle as forgiveness. We saw in chapter three that true brotherhood, for Blake, is a different thing from the apparent benevolence or false pity that masquerades as brotherhood. Brotherhood may entail "severe contentions of friendship & the burning fires of thought" (J 91.17). A sharp division into spiritual classes is a condition for the rescue of any individual from classes; error must be consolidated before it can be cast into the lake. Blake stigmatizes as "religion" any attempt to reconcile the classes, for it blurs the perceptions on which our liberation depends. Blake's Jesus, therefore, is a shepherd with a sharp eye on his mixed flock and a warrior with sharp spiritual weapons. "Note. Jesus Christ did not wish to unite but to seperate them, as in the Parable of sheep and goats! & he says I came not to send Peace but a Sword" (MHH 17).

As one grows in spiritual power one wastes no more time on the past. The past is the realm of the dead, and our serious spiritual business must go forward without reverence or nostalgia. Blake calls the entire fallen world "Eternal Death" in part because it is determined by the dead events of the past and their traces in our memories. He could have written Marx's famous sentence, "The tradition of all the dead generations weighs like a nightmare on the brain of the living."[11] But when we dead awaken to eternal life we shall turn abruptly from this world like the bereaved disciple whom Jesus told to "Follow me; and let the dead bury their dead" (Matt. 8:22). Blake's comparable injunction is to "Drive your cart and your plow over the bones of the dead" (MHH 7). The plow, in fact, could stand as an emblem of the double aspect of redemption, harsh and merciful, for it both cuts across the dead and quickens the earth as it passes.[12]

The state of mind prepared for such a drastic break with the past is of course the main target of Burke's reply to Dr. Price. One of the most celebrated passages of the *Reflections* defends those charters to which men "submit themselves, their heirs and posterities for ever," and he calls society a contract binding "those who are living, those who are dead, and those who are to be born."[13] Blake's view is the spiritual equivalent of Paine's reply to Burke, and of the slogan of Dissenters and American Revolutionaries: "The earth belongs to the living."[14]

* * *

To describe history as a mere chain of events and to associate it with death and vengeance is to rule out any theory of history per se. No event is of greater importance than any other, as no link is more important than any other in a chain. Yet Blake gave a good deal of thought to human history and seems to have considered it of great significance. He lived, of course, through several decisive historical events, events that were felt to be decisive even as they took place, and he seems to have invested some of them with great hopes, at least during his early years. Even in his mature and fully developed system history has a not entirely negative place. Blake is especially interested in the events of the Old Testament, many of which dot the pages of his long later poems. His attitude toward them is rather like that of Christian exegetes who found in them types or shadows of the Christian message. Blake's typology has a broader range of antitypes, and he sometimes treats both Testaments, as other radical Protestants had before him, as sources of analogies for modern English events and for his universal spiritual archetypes. Typology is still only a rudimentary notion of history; it gives history a direction but flattens it into a set of congruent structures, and at most reveals the divine hand behind it, compared to which all events are indeed mere fleeting "shadows."[15]

Blake insists nevertheless that history must in some sense be preserved. When a moment opens into eternity, or when collective man forgives and forgets his wearisome past, the moment and the past are not obliterated beyond recovery. Perhaps he is inconsistent in this, but Blake maintains that every moment is somehow saved:

> For Los in Six Thousand Years walks up & down continually
> That not one Moment of Time be lost & every revolution
> Of Space he makes permanent[.]
>
> (J 75.7-9)

It may be that we are to see the creative Los as a builder or gatherer of the higher history Blake imagined, like a curator of an eternal museum, a possibility we shall take up in more detail in chapter eight. It also suggests the merciful quality of creation, for Jesus, through the imagination, will strive to save all the little ones who ever lived. In any case the gathering in of the moments is made easier by the capacity of one moment to contain all the others:

> Then Eno a daughter of Beulah took a Moment of Time
> And drew it out to Seven thousand years with much care &
>   affliction
> And many tears & in Every year made windows into Eden[.]
>
> (FZ 9.9-11; cf. J 48.30-37)

So we return to the idea that through a visionary apprehension of eternity we can redeem all of time, and that it makes no difference in which moment we choose to do it.

Though the difference between a moment ripe in itself and a moment in which our imagination is ripe for acting is only the sort of shifting emphasis between subject and object we find everywhere in Blake, the emphasis nonetheless falls often enough on the objective ripeness or privilege of certain moments to raise the question nevertheless of time's shape. Blake

seems to have found meaning in the apparently prosaic prov-
erb, "Think in the morning, Act in the noon, Eat in the eve-
ning, Sleep in the night" (MHH 9), and everywhere we find a
concern for timely action, needless postponement, wise wait-
ing, or impetuous impulse in the life of both the individual
and the human race.

If some moments are privileged then time is not a flat un-
differentiated stretch but a pattern or rhythm. We naturally
think of cycles, with the visionary moment at the top and
darkness and blindness below. Blake once says "the times re-
volve" (FZ 122.4) and when he uses "revolution," even in a
political context, he means more a revolving than a revolting.[16]
He takes over Plato's definition of time as a revolving image
of eternity (Timaeus 38a), an "image of infinite / Shut up in
finite revolutions, . . . / . . . a mighty circle turning" (Eur 10.21-
23). When Blake describes the series of illuminated moments
in history, however, his imagery is not explicitly cyclical. It is
possible that he wants to reserve the spatial image of a circle
or wheel for fallen time as a whole, on the premise, as we
shall see, that space is a degraded form of time, while using
a more specifically temporal metaphor for the sequence of re-
demptive moments. That might explain his frequent use of
the pulse or rhythmical beat as the measure of time. Los beats
on his anvil to redeem the time. It might also explain the
passage in which the sons of Los, in building our conception
of time with its divisions and subdivisions, make the moment
equal to "a pulsation of an artery." That smallest human unit
of time, like the moment Eno draws out, contains eternity and
all history:

> Every Time less than a pulsation of the artery
> Is equal in its period & value to Six Thousand Years.
> For in this Period the Poets Work is Done: and all the Great
> Events of Time start forth & are concievd in such a Period
> Within a Moment: a Pulsation of the Artery.
> (M 28.62-63; 29.1-3)

Whatever the mode of measurement, Blake has two ac-
counts of the overall shape of history. One of them repeats
the description of Eno drawing out the moment (to 8,500

rather than 6,000 years) with the major difference that instead of an eternal window every year (which could mean every moment) there is "a door to Eden" every 200 years (j 48.26-37). In *Milton* we learn that 200 years equals one "Period" and a Period is divisible into "Seven Ages" (m 28.44-58). That comes to 28 or 29 years for an Age, or about a generation of human life. Every seven generations, then, there is a door to eternity for some prophetic figure to open and presumably redeem his Period, if not all of time. Seven, of course, is the Hebrew modulus of time, the week, at the end of which is the Sabbath, the day of the Lord, the door to eternity. As the weekdays are themselves indistinguishable, so we may assume that no development, no significant tightening or slackening of pace, takes place until the year of the eternal opportunity arrives.

Blake variously allots 6,000, 7,000, and 8,500 years to human history. The first two are traditional, and their difference is the millennium that precedes the end of time, which may or may not be taken as part of history itself. History is a week of millennia, followed by the Eternal Sabbath. Eno's figure of 8,500 years (mentioned again at j 83.52) is more mysterious. It may represent an inclusive week, with an extra thousand years to suggest an eternal "millennium" to follow the historical one, plus the apocalyptic "dividing of time."[17]

In these numbers we find little to indicate an overall shape of historical time, only a regular beat that will continue until some significant number has been counted off and then, apparently, stop. More hopeful, on its face, is Blake's other description of history, the Seven Eyes of God. Here, at least, the seven epochs have names that we might decipher into a substantive account of historical development, but their names, alas, raise more questions than they settle: Lucifer, Molech, Elohim, Shaddai, Pachad, Jehovah, and Jesus. I have relegated the details to the appendix, but it is clear on inspection that the first six Eyes are negative figures in Blake, variants of Satan or Urizen, and only the seventh, as we might expect, is hopeful. Traditional periodizations of history into seven ages, by Augustine, Luther, and English radical Protestants, among others, usually entail some development toward greater spiritual growth, although there may remain a great difference between the Incarnation and the events that bound the other ages. Blake may have known some of these, and assumed a direction to be implicit in his seven, but there is not much for us to go on. He says little or nothing to define the Eyes, and the passages in which they appear are only slightly integrated into their contexts. We are left, then, only with the sense that former ages may have differed from each other, but they were all bad, and only the coming of Jesus brought anything new, though that was nearly two thousand years ago.

As Milton descends to Blake in his garden (M 37.13f), Blake sees in him twelve "dishumanized" gods of Ulro and twenty-seven heavens and their churches.

> And these the names of the Twenty-seven Heavens & their
>   Churches
> Adam, Seth, Enos, Cainan, Mahalaleel, Jared, Enoch,
> Methuselah, Lamech: these are Giants mighty Hermaphroditic
> Noah, Shem, Arphaxad, Cainan the second, Salah, Heber,
> Peleg, Reu, Serug, Nahor, Terah, these are the Female-Males
> A Male within a Female hid as in an Ark & Curtains,
> Abraham, Moses, Solomon, Paul, Constantine, Charlemaine
> Luther, these seven are the Male-Females, the Dragon Forms
> Religion hid in War, a Dragon red & hidden Harlot[.]
>
> (M 37.35-43)

In *Jerusalem* the same list appears, again to the "I" of the poem, this time in South Molton Street (J 74.55, 75.10-18). A "heaven" seems to be the thought-horizon of an era, projected upward as all religions demand, as if on the ceiling of a church building, while "church" is used in its Swedenborgian sense, according to which Adam was "the Most Ancient Church," whose members had the closest apprehension of God, and the next nine, Seth through Noah, "signified so many churches," differing from one another in their "perceptions."[18] Although this is certainly a sequence in time, and points toward a culminating twenty-eighth church (that is, a fourth "week" which will transform what is first seen as "Thrice Nine" at 37.18), Blake spatializes them more than

Swedenborg did, and even imagines them as having an ark and curtains like the temple of Jerusalem. There is little further appreciation of history here, but paradoxically an exacting concern for reciting, at personal revelatory moments important in both poems, the names of all phases of history in their proper order. Put another way, we have an epitome of history as if from a standpoint above it, yet devoted to its "details" as if getting it straight is essential to redeeming it. It is both meaningless and all-important.

It is interesting that Blake's model of history has quite a different shape from the Joachite theory that so influenced mystical Protestantism, including the Jacob Boehme he so admired. Joachim of Flora professed a threefold division of history based on the inevitable exfoliation of the Trinity. The first age is the Age of the Father or Law, a time of servitude and fear; the second is the Age of the Son or Gospel, a time of faith and filial obedience; the third, now almost upon us, is the Age of the Holy Spirit, a time of love and spiritual liberty for God's children. The new age will be a high noon of spiritual illumination compared to the starlight or twilight of the former two, and God will no longer be above us in heaven but will dwell among us and within us, teaching us the "Everlasting Gospel." Boehme specified the three ages further, adducing a plant for each: the Age of the Nettle (the thorns of Law), the Age of the Rose (the blood of Christ, crowned with thorns), and the Age of the Lily (of the Song of Solomon and the Annunciation of the Holy Ghost). He also predicted that the lilies would bloom "in the north."[19]

If anything, at least after the stalling of revolutionary momentum in France and England, Blake's overall sense of human history seems to have been that things were getting worse; on the other hand, things must get worse before they get better, so the worst of times was also the best of times.[20] This accords with his insistence that the task of the poet-prophet is to consolidate error so it may be cast out, a task done in part by provoking the enemy, who is a cunning dissimulator, into an epiphany of his true nature. It is almost a spiritual *politique de pire*, but "worse" is really the maximum contraction, the limit of opacity, and thus a kind of clarity.

The goal is to wage mental war so "That he who will not defend Truth, may be compelld to / Defend a Lie, that he may be snared & caught & taken" (M 8.47-48). Such a war, of course, involves self-sacrifice on the part of the warriors, for their Selfhoods are part of the enemy. So it is that the Seventh Eye of history, Jesus, instigated a process through his transgressions of the Law whereby "the Body of Death was perfected in hypocritic holiness," that is, revealed for what it is, while soon the elect will be "Astonish'd at the Transgressor" and recognize him as their Savior (M 13.25-34).

Even a "materialist" like Karl Marx, with fewer illusions than Blake might have cherished about the imminence of a European revolution, placed great weight on the educative, even revelatory, effect of violent class struggle. "By making its burial place the birthplace of the *bourgeois republic*, the proletariat forced this republic to appear in its pure form, as the state whose avowed purpose it is to perpetuate the rule of capital and the slavery of labour."[21]

Partly because he could see the confinement of the American Revolution to America, the perversion of the French Revolution, and the repression of the English reform movement, disappointing though they were, as having nonetheless sharpened and clarified the spiritual (Marx would say ideological) conflict, Blake was not "disillusioned" with history or politics in the usual sense of the word. In saying this I am of course taking a stand in the long debate over Blake's possible turn or reversal because of political despair, but my stand is somewhere between, and somewhat apart from the two poles into which the debate has largely resolved itself: the "disillusionment" theory, whereby Blake is assimilated to the model of the Lake Poets, and the "transcendence" theory, which claims Blake was "above" politics from the beginning, concerned only with eternal truths. I think Blake was unhappy with the outcome of the French Revolution, and probably as a result revised some of his symbolism (notably the so-called "Orc cycle"), but as he was never uncritically committed to the Revolution as such, which he probably did not see as a monolithic event anyway, it is vain to seek a clear revulsion from it. There is no "Kronstadt" for Blake, whatever he may have thought of the September Massacres or the invasion of Switzerland. The parallel to Blake is not Wordsworth and Coleridge, nor the western fellow travelers who broke ranks with the Communist Party in 1921 or 1939 or 1956, but, in a way, to the leftist critics of the Russian Revolution like the anarchists Peter Kropotkin and Emma Goldman, the socialist Rosa Luxemburg, and the council communist Anton Pannekoek. Compared to them, no doubt, Blake was an innocent in politics (Lenin said the same of Kropotkin), but if so he was less innocent before, and more innocent after, the Kronstadts of his day than many have assumed who cannot conceive of a stance both socially *engagé* and politically independent.

We should distinguish, in other words, between Blake's possible faith in the happy outcome of history, imminent or eventual, and his possible faith in the revolutionary politics of his time. Looking at the narrower subject first, we can have no doubt that Blake welcomed the American and French Revolutions and saw them as either a sign or vehicle of a general apocalypse or *apocatastasis*, and there is no question that he later felt disappointed in the course these revolutions took. The question is whether Blake departed from his prevailing mode of thought out of enthusiasm for France (the American War occurred when Blake was in his early twenties and had not yet formulated his characteristic ideas). Frye argues that Blake's symbolism is all of a piece, and that "it is therefore unlikely that the outbreak of the French Revolution made any essential change in his thought at the age of thirty-two."[22] Hirsch disagrees: "it cannot be reasonably doubted that the Revolution of 1789 was the occasion for a radical change in Blake's valuation of actual life."[23] Frye's view rests on the assumption that Blake took revolutions as epiphenomena of spiritual doings, while Hirsch claims Blake had faith for a while in "the inherent divinity of the natural order" in which revolutions occur.[24] Without entering into the details of the dispute we will consider briefly Blake's treatment of the figure crucial to his idea of revolution, Orc, the spirit of energy and desire, to see if Blake presents him simply as the savior or comprehends him critically.

Great rhetoric is given to the rising fiery rebel in his first appearance, in *America*:

> The morning comes, the night decays, the watchmen leave their
>   stations;
> The grave is burst, the spices shed, the linen wrapped up;
> The bones of death, the cov'ring clay, the sinews shrunk & dry'd.
> Reviving shake, inspiring move, breathing! awakening!
> Spring like redeemed captives when their bonds & bars
>   are burst[.]
>
> (A 6.1-5)

And at the end of the poem the fires of Orc have spread to France, Spain, and Italy, signal of a universal *ekpyrosis* before the apocalypse, the consummation of the sensory barriers to vision:

> But the five gates were consum'd, & their bolts and hinges melted
> And the fierce flames burnt round the heavens, & round the
>   abodes of men[.]
>
> (A 16.22-23)

This is a high claim to make, but it is countered in part by Orc's own admission of his serpentine character—"I am Orc, wreath'd round the accursed tree" (8.1)—with the implication that he, like a serpent, has a cyclical existence. In Blake's later works, Orc has a minor role, and the redemptive agent is the prophet and artist Los. That is certainly a shift, and it may be, as Erdman judiciously phrases it, that Blake was "somewhat sorry" to have defended Orc in 1776 and 1793, because the times were not ripe for him,[25] but if we take the cycle and serpent imagery seriously we cannot say Blake was ever an uncritical Jacobin. These considerations support Frye's view that the French Revolution may have inspired a shift of emphasis in Blake's thought, but not a break.[26]

Even after Robespierre and Napoleon, Frye adds, Blake did not abandon all hope of an apocalypse. "As Blake never abondoned his belief in the potential imminence of an apocalypse, he did not, like Wordsworth and Coleridge, alter the essentially revolutionary pattern of his thinking."[27] Hirsch, on the other hand, claims that Blake's disappointment with France is "precisely the same" as the crisis Wordsworth and

Coleridge went through; Blake despaired of collective human action and sought, like Coleridge, an "individual solace in the perfection and divinity of the nonhuman world."[28] It is quite clear, Hirsch notwithstanding, that the apocalypse that concludes *Jerusalem* is collective, indeed universal: it is Albion and not Los who finally awakens and rises. Whether it is by collective human agency that the new dawn will arrive, however, is a separable question. Occasionally Blake seems to counsel patience, waiting upon the Lord. But for Blake there is no Lord to wait upon, no agency but the human to rely on for social or spiritual change. It may be that human action as we have witnessed it in history up to and including the revolutions cannot bring about a radical change. What follows from that, however, is not that all action is hopeless and all redemption is private (I think private redemption is a contradiction in Blakean terms), but that a new kind of action is needed. We have seen that for Blake forgiveness is an action of the most genuine sort, and so are prophecy and the creation of art. In the shift from Orc to Los Blake is not renouncing all collective action in this world in favor of a separate and transcendent peace, but is redefining the kind of action and actor that are needful. The "heroic" actions of Washington and Lafayette certainly have not brought us to the New Jerusalem, for violence begets violence, not the peaceable kingdom.[29] We need something new.

Blake was no political theorist, and seems to have only glanced at possible modes and principles of political action that would not repeat the dreary errors of the past. Propaganda, prophecy, education through art—the task of Los— were central in his thinking. A movement for change in which vengeance has no part—the task of Jesus—was also essential. Patience and careful timing Blake also seems to have stressed, as when he reminds us of the "fury premature" of Calvin and Luther.[30] These notions are not much to go on, but they are not naive, and have by no means lost their point today. Theorists of revolution still debate these principles, as they must, and speculate on ways to organize people to act on them. Two centuries of practice have seen many models of "revolution" other than the Jacobin. Even the refusal to take vengeance has found a place in the theory and practice (not always un-successful) of revolutionary nonviolence. Whatever positive courses of action we might infer from Blake's mature outlook, however, the point is that it is too narrow a view of political action and too easy an assimilation to familiar dualistic patterns to pronounce that Blake sought an individual transcendent solution. His continuing incorporation of historical events into his late poems, which Erdman richly documents, show at least an anxious scanning of the public world for possibilities and portents. Though he may have had some dark moments—and the times were very dark in Pitt's reactionary England—Blake maintained his vision of a collective transformation of this world.

* * *

The world we apprehend through our fallen senses, the world, that is, we construct on Lockean premises, is a world based on sight. The eighteenth-century theorists of mind and imagination assimilated the sensory powers to an optical paradigm derived from the "objective" laws of binocular vision. Blake, for all his stress on "vision" and his use of notions like the Seven Eyes of God, seems to have fought against this paradigm of what Thomas Frosch calls the "perspectival eye" in at least two ways, by reconstructing sight so that it is no longer detached from its object but is "in touch" with it, and by stressing the redemptive role of the ear and hearing.[31]

The perspectival eye, according to Frosch, is responsible for the apparent division of our world into three dimensions. "With its detached observation, its horizoned field, and its compartmentalization of experience into discrete pictures, it institutes our schismatic categories of space: above and below, here and there, before and behind, the outer of the bodily eye and the inner of the mind's eye." The subject-object split is the most serious consequence, for it leads to the development of the Self simultaneously with the alienation of the environment. "Just as the inquisitional eye of observation produces ever greater distance, taking the withered sense object into the void of mental abstraction, so the eye of self-observation withers man's imaginative form, his creative activity, and finds its terminus in stasis, emptiness, and despair." Such an eye, too, remains a passive victim of a static space extending indefinitely in all directions.

The redeemed sense of sight, seeing the infinite in all things, will see all things as intimately related, indeed as inseparable from itself. The sense of touch, which in the fallen world resides only in the tongue (the only one of the four localized senses that must touch its object to perceive it) and the sexual organs, will be restored to its proper role in all the senses. "Touch summarizes all the sensory modes that are suppressed by the perspectival eye; and it is also the unifying faculty of the redeemed senses, the one through which they, quite literally, come in contact with each other."[32]

Access to redemptive "vision," however, often seems to come through the ear. Indeed, Blake is quite willing to extend the incongruent idea of aural vision to concrete poetic action:

> And in the Nerves of the Ear, (for the Nerves of the Tongue
> are closed)
> On Albions Rock Los stands creating the glorious Sun each
> morning[.]
>
> (M 29.40-41)

Even if we are meant to think of the sun here mainly in its function as measurer of the day, having thus a temporal aspect, it is a striking image. Los generally propagates his emanations "in the Auricular Nerves of Human Life," now symbolized by the fallen Albion's ear (FZ 4.1). That ear is deaf to the once vocal and melodious world:

> A Rock a Cloud a Mountain
> Were now not Vocal as in Climes of happy Eternity
> Where the lamb replies to the infant voice & the lion to the man
> of years
> Giving them sweet instructions Where the Cloud the River &
> the Field
> Talk with the husbandman & shepherd.
>
> (FZ 71a.4-8)

It is by a call or a song that Albion will awaken (J 4.5), by "vocal wind" and "vocal harmony" that Vala (like the beloved in the Song of Solomon) responds to Luvah (FZ 126.35, 127.3), and by songs that both Milton and Los are prompted to descend to their work of salvation (M 14.10f, 20.56f).

We may see in this emphasis on hearing an extension of the convention that all poetry, no matter how bookish, is song, and a reflection of Blake's "vocation" as a poet. Remembering that Blake was by profession an engraver and designer, we may find it odd, however, that Los, the redemptive figure who sometimes represents Blake himself, is invariably associated with the ear. The hammer and the anvil, we may note, are two bones of the inner ear. (Urizen, who acts the villain, is associated with the eye.) One of the most interesting new currents of Blake interpretation is the question of an "auditory" or "tactile" style of pictorial representation, a style free of conventions of spatial location, perspective, stable shapes, source of illumination, and so on.[33]

The privilege Blake accords time and the ear over space and the eye would correspond to a reliance on history, or on a providence in history, as the field of redemption and not, say, on the static constitution of society, on a sacred place, on nature, or on a remote transcendent God. If Blake's organization of history is not progressive, it is clear enough that he thinks that a series of events will some day issue in the redemption of society. Even Blake's eternity is a dynamic one, and as such it seems more the quintessence of time than an escape from it. It may help place Blake in a relevant ideological context to recall that Plato, whose authoritarian utopia has served as a model for aristocratic and conservative thought, saw time as a fallen mode of being and history as a downhill slide from the golden age. Herbert Marcuse quotes a Nazi apologist, Möller van den Bruck, to illustrate the uses to which a veneration of space may be put:

> Conservative thought . . . can be understood only from the spatial viewpoint. Space is sovereign, and time presupposes it. . . . Things grow in and emerge from this space. In time, they rot. . . . All revolution is background noise, a sign of disturbance; it is neither the walk of the creator through his workshop, nor the fulfillment of his commands, nor agreement with his will.[34]

Joseph Gabel has argued that a common factor in schizophrenia, authoritarian political theory, and capitalist "reification" and alienation is the spatialization of the temporal order, such as the freezing of time at a past or future moment.[35]

Blake may be placed, or rather he placed himself, in an old tradition. In the opposition between the Greek and Hebrew strands of western thought he clearly decided on the latter. His devotion to the Bible and his contempt for classical forms and themes, for Muses born of memory and "the detestable Gods of Priam," have been well discussed by Northrop Frye and others.[36] Part of his Hebraism, we may now claim, lies in the Hebraic sense of history and distrust of visual icons, in contrast to the calm Hellenic *theoria* or contemplation of unchanging aesthetic forms. Blake's choice of Hebrew over Greek reflects his choice of time and hearing over space and sight.

The claim that Greek thought-forms were dominated by space and Hebrew thought-forms by time is pressed by Thorleif Boman in his book *Hebrew Thought Compared with Greek*.[37] Western time-expressions down to the present day are derived from spatial terms: line, circle, point, "before" and "after," etc. Plato and Aristotle saw time as the scene of decay and honored geometry above all knowledge. The Hebrews did not use spatial metaphors to describe or measure time, but relied on regular alternations of natural events for their calendar: the rhythm of light and dark, warm and cold, or the phases of the moon.[38] The smallest unit of time in ancient Hebrew is the *regha'*, which translates as "beat" or perhaps "pulse-beat," not as a short extent of space (136). It is hard to resist comparison here with Blake, who wrote of "pulsations of time, & extensions of space" (J 11.2), and whose smallest unit, we saw, was the "pulsation of an artery."

Historical time, for the Hebrews, was not an even-flowing medium containing more or fewer events, but a function of events themselves, their "occurrence" rather than their standard of measure (144). Yahweh revealed himself by deeds, not by ideas, and these deeds are absorbed into the people of Israel the way the actions of our life, and not our numerical age, define our sense of who we are. Qualitative or psychological time is more important than "objective" (really spatial) time. Greek history is a set of recurrent typical events, while

Hebrew history is a sequence of unique, if typologically in-
terpretable, events building toward an eschatological climax.

The Israelites were correspondingly poor in visual descrip-
tion, especially of static things. They were able to describe the
"impression" of a thing, but not, like the Greeks, its "appear-
ance." A description of a building in the Bible is really a
description of how it is made. "For the beauty of nature," too,
"the Israelite has little feeling; beautiful and powerful nature
praises its creator" (88), whereas the Greeks excelled in de-
scribing and portraying natural objects. Finally, the Hebrews
forbade any "graven image" of God or high religious matters.

Blake was a Christian, and Christianity was an outgrowth
of Judaism in a culturally Hellenic milieu. The resulting syn-
thesis was not stable. The eschatological and hence revolu-
tionary time-sense of the Hebrew sects absorbed with difficulty
the timeless, tolerant, and aesthetic attitudes of the Mediter-
ranean world. "In the earlier Christian centuries," Frye writes,

> the dethroned "pagan" tradition began slowly to form a liberal
> opposition, modifying, relaxing, and expanding the revolutionary
> narrowness of the Christian myth. . . . Again, the Christian myth,
> by remaining so close to the oral tradition, had thrown a strong
> emphasis on the ear, on the hearing of the word, on the receptivity
> to authority that binds a society together. In the word "idolatry,"
> and in its recurring iconoclasm, Christianity expressed its antag-
> onism to the hypnotizing power of the external visible world. It
> was, again, a more liberal expansion of Christian culture that de-
> veloped the visual arts, including the arts of the theatre, so much
> disliked by the more rigorous Christians, including Pascal and
> many of the Puritans.[39]

In the history of Christianity, then, we might see a permanent
antagonism between the Hebraic ear-oriented temporal sense
and the Hellenic eye-oriented spatial sense. At the time of the
Reformation the antagonism grew intense, with the Reform-
ers recurring, quite consciously, to a more primitive Hebraic
basis. Puritans considered themselves Old Testament Chris-
tians, as their Christian names, to go no further, attest. Cath-
olics and Anglicans displayed relics and performed rituals;
Protestants sang hymns and broke icons.[40] In the Elizabethan
world picture, society was a stable body politic or a dance of

harmonious elements; to the Puritans it was a ship in need of a rudder and stout sailors.[41] The old Christian inherited his "place" in the hierarchy of his ancestral community; the new Christian heard his "vocation" or "calling" and set forth on his life's pilgrimage.

Blake was not a Puritan. He saw society as an organism (though without a "primate" or head), relished the human body, and made his living as a graphic artist. But he had inherited, perhaps through the surviving subculture of revolutionary Protestantism, much of the Hebraic thrust of the English Puritan Reformation. His project, in a sense, was to reconcile this inheritance with the more artistically satisfying Hellenic tradition, and to make, in William Carlos Williams' words, "the ear and the eye lie / down together in the same bed."[42] Yet, the ear always had priority. Blake's crusade was not like the degraded, spatialized attempt to reconquer the old Jerusalem, for that Jerusalem, as Hegel says, is only the grave of the higher consciousness we have lost.[43] His was a pilgrimage in time, a continual laboring at the rhythmic anvil of creation. To that rhythm we are to build the new Jerusalem in the green and pleasant land where we happen to be sojourners.

8

Blake's Apocatastasis

It will be in keeping with the theme of this chapter to begin it by doing what we can to redeem one of the most scandalously intractable passages of *Jerusalem*.

> Here Los fixd down the Fifty-two Counties of England & Wales
> The Thirty-six of Scotland, & the Thirty-four of Ireland
> With mighty power, when they fled out at Jerusalems Gates
> Away from the Conflict of Luvah and Urizen, fixing the Gates
> In the Twelve Counties of Wales & thence Gates looking
>   every way
> To the Four Points: conduct to England & Scotland & Ireland
> And thence to all the Kingdoms & Nations & Families of
>   the Earth[.]
> The Gate of Reuben in Carmarthenshire: the Gate of Simeon in
> Cardiganshire: & the Gate of Levi in Montgomeryshire
> The Gate of Judah Merionethshire: The Gate of Dan Flintshire
> The Gate of Napthali, Radnorshire: the Gate of Gad
>   Pembrokeshire
> The Gate of Asher, Carnarvonshire the Gate of Issachar
>   Brecknokshire
> The Gate of Zebulun, in Anglesea & Sodor. so is Wales divided.
> The Gate of Joseph, Denbighshire: the Gate of Benjamin
>   Glamorganshire
> For the protection of the Twelve Emanations of Albions Sons
>
> And the Forty Counties of England and thus divided in the Gates
> Of Reuben Norfolk, Suffolk, Essex. Simeon Lincoln, York
>   Lancashire
> Levi. Middlesex Kent Surrey. Judah Somerset Glouster Wiltshire.
> Dan. Cornwal Devon Dorset, Napthali., Warwick Leicester
>   Worcester
> Gad. Oxford Bucks Harford. Asher, Sussex Hampshire Berkshire

Issachar, Northampton Rutland Nottgham. Zebulun Bedford
    Huntgn Camb
Joseph Stafford Shrops Heref. Benjamin, Derby Cheshire
    Monmouth;
And Cumberland Northumberland Westmoreland & Durham are
Divided in the Gates of Reuben, Judah Dan & Joseph

And the Thirty-six Counties of Scotland, divided in the Gates
Of Reuben Kincard Haddntn Forfar, Simeon Ayr Argyll Banff
Levi Edinburh Roxbro Ross. Judah, Abrdeen Berwik Dumfries
Dan Bute Caitnes Clakmanan. Napthali Nairn Invernes Linlithgo
Gad Peebles Perth Renfru. Asher Sutherlan Sterling Wigtoun
Issachar Selkirk Dumbartn Glasgo. Zebulun Orkney
    Shetland Skye
Joseph Elgin Lanerk Kinros. Benjamin Kromarty Murra
    Kirkubriht

(J 16.28-58)

Though the abbreviations in this list, such as "Camb" or
"Heref," may suggest it is meant to be skimmed or only con-
sulted, like a telephone directory, I think the reader should
pass through this wilderness slowly, taking in its full tedium
and refractoriness, and not rush through it to the promised
meaning. Refractoriness is part of its point: the obstinacy of
Britain is here fixed in obstinate verse, onomatopoeic in al-
most the root sense of "name-making." Wilderness, too, is
part of its point: to flee out of Jerusalem is to wander in the
wilderness, against the day of redemption when each county
shall return through the gate Los has fixed within it.

"No defence on poetic grounds of such a list is possible,"
according to Harold Bloom, "but a great poet can be pardoned
his few descents into excessive literal-mindedness."[1] Bloom
compares it with the Bible's genealogies, Spenser's pageant of
British kings, and Milton's geographical place names as pre-
cedents for a kind of *poétique de pire*, whereby we enjoy the
next passage the more for having felt miserable during this
one. Of the next passage Bloom writes, "This fine recovery
is dependent on the merciless listing that precedes it" (E 933).
It is hard to disagree with this, but it is not sufficient as a
theodicy of wildernesses. As an epic *topos* or commonplace
the list goes back to Homer, who doubtless had better reasons

for his "descent" to a 266-line Catalogue of Ships in the *Iliad* than that it would feel good when it stopped. Homer seems to have been moved by an urge toward total comprehensiveness and the memorial preservation of historical details, and so was Blake. Spenser and Milton passed on this incorporative, encyclopedic tradition to their heir and rival, who reduced it, with warrant from the Old Testament (Num. 1-2, Josh. 12-21), to its bare essentials. For reasons we shall explore in this chapter, it was important to Blake that everything be named, that we say the names over, that they find a permanent place in "the rounded catalogue divine, complete," of his redemptive epic.[2]

If the listing of the counties is "merciless" (and it may have been too much even for Blake, who spares us the Irish counties until plate 72 much later), the "fixing down" of the counties and the fixing of the gates in them are acts of mercy. By assigning counties to the Twelve Tribes, Los has gone beyond the boundary-fixing of Joshua and traced the scattered tribes of Britain back to their spiritual roots in Jerusalem. The gate he establishes in each county is its way back to the ancient spiritual liberty it lost when Albion fell, its window on eternity. Disconnected from this spiritual center, Albion is only a shadow of his former substance, a body without a soul (J 71.1-5).[3] Los's act corresponds to the finding of the Limits of Opacity and Contraction by the Divine Hand of Mercy (J 42.29-34; M 13.20); this limit might be called the Limit of Dispersal, or of Diaspora. Wales is listed first, not only because she has a convenient number of counties (one for each tribe, and a tithe of Britain's total of 120),[4] but because she can "conduct to England & Scotland & Ireland" the ancient spirit through her famous bards.

It is almost as if Blake has put the Bible under a map of the British Isles in order to buoy them up, to keep them from sinking into nonentity. In Emily Dickinson's words, "Mortality's Ground Floor / Is Immortality."[5] The Bible is an imaginative *terra firma* where everything is already fixed reliably and permanently, even eternally—a Rock of Ages in a Sea of Chaos. Albion sleeps on top of it, on

a Couch of Repose,
With Sixteen pillars: canopied with emblems & written verse.
Spiritual Verse, order'd & measur'd, from whence, time shall
     reveal.
The Five books of the Decalogue, the books of Joshua & Judges,
Samuel, a double book & Kings, a double book, the Psalms &
     Prophets
The Four-fold Gospel, and the Revelations everlasting[.]
                    (J 48.6-11)

Blake's pleasure in lists is evident even in his description of
the prototype of all lists.[6]

Anyone who read his poem, Blake may have thought, would
necessarily live in one of the counties Los fixes. He or she
would feel singled out, even given a special "gate" of uncertain
but deep significance, and be brought to attention. Even you
who dwell in Clakmanan, listen: these words are of your eter-
nal salvation! The same intention seems to govern the four
prose addresses interspersed in *Jerusalem,* directed in turn to
the public, the Jews, the deists, and the Christians. Everyone
is important, no one need despair, for there is a way back for
every minute particular of Albion. As Blake's real audience
shrank to nothing, his putative or internal audience grew until
it coincided with all humanity.

                    *   *   *

The very exhaustiveness of Blake's lists bespeaks his desire
that everyone be saved. Whether he thought that everyone
would be saved, or only that everyone *could* be saved, is not
entirely clear. As I suggested in chapter three, the pitch of
his work is toward universal salvation, or Universalism, the
doctrine of the predestined salvation of all intelligent beings,
including Satan, the fallen angels, and the worst of sinners.
We might doubt if the elision of moral freedom suggested in
this doctrine would appeal to Blake; it might be more accurate
to call him a general redemptionist, one who opposes pre-
destination of any sort and believes everyone *may* be saved by
human effort and ever-proffered grace.

Blake sometimes seems inconsistent on the question of Sa-
tan's salvation. In *Milton,* Satan is Urizen drawn into gener-

ation, and Urizen is redeemable. Leutha, Enitharmon, the Lamb, and finally Milton intercede in one way or another to save him, "to loose him from my Hells," as Milton says (M 14.31). At several other places in *Milton* and elsewhere, Satan is a negation, a Spectre, a Selfhood, which must be destroyed.[7] "Christ comes as he came at first to deliver those who were bound under the Knave not to deliver the Knave He Comes to Deliver Man the Accused & not Satan the Accuser" (VLJ, E 564). The question is whether Satan is a state (Blake's usual claim) or an individual, a distinction as important in early formulations of Universalism (by Origen, for example) as it is in Blake. "Satan is the State of Death, & not a Human existence" (J 49.67). So too Blake usually speaks of "Eternal Death" as a condition we may awaken from, but occasionally he expresses the hope "that Death himself may wake / In his appointed season when the ends of heaven meet" (M 29.45-46).

Universalism, though a heresy to Roman Catholicism and to most Reformers, has at least a prima facie scriptural warrant. The word "all" recurs in crucial passages, such as: "God hath concluded them all in unbelief, that he might have mercy upon all" (Rom 11:32). The orthodox must argue that a clause like "who believe in Christ" is understood to limit the "all." With such restrictions this and the other proof texts of Universalism, they would claim, can be brought into line with exclusionary doctrines. Of central interest is the Christological doctrine of the Second Adam, perhaps originally a gnostic idea, which assumes the undoing of the Fall at the end of time. "Therefore as by the offense of one judgement came upon all men to condemnation; even so by the righteousness of one the free gift came upon all men unto justification of life" (Rom. 5:18). "For as in Adam all die, even so in Christ shall all be made alive" (1 Cor. 15:22). Beside these we may set several passages that include even more than "all men." "That in the dispensation of the fullness of times he might gather together in one all things in Christ, both which are in heaven, and which are on earth; even in him" (Eph. 1:10). "And, having made peace through the blood of his cross, by him to reconcile all things unto himself; by him, I say, whether they be things in earth, or things in heaven" (Col. 1:20).

With "all things" gathered in Christ, the Second Adam, we are at the doctrine of the *apocatastasis*, the restitution or restoration spoken of in Acts 3:21 (and only there): "Whom [Christ] the heaven must receive until the times of restitution of all things, which God hath spoken by mouth of all his holy prophets since the world began." The "restitution of all things" goes beyond the question the disciples ask Jesus in Acts 1:6: "wilt thou at this time restore again [*apocathistaneis*] the kingdom of Israel?" To the traditional Jewish idea of a messianic restoration of the Promised Land, were added Greek cosmological speculations that help motivate the "all things" (though we should note that some scholars would drop the comma after "all things" and make the following clause restrictive). *Apocatastasis* was the technical term for the return of the stars to their original position after a cycle of equinoctial precession (25,800 years, the Great Year) or for the shining of the sun or moon after obscuration. "The Sun has left his blackness & has found a fresher morning / And the fair Moon rejoices in the clear & cloudless night" (A 6.13-14; cf. FZ 138.20-21). Neoplatonic writers used the term for the release of the soul from the material body, and sometimes for the downward cycle of the soul into the body. Philo combined the former usage with his allegorizing of the Old Testament; for him the Exodus from Egypt betokened the *apocatastasis* of the soul. Several Church Fathers, notably Origen and Gregory of Nyssa, defended the doctrine of *apocatastasis*. "The end is always like the beginning." Hell is really purgatory, a refining fire; our bodies will not perish but be transformed at the End. As part of the redemptive process, Origen posits the existence of "orders," much like Blake's "states," through which "every rational creature" can "travel" on its way to salvation, even after death.[8]

In this Christian cosmology we are near to a total allegorizing and psychologizing of the literal history and doctrine of the Bible: the orders our spirits pass through are ontological projections of states of mind or the soul in this life. The final step was taken in early modern times, if not sooner.

Gerrard Winstanley, who resembles Blake in so many other
ways, rails like him at the doctrine of the elect, and endorses
complete Universalism in explicit terms: "He [the preaching
clergy] saith some are elected to salvation and others are
reprobated; he puts some into heaven, thrusts others into hell
never to come out, and so he is not a universal saviour. That
is no salvation to the creation, mankind, while any part groans
for the true saviour; when he comes he will wipe away all
tears, he comes not to destroy any but to save all."9 Winstanley
denies the existence of any local heaven or hell, taking them
and all the topography of the Bible as representing something
spiritual: "even so mankind, the living earth, is the very gar-
den of Eden," the tree of knowledge is the imagination, the
tree of life is "universal love or pure knowledge in the power,"
and so on.10 Throughout his writings he speaks of states, or
"estates," with no external existence.

Detached in part from the nexus of radical Inner Light
beliefs, Universalism as a distinct theological issue found de-
fenders a century later in England and especially America.
Charles Chauncy of Boston was one of the most respectable
clergymen to take up the cause: in 1784 he published a book
arguing the ultimate reconciliation of all sinners to God.11
Later John Murray and Hosea Ballou founded the Univer-
salist Church and drew many followers, especially in upstate
New York. In Blake's England defenders of Universalism ex-
changed frequent pamphlets with attackers, and it is likely
that some of them came Blake's way. He might well have been
interested in a long series of debates sponsored by the Amer-
ican Universalist Elhanan Winchester, which drew large au-
diences, on the question "Which is the most consistent with
Revelation and Reason, the Arminian tenets of the Rev. Mr.
John Wesley, the Calvinistic Decrees upheld by the Rev. Mr.
Whitfield and others, the Theology propagated by the late
Emanuel Swedenburgh, under the title of the New Jerusalem,
or the Doctrine of Universal Salvation, maintained by the Rev.
Mr. Winchester?"12 Blake might also have been impressed by
a pamphlet Winchester published in 1792 called *The Ever-
lasting Gospel*; it was a translation of a German tract that argued
for the universal restoration.13 He would probably have been

pleased with the Universalist, or at least very generous, spirit one can find in Methodism, despite its great preoccupation with sin. "Thy goodness and Thy grace to me," one of Wesley's hymns reads, "To every soul abound; / . . . / Enough for all, enough for each, / Enough for evermore."[14]

Especially in its more radical millenarian form, the social bearings and ideological features of Universalism are fairly evident. Winstanley makes clear that he does not believe in a coming personal reign of Christ on earth, a reign that, however merciful and wise, would still be a theocracy. He tries to think beyond the conflicting thoughts of John of Patmos, whose Wrathful Lamb, bloody from its own sacrifice, sits on a throne surrounded by militant angels. The division of the elect from those marked by the Beast, so prominent in Revelation, does not excite Winstanley's repressed resentment or thirst for revenge as it did, and does, so many lower-class Christians. He will not simply turn the world upside down, leaving its structure unchanged. He does not want a revolution in the original sense of the word, a circulation of elites (or elects), but rather a deliverance of everyone, ruler and ruled, from the "state" of rulership itself.

So it is with Blake's refusal to condemn the self-proclaimed elect to the perdition they consign everyone else to, for if he did so the elect would gain a convert. Blake even seems to reject the idea held by many Universalists that sinners "owe" a stint in hell before the general resurrection:

> . . . Doth Jehovah Forgive a Debt only on condition that it shall
> Be Payed? Doth he Forgive Pollution only on conditions of Purity
> That Debt is not Forgiven! That Pollution is not Forgiven
> Such is the Forgiveness of the Gods, the Moral Virtues of the
> Heathen, whose tender Mercies are Cruelty. But Jehovahs
>   Salvation
> Is without Money & without Price, in the Continual Forgiveness
> of Sins[.]
>
>   (J 61.17-22)

At certain testy moments Blake seems to damn a few people— "The Fool shall not enter into Heaven . . . Wo Wo Wo to you Hypocrites" (VLJ, E 564)—though it is arguable that he is really damning the states of folly or hypocrisy and not the individuals passing through them. He sometimes claims that the only unforgiveable sin is to refuse to forgive: "O Albion, if thou takest vengeance; if thou revengest thy wrongs / Thou art for ever lost!" (J 45.36-37). But then "forever" in Blake is equivocal, for eternity is in a moment, and it is never too late to repent.

Blake's distinction between a state, which, however personified, may be annihilated, and individuals who may inhabit them or pass through them and be saved, corresponds obviously enough to that between the office and the official, or between the "body politic" and the "body natural" of the king. Blake hated kingship but does not seem to have favored regicide; the point is to get rid of the whole institution, including the place of kingship in our minds. His few cryptic lines on Charles and Cromwell (M 5.39-41) do not prove it, but he probably thought it was a mistake for Parliament to have executed Charles to make him atone for his crimes; the crimes were inherent in the kingship and were passed on not only to the royal successor but to the Lord Protector himself. Killing Louis will not prevent a Robespierre, nor killing Nicholas a Stalin. "The iron hand crushd the Tyrants head / And became a Tyrant in his stead" (E 490).

In its listing and redeeming functions, *Jerusalem* and to a lesser degree *Milton* and *The Four Zoas* correspond to the "book of life" of Revelation 20:12-15.

> And I saw the dead, small and great, stand before God; and the books were opened: and another book was opened, which is the book of life: and the dead were judged out of those things which were written in the books, according to their works.

In Blake's *A Vision of the Last Judgment*, as he describes it, "On the Cloud are opened the Books of Remembrance of Life & of Death" (E 561). In Malachi 3:16 there is a "book of remembrance" for those who feared the Lord; these the Lord shall spare at the day of his return.

> And the sea gave up the dead which were in it; and death and hell delivered up the dead which were in them: and they were judged every man according to their works.

And death and hell were cast into the lake of fire. This is the second death.

To Blake death and hell are states to pass through, in this life and, perhaps, the next.

The last verse Blake could accept only if the lake of fire is taken as another state:

And whosoever was not found written in the book of life was cast into the lake of fire.

For everyone, by a kind of virtual representation, would find himself written in Blake's own book of life. To name the counties and countries and kings, the Seven Eyes of God and Twelve Sons of Albion and Twenty-seven Churches, is to rescue the whole of humanity. Reading Blake, we find ourselves named, not as if we are predestined by an external agency to be saved, but as eternal addressees, who may always, by internal action and with the help of one another, save ourselves.

* * *

I have skirted a problem we must face, if not solve, before we go much further. Orthodox Universalism, if we may use the phrase, assumed the literal death and resurrection of the dead, whether from a period in hell (now rather like purgatory) or immediately after this life. At the general resurrection all souls who ever lived would return to life and ascend to heaven. Now there are a few passages in which Blake sounds perfectly orthodox in this respect:

Many a woful company & many on clouds & waters
Fathers & friends Mothers & Infants Kings & Warriors
Priests & chaind Captives met together in a horrible fear
And every one of the dead appears as he had livd before
. . . .
. . . the children of six thousand years
Who died in infancy rage furious a mighty multitude rage
furious[.]
(FZ 122.38-41; 123.7-8)

This passage is troubling for its vengefulness—these innocents are enraged against the warriors and tyrants who slaughtered them—but it is not the Last Judgment. More in keeping with universal forgiveness, but no less evidently a resurrection of the dead, is the arrival of the much-denounced infernal trinity of Bacon, Newton, and Locke at the chariot races in heaven with Milton, Shakespeare, and Chaucer (J 98.9). The question, as W.J.T. Mitchell points out, is whether the word "Last" in "Last Judgment" means last in time or ultimate in significance.[15] Is it history or mystery? So much of Blake rests on an Inner Light or "anacalyptic" reading of biblical events that it seems only right to try to read his passages of seemingly orthodox literalness in the same way. Before the accusing consciences of living tyrants or of our own tyrannical selfhoods rages the memory of innocents murdered through all of time. In our redeemed reasons the exemplars of fallen reason will be purged of error and rejoin the prophets of imagination. In his description of his *Vision of the Last Judgment,* the extant pen-and-watercolor versions of which seem orthodox enough, Blake seems to refer the whole elaborate eschatological drama to a peripeteia of a psychomachia, an "ultimate" moment in our personal, and perhaps also collective, spiritual lives: "whenever any Individual Rejects Error & Embraces Truth a Last Judgment passes upon that Individual" (E 562).

Is it then only in the memory of those living, enshrined in a "book of remembrance," that those who have died live on, or do they return in any more literal sense, in body or spirit? When Blake writes that he may converse with his friends in eternity and take down his poems "from immediate dictation" (Letter to Butts, 25 April 1803, E 729), we may still take this metaphorically, as he seems to do himself on other occasions: "Thirteen years ago I lost a brother & with his spirit I converse daily & hourly in the Spirit & See him in my remembrance in the regions of my Imagination. I hear his advice & even now write from his Dictate" (Letter to Hayley, 6 May 1800, E 705). Near his own death, however, he can write of a future state in terms that equally admit of a literal afterlife and of a place in the collective mind of humanity:

> Flaxman is Gone & we must All soon follow every one to his Own Eternal House Leaving the Delusive Goddess Nature & her

Laws to get into Freedom from all Law of the Members into The
Mind in which every one is King & Priest in his own House God
Send it so on Earth as it is in Heaven

> (Letter to Cumberland, 12 April 1827, E 784)

We do not need to decide this question, if deciding means
ruling out one choice, for Blake may well have believed in
certain orthodox Christian notions at the same time that he
recast them into very different notions of his own. The mys-
tery need not entirely erase the history. That the Last Judg-
ment is a kind of conversion experience is the main thing to
us, and to Blake. One suspects that if in an orthodox sense
Blake is "famed in Heaven," as he wrote in another letter (to
Flaxman, 21 September 1800, E 710) and his works are "the
delight & Study of Archangels," it is because he devoted him-
self to what heaven and archangels "mean" in our minds dur-
ing this life.

*   *   *

Let us turn now to the great rescue mission of Los. His main
task in *Jerusalem* is to build the city of Golgonooza and fill it
(and to fill it *is* to build it) with everything that ever existed,
including errors and terrors. The errors and terrors are given
form so they may be annihilated; the finger of God goes forth
upon the furnaces in Los's smithy, "Giving a body to Falshood
that it may be cast off for ever" (J 12.13). This may account
for the unpleasant presences in a passage about Golgonooza
which otherwise dwells poignantly on what must be preserved:

> . . . Los walks round the walls night and day.

> He views the City of Golgonooza, & its smaller Cities:
> The Looms & Mills & Prisons & Work-houses of Og & Anak:
> The Amalekite: the Canaanite: the Moabite: the Egyptian:
> And all that has existed in the space of six thousand years:
> Permanent, & not lost not lost nor vanishd, & every little act,
> Word, work, & wish, that has existed, all remaining still
> In those Churches ever consuming & ever building by the
>   Spectres
> Of all the inhabitants of Earth wailing to be Created:
> Shadowy to those who dwell not in them, meer possibilities:
> But to those who enter into them seem the only substances

For every thing exists & not one sigh nor smile nor tear,
One hair nor particle of dust, not one can pass away.
(J 13.55-14.1)

Looms and mills and prisons and workhouses are the disor-
ganized or "conglomerating" (13.52) forms, or un-forms, of
social life, the terribly wrong ways people have gotten them-
selves together during the ages of the twenty-seven Churches.
Through all the ages everyone oppressed in them (that is,
everyone without exception) still exists in at least spectral
form. In a sense, perhaps, that is because they never really
existed, for without brotherhood man is not, however sub-
stantial these shadowy churches seem. They are products of
the "States that are not, but ah! Seem to be" (M 32.29).

What Los does with these specters is "create" them. Though
the idea here seems to derive from Platonic notions of gen-
eration, no "honey of generation" (in Yeats's phrase) is nec-
essary to lure them into this life; they wail to be created. Los
in both senses of the word "draws" them into life, as gener-
ation is a vehicle for an aesthetic tenor. In *Milton* the task of
drawing is assigned to a son of Los named Antamon,

> . . . who takes them into his beautiful flexible hands,
> As the Sower takes the seed, or the Artist his clay
> Or fine wax, to mould artful a model for golden ornaments.
> The soft hands of Antamon draw the indelible line:
> Form immortal with golden pen; such as the Spectre admiring
> Puts on the sweet form; then smiles Antamon bright thro his
>   windows[.]
>
> (M 28.13-18)

His recasting of the doctrine of the incarnation of souls is
not Blake's only improvement of Plato here. Plato extended
his hierarchical model of the good society (with the elect in
charge) to his metaphysics. In the *Parmenides* (130c-d) Socrates
concedes, despite some doubts, that it would be absurd to
believe that there is a form (*eidos*) of hair or mud or dirt or
anything else vile or worthless. But universalist Blake, whose
God became a worm to nourish the weak (E 599), will not
allow a hair or particle of dust to go unhoused in a permanent
form.[16] When he has the tender voices of Beulah claim that

"not one sparrow can suffer, & the whole Universe not suffer also" (J 25.8), he invokes as Hamlet does Jesus' example of universal Providence (Matt. 10.29), and as Hamlet defies augury, the bird-watching of Greek and Roman predestinarians, Blake defies Plato's contempt for the masses and for mass-nouns like "hair." Jesus in Matthew's next verse insists "the very hairs of your head are all numbered."

Golgonooza is a city of art, a kind of museum in which Blake shores eternal forms against the ruins of time. The Bible is the great original here as well, for it is a book of forms. "The Old & New Testaments are the Great Code of Art" (E 274). The canopy of Albion's couch of repose held emblems as well as Scripture; the whole thing was "a sublime Ornament" of gold and jewels. Immediately following our passage on the counties of Britain come these splendid lines:

> All things acted on Earth are seen in the bright Sculptures of
> Los's Halls & every Age renews its powers from these Works
> With every pathetic story possible to happen from Hate or
> Wayward Love & every sorrow & distress is carved here
> Every Affinity of Parents Marriages & Friendships are here
> In all their various combinations wrought with wondrous Art
> All that can happen to Man in his pilgrimage of seventy years
> Such is the Divine Written Law of Horeb & Sinai:
> And such the Holy Gospel of Mount Olivet & Calvary[.]
>
> (J 16.61-69)

In these lines Blake seems to take a less extreme stance. The Bible, which puts a floor under the fall of Albion by giving form to every otherwise inchoate action or emotion that might occur in his limbs—"piteous Passions & Desires / With neither lineament nor form but like to watry clouds" (M 26.26-27)—does so not by naming each individual but by representing every kind of individual (or situation or action). This comes close to a Platonic theory of art after all, Los's halls being the realm of the archetypes that nourish existent things, and even to the neoclassical theory of general ideas that Blake characteristically denounces. That Blake wants it both ways—every individual and every kind—may account for his identifying eternal forms with "Individual Identities" that "never change nor cease":

> The Oak is cut down by the Ax, the Lamb falls by the Knife
> But their Forms Eternal Exist, For-ever, Amen Halle[l]ujah[.]
> (M 32.23, 37-38)

Blake does not say what, if it is not a form, "the Oak" is. To any particular oak or lamb the eternal existence of its form may not seem much to sing Hallelujah over as it falls by the ax or the knife.

A similarly exhaustive catalog of human, and not only human, types, though operating at a lower theological pressure than the Bible, may also be found, according to Blake, in the prototype of the English epic, Chaucer's *Canterbury Tales*.

> The characters of Chaucer's Pilgrims are the characters which compose all ages and nations: as one age falls, another rises, different to mortal sight, but to immortals only the same; for we see the same characters repeated again and again, in animals, vegetables, minerals, and in men; nothing new occurs in identical existence; Accident ever varies, Substance can never suffer change nor decay.
>
> Of Chaucer's characters, as described in his Canterbury Tales, some of the names or titles are altered by time, but the characters themselves for ever remain unaltered, and consequently they are the physiognomies or lineaments of universal human life, beyond which Nature never steps. Names alter, things never alter. I have known multitudes of those who would have been monks in the age of monkery, who in this deistical age are deists. As Newton numbered the stars, and as Linneus numbered the plants, so Chaucer numbered the classes of men. . . .
>
> . . . Chaucer's characters live age after age. Every age is a Canterbury Pilgrimage; we all pass on, each sustaining one or other of these characters; nor can a child be born, who is not one of these characters of Chaucer.   (E 532-33, 536)

As the comparison to Newton and Linnaeus suggests, Blake does not give to Chaucer the renovating and redemptive powers of the Bible. Chaucer is an organizer of the forms "beyond which Nature never steps," whereas the Law and the gospel, like Los's halls, organize spiritual forms as well. The difference may lie in the subjects of each book: Chaucer presents

every possible character while Scripture presents every pos-
sible story, every action and passion, "every little act, / Word,
work, & wish," every event of the spirit.

Rather more in the mode of strict than of "representative"
Universalism is the drive to save all of history.

> For Los in Six Thousand Years walks up & down continually
> That not one Moment of Time be lost & every revolution
> Of Space he makes permanent[.]   (J 75.7-9)

"Revolution of space" is an arresting phrase. It reminds us
that terms we use for time are often drawn from those more
"at home" in space; only fallen time, or time seen with a fallen
"spatialized" eye, can be described or measured as cycles of
revolving wheels. Time that revolves is really a form of space.
Los's task here is to give time a form in a sort of higher space,
his sculptured halls.

Then follows the telegraphic chronicle we quoted in the
last chapter:

> And these the names of the Twenty-seven Heavens & their
>   Churches
> Adam, Seth, Enos, Cainan, Mahalaleel, Jared, Enoch,
> Methuselah, Lamech; these are the Giants mighty,
>   Hermaphroditic
> Noah, Shem, Arphaxad, Cainan the Second, Salah, Heber,
> Peleg, Reu, Serug, Nahor, Terah: these are the Female Males:
> A Male within a Female hid as in an Ark & Curtains.
> Abraham, Moses, Solomon, Paul, Constantine, Charlemaine,
> Luther, these Seven are the Male Females[.]
>   (J 75.10-17)

To name them is to preserve them (we shall pass over their
categorization into three types of hermaphrodite) but in this
case they are preserved in exemplary form in order to be
gotten round, to be seen through, to be made porous to the
redemptive imagination. Jesus breaks through them and
"Opens Eternity in Time & Space." In other words, to be
made to see the whole dreary, repetitive round of it is to free
us imaginatively from it.

> Thus are the Heavens formd by Los within the Mundane Shell
> And where Luther ends Adam begins again in Eternal Circle

To awake the Prisoners of Death . . .

(J 76.22, 23-25)

The "Prisoners of Death" can refer, of course, to us the living, who read Blake, who view the halls of Los, but it also seems to name everyone who ever lived during the whole of history, "the children of six thousand years," the specters laboring in "The Looms & Mills & Prisons & Work-houses of Og & Anak." Blake remains equivocal. He allows us to translate his visions into more acceptable terms while preserving the metaphysical pathos of a traditional if heretical theology.

There may be other ways to take this. Donald Ault compares Los's salvation of all people, all acts, and all moments with Alfred North Whitehead's idea of "objective immortality" of all events in space and time, which Whitehead in turn compares with God's "tender care that nothing be lost." Thomas Carlyle expresses a similar idea, which he borrowed from J. G. Fichte: "The true Past departs not. . . . no Truth or Goodness realized by man ever dies."[17] I think the best way for us to take Blake's teaching here, whatever he may have had in mind, is to see the resurrection of all mankind as a figure for our recuperation of lost human history, for our imaginative penetration of the abstract fog that hides it, indeed, for a kind of spiritual archaeology. Such a science would excavate history from the memory holes to which some societies consciously consign it or from its recycling by other societies as the merely "historical" or "quaint" feature of a consumable commodity.

Ault denies that the redemption of time has to do with memory; it is rather a visceral feeling about the past, an intuition of its presence. He is right if "memory" is taken as it often is in Blake as a "ratio" of the fallen intellect, "the rotten rags of Memory" to be cast off through inspiration (M 41.4), but there is a higher and deeper kind of memory in Blake that is akin to inspiration or vision. For in eternity, at the apocalypse, what we shall be doing is rather like what Los does in this fallen world—"creating exemplars of Memory and of Intellect" (J 98.30).

These two levels of memory invite comparison with Proust's distinction between *mémoire volontaire* and *involontaire*: the rising up in vivid reverie of a forgotten childhood scene would be well described as a resurrection of the dead child. Walter Benjamin makes a similar distinction in his disparagement of historicism. "To articulate the past historically does not mean to recognize it 'the way it really was' (Ranke). It means to seize hold of a memory as it flashes up at a moment of danger." So with Blake's Los: "At last when desperation almost tore his heart in twain / He recollected an old Prophecy . . ." (M 20.56-7). These memories, which come to us unbidden and with an affinity for the present need that we could not consciously have foretold, must be preserved from the distortions or amnesia propagated by the ruling classes.

> In every era the attempt must be made anew to wrest tradition away from a conformism that is about to overpower it. The Messiah comes not only as the redeemer, he comes as the subduer of Antichrist. Only that historian will have the gift of fanning the spark of hope in the past who is firmly convinced that *even the dead* will not be safe from the enemy if he wins. And this enemy has not ceased to be victorious.

And so something must be said for the chronicler who cites everything and refuses to give history a shape; any of it or all of it might be necessary in the emergencies ahead, and each moment of danger will dictate a different shape to the past. When the state of permanent emergency that is our history finally passes, then perhaps we will have the God's-eye view Otto Ranke aspires to.

> A chronicler who recites events without distinguishing between major and minor ones acts in accordance with the following truth: nothing that has ever happened should be regarded as lost for history. To be sure, only a redeemed mankind receives the fullness of its past—which is to say, only for a redeemed mankind has its past become citable in all its moments. Each moment it has lived becomes a *citation à l'ordre du jour*—and that day is Judgment Day.[18]

We may think of Blake as a general who wants all his Christian soldiers to be cited for bravery in the dispatches, in the Book of Life, so that dead or alive they will be immortalized. Blake's lists, his conscientious surveying of human history in order to rescue any strayed sheep, bespeak a general's or a God's perspective, and in this he differs from Benjamin, for whom such a view is, perhaps forever, premature. For Blake, to conceive of human history as the same dull round of twenty-seven Churches or 120 counties is to make the leap into apocalyptic readiness. Had Benjamin lived in an England thick with history and loud with Burke's defense of it (admittedly a conformist history of the kind Benjamin was out to sabotage) and not in a Europe on the brink of a fascist pulverization, he might have been less anxious about history's disappearance.

For his part Blake seems to have seen history in two ways. He sees it as a ruling-class affair only, as though the lower classes have had no "Churches," no traditions and institutions, of their own, and did not fight back and change the course of history, but played the parts only of victims, the same in every era; or he sees periodic eruptions of the people (Orc) followed by relapses into tyranny and oppression. Recycling history may be useful in moments of despair, but redemption seems to be a total escape from it.

* * *

If even hairs and particles of dust take their places at the universal *apocatastasis*, we might expect our poet to announce that the language itself, and all the arts, will arrive at the muster of eternity in their eternal dress. If we are to be gathered within the Second Adam, we might expect to learn the Adamic prelapsarian speech and to hear our names called out in the divine *Ursprache*.

Blake says very little about what this language might be, but English, he makes pretty clear, is a kind of minimal language just this side of inarticulateness, a limit like the other limits Los or Jesus finds to put a floor under the Fall. This one might be called the Limit of Dumbness. "I call them by their English names," Blake says *in propria persona*—"them" referring to another list, the twenty-four cities of Albion—

English: the rough basement.
Los built the stubborn structure of the Language, acting against Albions melancholy, who must else have been a Dumb despair.
(J 36.58-60)

If English is a rough basement, we may note, it is not only the ruin of a once glorious linguistic mansion but the foundation of its reconstruction. "The Ruins of Time builds Mansions in Eternity" (E 705). But what the primal and final language may be, and whether it is even a language in the usual sense, we are left to infer.

It is as ruins of a primal language, I think, that we may take one of the most distinctive, and sometimes most irritating, features of Blake's work, his invented names. Los, Orc, Thel, Oothoon, Urizen; Golgonooza, Bowlahoola, Allamanda; Udan Adan, Entuthon Benython—these serve as constant reminders that something we have not heard of before is going on in Blake's universe, something involving categories and characters of greater priority or depth than any cultural sphere we know, including the Bible. For if the counties of Britain, named in the rough makeshift mortal pidgin of English, are attached to a set of names in the prior, more original, language of Hebrew, even the Hebrew names throughout Blake's epics are late and degenerate compared with the tongue of the remote times, of the "Names anciently rememberd" but now scorned or forgotten (J 5.38). Even this seemingly original tongue contains distinctions of priority, which would suggest infinite regression were the earlier terms not declared to be eternal. "Los was the fourth immortal starry one. . . . / . . . Urthona was his name / In Eden"; "Los . . . is the Vehicular Form of strong Urthona" (FZ 3.9-4.1; J 53.1; cf. J 35.7-9). "Orc is the generate Luvah"; "Terrified Urizen heard Orc now certain that he was Luvah" (M 29.34; FZ 80.43). The distinction between eternal and generate names has as its epic precedent the divine and mortal languages of Homer: "the great deep-eddying river / Who is called Xanthos by the gods, but by mortals Skamandros"; "a singing bird whom in the mountains / the immortal gods call chalkis, but men call him kymindis" (*Iliad* 20.73-74, 14.290-91; trans. Lattimore). At least Urthona and Luvah, then, appear to be names in the *Ursprache*. That they sound like "earth-owner" and "lover" may only show how stubbornly the structure of English has preserved the original sounds.

It has recently been suggested that the most fruitful way to interpret the names is not, to use Ferdinand de Saussure's terms, diachronically, searching for etymologies, but synchronically, as a self-contained system. "The autonomy of mythic names and their formulaic arrangements imply that they function collectively as a principle of structure in Blake's works and not a principle of conceptual reference."[19] This faces us in the right direction, and reminds us that the search for etymologies in Blake's sources, however enjoyable a scholarly pursuit, will mislead us if we take them as constituting the meaning of a name. (A Blakean name, moreover, being consciously invented, can hardly be said to *have* an etymology like that of a word in any natural language, evolving "unconsciously" over centuries among millions of speakers.) It is better to take them as the surviving vocabulary of a lost tongue (we might call it Golgonoozish), words with internal relations to each other, showing preferences for certain sounds (for example, the "oo" vowel), ways of prefixing, repetition, and the like. This approach is equally misleading, however, if it makes us deaf to the implicit claim that this language is an ancestor of English, or was present in Los's mind as he made English for Albion to speak. The most important names, to put it another way, bear marks of "ancient Englishness" (or sometimes of Greek or Latin or Ossianic Gaelic) or of what we might call "etymologicity." They hint that antiquarianism has a purpose, as Blake often acknowledged, but Blake scholars who seek the "origins" of the names are doing the mirror opposite of what the names themselves invite us to do: trace English back to Golgonoozish. So our words "earth" and "owner," the Roman-Welsh names Arthur and Uther,[20] the Ossianic U-thorno, and so on, may all be traceable back to "Urthona."

At the general restoration we will speak a restored tongue. And it is by speech, restorative if not restored, that the sleeping Albion is awakened. "Her voice [that of contrite England] pierc'd Albions clay cold ear. he movd upon the Rock. / The Breath Divine went forth upon the morning hills, Albion mov'd / Upon the Rock" (J 95.1-3). Before this, faithful to his post, "in the Nerves of the Ear . . . / On Albions Rock Los stands creating the glorious Sun each morning" (M 29.40-41), as if

Albion can somehow hear the light. As Urizen, regent of the eye, and Los, master of the ear, join in harmony with the other senses, the language will add the character of vision to its aural essence. "And [the Zoas] conversed together in Visionary forms dramatic which bright / Redounded from their Tongues in thunderous majesty, In Visions / In new Expanses" (J 98.28-30). The "Visionary forms dramatic" seem to be what Albion utters on waking, "speaking the Words of Eternity in Human Forms, in direful / Revolutions of Action & Passion" (J 95.9-10). It is a language of aural hieroglyphics, of moving pictures (we remember the "emblems & written verse" on Albion's couch), a vehicle for the direct conveyance of experience from speaker to speaker. It is the unmediated, spontaneous version of the bright sculptures of Los, with "every pathetic story," the free expenditure of the treasury Los has stored up.

It is interesting that the word Blake prefers for his restored speech-acts is "converse." In Blake's fallen world, of course, there are not many dialogues we could call conversations in any normal sense. Much of the speaking is calls, cries, lamentations, howlings, ragings, cursings, and "threat'nings loud & fierce" (J 8.29), with occasional chantings of songs; what dialogues there are resemble formal debates or Homeric vauntings, exchanges of monologues, taking the impress of each other along the narrowest register. The occasional genuine conversations sound very different from those: they are usually about important spiritual matters, sober in tone, with no interference from the Selfhood. Indeed, when Milton ("His real Human" portion sleeping above) speaks with the Seven Angels he begins by confessing error; it seems a precondition to real conversing. The Angels instruct him and "thus they converse": Blake uses "converse(d)" three times in *Milton* 32. At a universal council the Eternals discuss high matters and then return to their stations, "And many conversed on these things as they labourd at the furrow" (J 55.48). These conversations are enactments of eternity in this life, while in eternity itself (though I may be pressing a distinction without a difference) our main activity will be conversation.

Blake describes his *Vision of the Last Judgment* as of "Paradise with its Inhabitants walking up & down in Conversations concerning Mental Delights[.] Here they are no longer talking of what is Good & Evil or of what is Right or Wrong & puzzling themselves in Satans Labyrinth But are Conversing [as opposed to "talking"] with Eternal Realities as they Exist in the Human Imagination" (E 562). I think the same correlations of talking or puzzling about morality with wandering in a maze, and of conversing about mental realities with walking in a garden,[21] may be found in Milton's confession to the Angels. He sees his Spectre as an "idiot Reasoner" wandering through the "Heavens" he (with his Calvinist tendencies) helped build, the Spectre being Milton himself as we meet him in the opening of the poem, "who walkd about in Eternity / One hundred years, pondring the intricate mazes of Providence" (M 2.16-17).[22]

We must turn, in any case, to resonances of "converse" and "conversation" as Blake met them, before he gave them his own nuance. In every case in Blake the primary sense is "talk with one another" or "discuss," but there are secondary senses that derive from the Bible. As he begins to converse Milton says, "I have turned my back upon these Heavens"; to turn (one's) back is to convert; thus to converse you must convert. Only a hint of this is present (neither "conversion" nor "convert" is found in the poems), but it is enough to underline the spiritual provenance of conversations. More important is the sense of "conversation" found several times in both Testaments as "conduct" or "mode of life." Psalm 37:14 speaks of "upright conversation." Paul warns Christians to "Let your conversation be as it becometh the gospel of Christ" (Phil. 1:27), and cast off "the former conversation the old man" (Eph. 4:22). The proper place for a Christian's conversation— and this may have prompted Blake—is in heaven: "For our conversation is in heaven" (Phil. 3:20). "Conversation" in this sense is nearly equivalent to "walk"—"For we walk by faith"; "we should walk in newness of life" (2 Cor. 5:7; Rom. 6:4).[23] So John Bunyan explains in a note to *Pilgrim's Progress* that when Apollyon wounds Christian in his head, hand, and foot, it means "Christian wounded in his understanding, faith and conversation."[24] And so "Los in Six Thousand Years walks up & down continually" at his labors (J 75.7) and Blake's restored conversers walk up and down as they discourse—a Christian transfiguration of the Peripatetics.

Just what we talk about in heaven Blake explains no further than he does in the passages we have quoted, but as to whom we talk to he has some startling ideas. For one thing, we converse with lions. In the apocalyptic conclusion of *The Four Zoas*, the newly risen Man

> ... walks upon the Eternal Mountains raising his heavenly voice
> Conversing with the Animal forms of wisdom night & day
> That risen from the Sea of fire renewed walk oer the Earth

> For Tharmas brought his flocks upon the hills & in the Vales
> Around the Eternal Mans bright tent the little Children play
> Among the wooly flocks The hammer of Urthona sounds
> In the deep caves beneath his limbs[.] renewd his Lions roar
> Around the Furnaces & in Evening sport upon the plains

—presumably with the flocks. For their part the lions have a few questions, as well they might:

> They raise their faces from the Earth conversing with
>   the Man.

> How is it we have walkd thro fires & yet are not consumd
> How is it that all things are changd even as in ancient times
> (FZ 138.30-40)

Terrific lions and tigers show up at the pre-apocalyptic finale of *Milton*, prepared with all other animals to "go forth to the Great Harvest & Vintage of the Nations" (M 42.38-43.1), and they head the list of nine creatures "humanizing" at the end of *Jerusalem*. This list, happily a brief one of typical animals from lion to worm, tells us that the main point is the human form divine of all animals, including the seemingly most obstinate; they are eternal realities of the human imagination, animal forms of human wisdom. And not only animals. Earlier in *The Four Zoas* we learn how "all things" were, and presumably how they will be at the general restitution, in contrast to the fallen present:

> A Rock a Cloud a Mountain
> Were now not Vocal as in Climes of happy Eternity
> Where the lamb replies to the infant voice & the lion to the man
>   of years

Giving them sweet instructions Where the Cloud the River &
　the Field
Talk with the husbandman & shepherd.

(FZ, 71.4-8)

"Sweet instructions" is a happy phrase for poetry, *dulce et utile*;
these lambs and lions speak in eclogues and georgics. But
even rocks will converse with us, instructing us how it is with
rocks, and, for these are humanized forms, how it is with us
in our rocklike states. "All Human Forms identified even Tree
Metal Earth & Stone" (J 99.1). For the mind has mountains,
and rocks and stones and trees, and we may either disown
them in fear, in which case they will become the hostile Other
of nature, Thel's "land unknown" full of sorrows and tears
which she enters when her conversations fail, or we may reas-
sume them in an imaginative embrace.

This is Blake's version of the myth of prelapsarian harmony
or Adam's "dominion" over the animals, by way of the Kab-
balah, whose Adam Kadmon contained all things before the
Fall. "Your tradition," Blake tells the Jews, "that Man con-
tained in his Limbs, all Animals, is True & they were separated
from him by cruel Sacrifices" (J 27). Animal (and human)
sacrifice was brought to an end, Blake goes on to say, when
Jesus took on an animal form of wisdom as the Lamb of God
in willing self-sacrifice. This is also Blake's version of the myth
of Orpheus, who sings sweet georgics to animals and stones,
harrows hell, and dies a sacrifice to nature. Blake is here at
the mythic roots of poetic personification. The archetypes of
Adam, Orpheus, and Jesus all define the relationship between
restored speech and restored nature, whether naming-day in
Eden, the primal Orphic songs, or the incarnation of the Word
in human and animal form.

Blake's vision of restored "natural" speech gives us a frame-
work for that terrifying and elusive poem "The Tyger." In
working through the imagery of the questions we may fail to
register the crucial fact that the tyger says nothing. It is not
a conversation. In its counterpart poem, "The Lamb," there
is a suggestion that the lamb speaks between stanzas. "Dost
thou know who made thee?" "No, I don't." "Little Lamb, I'll

tell thee." At least there is a movement from question to sweet instruction, prompted by the lamb's willingness to listen and appear interested. The tyger, if he knows, stays not for an answer, and leaves his questioner "pondring the intricate mazes of Providence," wandering in the forest of *aporia*. That we should wonder why the tyger says nothing may itself be wondered at, but it is one of the benefits of walking up and down in Blake's epics that we leave them with fresh questions about tygers, and about poems.

* * *

We may see at work in *Jerusalem*, finally, a dramatization of linguistic *apocatastasis*, a rescuing of words from Satan's labyrinth, even a conversion of Satanic words into verbal weapons against him. "Enthusiasm" was discussed in chapter two. Here are three more examples.

One of the grisly sports the Daughters of Albion enjoy is "circumscribing" the senses of London's inhabitants, who "Feel their Brain cut round beneath the temples shrieking / Bonifying into a Scull" (58.7-8); "London feels his brain cut round: Edinburghs heart is circumscribed!" (66.64); "the Senses of Men shrink together under the Knife of flint" (66.83), "while they circumscribe his Brain, & while they circumscribe / His heart, & while they circumscribe his Loins!" (90.3-4). Los, ever at his post, combats circumscription with circumcision. If the Daughters appear as formidable and alluring virgins to the lobotomized males, Los rejoins that "Establishment of Truth depends on destruction of Falshood continually / On Circumcision: not on Virginity" (55.65-66). He fights with a surgery of his own "the Sexual Religion in its embryon Uncircumcision" (44.11). Without going further into the meanings of circumcision in Blake,[25] we can see a simple contrast of similar terms: circumscribing is a fallen parody of circumcising. Yet at the apocalypse the parody is elevated to parity with its original, for the human senses will expand while "Circumscribing & Circumcising the excrementitious / Husk & Covering" (98.18-19). The word itself is redeemed from its own excrementitious husk.

"Contemplation" in Blake is always bad. Urizen writes his "secrets of dark contemplation" (u 4.26), but his "dire Contemplations" only produce chaos (*The Book of Ahania* 3.7). Los sees Urizen as a "contemplative terror, frightend in his scornful sphere" (fz 52.27; cf. 24). In *Jerusalem* the Spectre of Albion seems to hypnotize the "unfortunate contemplator" and devour him (j 29.23). Los later seeks out the invisible criminals who have imprisoned his countrymen "Among the winding places of deep contemplation intricate" (45.22). Again the point is clear: contemplation, an inward-turning and rational undertaking, Milton's intricate mazes, is set against the faith and creative power of Los. But as the Last Judgment passes over Albion he comes out of himself in love for another: "Albion stood in terror: not for himself but for his Friend / Divine, & Self was lost in the contemplation of faith / and wonder at the Divine Mercy" (96.30-32). Faith is so strong it can redeem its opposite.

With a third term, used more frequently than either of these, Blake makes the same maneuver, this time with a more aggressive, sometimes sarcastic, tone, but he anticipates his rhetorical strategy twice with a doctrinal statement. The word is "demonstration," which like "contemplation" is always a mistaken basis of existence. Demonstration is an activity of the reason, ignorant and myopic, cruel in what it does to the minute particulars of life, and vague and indefinite in its reliance on unimaginative, "unhewn" rocks—rocks not of faith but of unbelief. As he collapses in the opening of *Jerusalem* Albion announces his desperate belief that "By demonstration, man alone can live, and not by faith" (4.28). He realizes soon enough what his new rational philosophy has done to his children—"I have educated you in the crucifying cruelties of Demonstration" (24.55)—but he subsides again, and Los surveys the damage done "By Demonstrations the cruel Sons of Quality and Negation" (38.67): "O Demonstrations of Reason Dividing Families in Cruelty & Pride" (57.11). Urizen the architect then makes Albion's sons build Stonehenge of rocks, "of Reasonings: of unhewn demonstrations" (66.3; cf. 55.56).

The climax of this leitmotif comes late in the poem, where Los states some home truths and then says of them, "These are the Demonstrations of Los, and the blows of my mighty Hammer" (90.57). Like Nietzsche, Los philosophizes with a hammer. If it is demonstrations you want, I will give you demonstrations! (In another sense that is just what he does, since the truths he states are undeniably generalizations, not minute particulars.) This fine effect is perhaps somewhat undercut by its anticipation in two earlier passages, but they give us terms for Los's strategy, and Blake's. The Living Creatures, at the work of redemption, cry, "Compell the Reasoner to Demonstrate with unhewn Demonstrations / Let the Indefinite be explored, and let every Man be Judged / By his own Works" (55.56-58). This is one way of putting the *reductio ad absurdum* tactic Blake employs from "There is No Natural Religion" on: let us grant your premises and see what comes of them. If only excrement comes, we will cut it off by circumcision. Earlier, however, Blake puts it more personally and dramatically. Los sees the finger of God "by mathematic power / Giving a body to Falshood that it may be cast off for ever. / With Demonstrative Science piercing Apollyon with his own bow!" (12.12-14).[26] Apollyon's bow of demonstration can be shot by a greater Archer. Satan, who invented artillery (PL 6.482f), faints beneath it in *Milton* (5.2). To redeem one of Satan's words is to hoist him with his own petard. "O all-powerful Human Words! / You recoil back upon me in the blood of the Lamb" (J 24.1-2).[27] Words are packets of energy that will explode if you abuse them, as all energy is from the intellectual fountain, the Holy Ghost, the human Word divine. The rational devil may cite the Word for his own purposes, but the Word has reasons that the reason does not know.

APPENDIX

The Seven Eyes of God

Three times Blake lists the Seven Eyes of God, once in each of his longer "prophetic books." In *Jerusalem* 55.31-32 they are listed only by name, while the accounts in *The Four Zoas* and *Milton*, nearly identical, provide a characteristic or two for each Eye. Here is the version in *The Four Zoas*:

> . . . And those in Eden sent Lucifer for their Guard
> Lucifer refusd to die for Satan & in pride he forsook his charge
> Then they sent Molech Molech was impatient They sent
> Molech impatient They sent Elohim who created Adam
> To die for Satan Adam refusd but was compelld to die
> By Satans arts. Then the Eternals Sent Shaddai
> Shaddai was angry Pachad descended Pachad was terrified
> And then they sent Jehovah who leprous stretchd his hand to
>   Eternity
> Then Jesus came & Died willing beneath Tirzah and Rahab[.]
>
> (FZ 115.42-50)

The context here and in *Milton* is the creation of space by Enitharmon to protect Satan from punishment. Whether or not Enitharmon was wise to do that, the Eternals in Eden ratify her "kind decision" and give a time of six thousand years to the space (M 13.12-17). The goal, presumably, is to redeem Satan through voluntary self-sacrifice, and so the Eternals send a series of "Guards" for that purpose. They all refuse to "die" for Satan until Jesus comes and "Died willing" beneath Satan's natural and spiritual representatives.

Blake may have had more immediate sources, as we shall see, but the natural recourse is to the Bible for this list of strange bedfellows. Some sort of rationale can be erected for each Eye, and in conjunction with other passages throughout Blake's work dealing with recognizable history, rough dates and characteristic features can be assigned to them. Northrop Frye's is the most notable attempt to do this.[1] I will not try to better his account but rather concentrate on the biblical motivations for the names to see if a general "historical" pattern emerges.

The prime source of the Seven Eyes is the prophecy of Zechariah. The angel shows Zechariah a candlestick with seven lamps and tells him "they are the eyes of the Lord, which run to and fro through the whole earth" (4:10). This vision is taken up by John of Patmos in his apocalypse: "And I beheld, and, lo, in the midst of the throne and of the four beasts, and in the midst of the elders, stood a Lamb as it had been slain, having seven horns and seven eyes, which are the seven Spirits of God sent forth into all the earth" (Rev. 5:6). Coleridge follows a long tradition in setting Zechariah's lamps around John's throne: "Wheeling round the throne the Lampads seven, / (The mystic Words of Heaven)."[2]

There is nothing in the biblical passages to suggest that the Eyes emerge or descend serially in time, as they might if they were words, but it is a natural enough exegesis in view of the seven days of creation and the speculations about future intervals in Daniel and other apocalyptic writings. There is also nothing to suggest that six of them are spiritual failures and even destroyers of the spirit, though we might well ask why God needs seven of them if they are all spiritually potent.

Bloom suggests that the choice of Lucifer as the first Eye was motivated by Isaiah 14:12: "How art thou fallen from heaven, O Lucifer, son of the morning!"[3] Blake, of course, also had *Paradise Lost* before him with its unrivaled account of Lucifer's defeat and fall. A more specific association of the Seven Eyes with Lucifer (or rather with Satan) lies in Job 1:7, where Satan comes to the Lord "from going to and fro in the earth," a phrase that Zechariah 4:10 echoes.[4] Lucifer is, of course, the paradigm of pride; it was out of pride, Blake says, that "he forsook his charge" of, in fact, annihilating pride. (Blake distinguishes Lucifer from Satan so that the latter may stand for the negative adversary still at work in the world.)

Molech, the second Eye, is the Ammonite god to whom children were sacrificed. He hardly seems to be an improvement on Lucifer, for he not only fails to sacrifice himself but demands the atonement of others. It is interesting that Blake elsewhere (J 89.30-31) names Molech as one of the "Generalizing Gods," thereby adding a twist to the motif of the Minute Particular or "little one" crushed by general laws. It is not clear, however, why Molech should be particularly "impatient," unless we are to take it to mean "unwilling to suffer" as Christ suffered (Christus Patiens) in his Passion.

Elohim, the third Eye, seems to recognize his obligation to sacrifice something, at least, for Satan, but vicarious atonement is only a variation on the same dismal theme, not a new departure. Even his product Adam refuses to die voluntarily. "Elohim," Damon points out, is the name of God generally used in the Bible from Adam to Abraham.[5] It is used of the Creator in Genesis 1 but not Genesis 2. We know from Crabb Robinson's memoirs, and it is implicit at several points in Blake's work, that Blake distinguished between Elohim, the creator of this fallen world, and Jehovah, a more favorable figure. It is significant that human history as traditionally conceived begins in the third period. The first two Eyes must then cover a time of prehuman fall, embracing not only the angels led by Lucifer but perhaps also the "Antediluvians" or giants Blake describes in *The Marriage of Heaven and Hell* (16, 17), who "formed this world into its sensual existence and now seem to live in it in chains." *The Book of Urizen*, the Genesis-myth that begins with the Lucifer-like Urizen, ends after many stages of collapse with shrunken human forms. We noted in the last two chapters, however, that Jesus seems to have put limits on the fall, and, in an episode inserted between Molech and Elohim in the *Milton* version of the Seven Eyes, Blake repeats the idea:

... and when Molech was impatient
The Divine Hand found the Two Limits: first of Opacity, then
    of Contraction
Opacity was named Satan, Contraction was named Adam.
                                        (M 13.19-21)

Perhaps then we may see this phase as a turning point in man's spiritual history, as the bottom of a U-shaped curve. Man cannot collapse, nor can Satan blind him, any further. After Elohim (who in the *Milton* version simply faints in

weariness) come Shaddai, who is angry, and Pachad (or Pa-
had), who is terrified. Shaddai, translated in the King James
Bible as "the Almighty," is the name of God prevalent from
Abraham to Moses, and so we may take him as a symbol of
the spiritual condition of man during that period.[6] It was
under Abraham, as Frye points out, that infant sacrifice was
abolished, and so we may take that condition as an improve-
ment over that of Molech.[7] El Shaddai is also the name of
God in the Book of Job, out of sequence but perhaps be-
longing to the time of the Patriarchs in its portrayal of inex-
plicable divine anger. Pachad, the fifth Eye, gives us even less
to go on. If we are to associate Shaddai with the God of
Abraham then we are probably to take Pachad as the "fear"
of Isaac, the King James translation of *pahad* in Genesis 31:42:
"the God of my [Jacob's] father, the God of Abraham, and
the fear of Isaac, had been with me." Though "fear" follows
Abraham, Isaac precedes Moses, and that calls into question
any attempt to assign definite times to the Eyes. Anger and
fear are a plausible pair of unregenerate states of mind, if
not aspects of the same state. There may be some progress
between wrath's propensity to sacrifice another (though per-
haps without the deliberate malice of Molech or Elohim) and
terror's conviction that oneself is the victim. Fear of the Lord,
in any case, could be the beginning of wisdom.

Jehovah, as we said, is sometimes a positive figure in Blake,
as in *The Marriage of Heaven and Hell* where he "dwells in
flaming fire" as the spirit of desire or imagination (E 35). Here,
however, he is leprous. In the Bible itself, it could be said,
Jehovah is both the stern lawgiver who demands sacrifices and
the self-sacrificer who, in the form of Jesus, descends to save
us from that law. He is a transitional figure, the last of the
series of cruel gods and the forerunner of the god of mercy
and forgiveness. Los longs for "the Forgiveness of Sins in the
merciful clouds of Jehovah," but the Jehovah who now reigns
has not yet chosen to turn his merciful side to man. Los recalls
God's intervention to save Isaac from his father's sacrificial
knife: "O when shall Jehovah give us Victims from his Flocks
& Herds"—his Son the Lamb of God—"Instead of Human
Victims" (J 63.27, 30-31). If we are right to see Jehovah as
ambivalent and pivotal, then his behavior in the Eye sequence

suggests an apocalyptic consolidation of error, its completion or "perfection" before it is cast off. In *The Four Zoas*'s version Jehovah "stretchd his hand to Eternity"; in *Milton* Blake adds "For then the Body of Death was perfected in hypocritic holiness, / Around the Lamb, a Female Tabernacle" (M 13.25-26). This Body of Death, we know, Christ resurrected, shedding the mortal cerements and rising through the sepulcher. As he destroyed the Body of Death, he also rent the veil of the tabernacle in the temple, entering it as a new high priest to dispense its hidden spiritual goods. And Jesus' message, of course, was the abrogation of the law of sacrifice and revenge in the continual forgiveness of sins.

Sometimes Blake speaks of an Eighth Eye of God, one not yet come, which when it does come will turn the week of Eyes into an eternal Sabbath of vision. In *Jerusalem* the Eternals "named the Eighth. he came not, he hid in Albions Forests" (J 55.33). Are we to consider Albion himself as the Eighth Eye, now lost in error but one day to awaken to vision and the unity of mankind? Is it the Second Coming of Jesus, whose numerical value in Greek is 888? Blake seems to have a more radical idea in mind: the Eighth Eye is Satan himself, the one for whom the other seven were sent. The voluntary self-sacrifice of Jesus has brought about the precondition for Satan's salvation, but the time of fulfillment has not yet come. Satan must first be "perfected" and revealed for what he is before he can be redeemed, before, that is, those who are caught in the state of Satan can be rescued from it.

> . . . you cannot behold him till he be revealed in his System
> Albions Reactor [Satan] must have a Place prepard: Albion
>   must sleep
> The Sleep of Death, till the Man of Sin & Repentance be reveald.
> Hidden in Albions Forests he lurks . . .
>
> (J 43.10-13)

The revelation of Satan will be the annihilation of Satan, the barrier to vision and mercy, and that will be his redemption as well, his reintegration into the Divine Humanity as the majestic intellect of Urizen giving light to the creations of love.

Blake's source for the Seven Eyes of God, if he had one,

has not turned up. They are identified in *Paradise Lost* as archangels—

> Th' Arch-Angel *Uriel*, one of the sev'n
> Who in God's presence, nearest to his Throne
> Stand ready at command, and are his Eyes
> That run through all the Heav'ns, or down to th' Earth
> Bear his swift errands over moist and dry,
> O'er Sea and Land
>
> (PL 3.648-53)

—but only in an infernal sense could this be taken as a source. There is no reason, on the face of it, that he had to have any more immediate source than the biblical passages we have cited, for surely Blake shows more than enough inventiveness in his use of biblical themes everywhere else in his poems to construct the Seven (or Eight) Eyes himself. The three accounts of the Seven Eyes, however, are not well integrated into Blake's symbolic structure; they have a sort of ad hoc or interpolated character. There are, too, some analogues sufficiently close to Blake's sequence to raise expectations that an exact source may be found. For our purposes the question is not important, but it will be worth a brief look at some analogues.

Neither Swedenborg nor Boehme, both of whom Blake studied, seem to assert a seven-phase providential history. Boehme has a number of sevenfold emanations or hypostases of God or Nature, but none resemble Blake's. The idea of the seven ages of man, of course, has been a commonplace at least since Augustine. Luther periodizes history in a way that suggests a general improvement through the first five (Adam, Noah, Abraham, David, Christ), an apocalyptic turn for the worse (the Pope), and then the Millennium. Gerrard Winstanley, in *The Mysterie of God* (1648), follows Luther's sequence, more or less, and stresses a pattern of progressive enlightenment, of an increasing specificity and clarity through seven "dispensations" of God: Adam ("Do not eat the fruit"), Adam to Abraham ("The seed of woman shall bruise the serpent"), Abraham to Moses ("It shall be Abraham's seed"), Moses to Jesus (the Law of Sinai), Jesus to the present (the

Incarnation in one man), the present "dividing of time" (God's appearance in the flesh of the Saints) during which the rage of the serpent grows, and the time shortly to come (the gathering of the Saints at the Last Judgment). This Protestant pattern, progressive and eschatological, influenced by Joachite speculation, prompts us at least to look for a direction or *telos* in Blake's sequence.

The names of Blake's Seven Eyes, however, bear little resemblance to these precedents, which are not called "eyes" in any case. Blake's first six are all versions of Lucifer, the fallen angel and king of this world, even though most of them have divine names. Since Adam, moreover, does not appear until the third Eye, it seems we have to do less with human history than with events in the Godhead (though of course for Blake there is ultimately no difference). These considerations point to older analogues in gnostic and cabalistic speculation.

The Christian gnostic Saturninus said that the world and man were created by seven demiurgic angels, feeble and rebellious artisans who made a mess of their work.[8] They resemble Blake's third Eye, the Elohim. Their names, according to Ophite gnostics, were Ialdebaoth, Horaeus, Astaphaeus, Iao, Sabaoth, Eloaeus, and Adonaeus. The last four of these, at least, seem derived from Hebrew, and the sixth is probably Elohim.[9] Whether Blake knew the gnostic writers or not, they seem to have ransacked the Old Testament in a similar way. "Gnostic teachers," R. M. Grant writes, "could easily conclude [from passages in Genesis and Exodus] that at least Yahweh and Elohim were angels, and that Yahweh was an unfriendly angel. By looking through some more of the Old Testament they could find the names of all seven hostile spirits. Relying on their own experience, on 1 Chronicles [21:1], and on apocalyptic literature, they could proceed to identify Yahweh with his adversary Satan."[10] In the Kabbalah there is an account of seven cosmic cycles or *shemittoth*, each cycle a product of one of the seven lower emanations or *sefiroth* of God, and each lasting seven thousand years. (In the fiftieth millennium they all return to God.)[11] These seven "*sefiroth* of construction" are the "seven eyes" God opens to contemplate the creative possibilities in himself.[12] In one version these are the seven emissaries that go forth from the eye of Microposopus the cosmic man.[13] But of the various names of these emanations only one corresponds to Blake, Pachad, Blake's fifth Eye and God's fifth *sefirah*.[14]

These gnostic and cabalistic traditions do not seem to be progressive or teleological and they seem to demote human history to epiphenomenal status. They are founded on a severe dualism with no bridge like that of the Incarnation and certainly not the ultimate merger of God and man that Blake taught. We might conclude, then, that Blake borrowed the terminology of his Seven Eyes from the Bible and the esoteric exegetical traditions found in gnosticism and the Kabbalah, but assimilated it to the more generally Protestant "histori-cistic" sequence that accumulates to a decisive and glorious conclusion.

I could find only one predecessor of Blake who claimed there are eight ages, but his work was well known in seventeenth-century England and may have survived as part of the tradition Blake knew. Henry Niclaes, born in 1502 in Münster, founded the Family of Man, a radical sect that interpreted scripture in an "inner" spiritual sense and held many doctrines common to "Holy Ghost" Christians. Familism had spread to England by 1570 and soon came to the authorities' notice. In 1645, when a thousand sects were blooming in the hothouse air of the Civil War, a hostile observer, Ephraim Pagitt, blamed many of them on Niclaes. Among Niclaes's many absurdities, Pagitt wrote,

> This deceiver describeth eight throughbreakings of light (as he termeth them) to have been in eight several times, from *Adam* to the time that now is, which (as he saith) have each succeeded other. The seventh he alloweth Jesus Christ to be the publisher of, and his light to be the greatest of all that ever were before him; and he maketh his own to be the last and greatest, and the perfection of all. . . .[15]

Blake, more modest, seems to assign his eighth Eye to Satan, as we have noted. Satan, however, is a part of each of us, our limit of opacity; when we open our eighth Eye we will see through the opaque Satanic selfhood that now envelops us. A prophet who exhorts us to open our eyes and see must claim implicitly that his are at least partly opened now. We may not go far wrong to follow Niclaes's hint and take Blake, the prophet howling in the wilderness of Albion's forests, as the apocalyptic eighth Eye himself.

This interpretation gains support from Blake's treatment of Milton as the "Eighth Image Divine" surrounded by the Seven Angels of the Presence, the first of whom is named Lucifer, while Milton's shadow descends to the fallen world (M 14.42-15.7). It is not clear whether we should equate these Seven Angels with the Seven Eyes, but they are surely related. The climax of *Milton* consists in an epiphany of Milton's Satanic portion (37.6-38.27), followed by Milton's renunciation of Satan (38.29-49), Satan's epiphany and final consolidation "Till All Things become One Great Satan" (38.50-39.2), and a second epiphany of Milton surrounded by the "Starry Seven" (39.3-13). Finally, "with one accord the Starry Eight became /One Man Jesus the Saviour. wonderful!" (42.10-11). Milton, already merged with his self-proclaimed heir Blake (15.49; 21.4), is now one with the awakening Albion or Universal Man and with Jesus the Savior. At the moment of apocalypse "History is now and England" and all who awaken become the eighth and final Eye that will transcend history and behold eternity.

NOTES

Preface

1. Robert N. Bellah, *The Broken Covenant: American Civil Religion in Time of Trial* (New York: Seabury Press, 1975), p.124.
2. "An Open Letter to Leszek Kolakowski," in *The Poverty of Theory* (London: Merlin Press, 1978), p.106. Having studied at the feet of Blake as well as Marx, Thompson is now the most prominent spokesman for the European nuclear disarmament movement in Great Britain.
3. *Search for a Method*, trans. Hazel E. Barnes (New York: Knopf, 1963), p.126 and *passim*.
4. See " 'London' and Its Politics," *ELH* 48 (Summer 1981), 310-38.

1. The Concept of Ideology

1. I am pulling together ideas from many sources in the discussion that follows. Two good brief histories of the idea are George Lichtheim, "The Concept of Ideology," in *The Concept of Ideology and Other Essays* (New York: Random House, 1967); and Emmet Kennedy, " 'Ideology' from Destutt de Tracy to Marx," *Journal of the History of Ideas* 40 (July-Sept. 1979), 353-68. Three works have convinced me of the value of the concept for literature despite their own disagreements: Fredric Jameson, *Marxism and Form* (Princeton: Princeton University Press, 1971); Terry Eagleton, *Criticism and Ideology* (London: New Left Books, 1976); and Raymond Williams, *Marxism and Literature* (Oxford and New York: Oxford University Press, 1977). Besides the seminal work of Georg Lukács, *History and Class Consciousness* (1923; English trans., Cambridge, Mass.: MIT Press, 1971) and its development by the Frankfurt School in Germany and America, Sartre's *Search for a Method* (1960; English trans., New York: Knopf, 1963) has been an inspiration. Just about every possible difficulty with the concept, in its Marxist usage, is put forth by Martin Seliger in *The Marxist Conception of Ideology* (Cambridge: Cambridge University Press, 1977). A judicious survey from Machiavelli and Bacon through Freud and Mannheim to the *Tel quel* group is Jorge Larrain, *The Concept of Ideology* (London: Hutchinson, 1979); it im-

plicitly rescues the Marxist notion from Seliger's strictures. The literature is large and growing larger; these are a beginning.

2. Sartre, *Search for a Method*, p.56.

3. Louis Althusser, *Lenin and Philosophy and Other Essays*, trans. Ben Brewster (New York: Monthly Review Press, 1971), p.222.

4. G. S. Kirk and J. E. Raven, *The Presocratic Philosophers* (Cambridge: Cambridge University Press, 1966), pp.168-69.

5. Althusser, *Lenin and Philosophy*, pp.195-219.

6. Gunther Kress and Robert Hodge, *Language as Ideology* (London: Routledge & Kegan Paul, 1979), is such a study; it avoids globalizing "ideology" to the point of including language itself.

2. Blake's Ideology

1. The phrase is Anthony Lincoln's, in *Some Political and Social Ideas of English Dissent* (Cambridge: Cambridge University Press, 1938), p.33.

2. John Dunn, "The Politics of Locke in England and America in the Eighteenth Century," in *John Locke: Problems and Perspectives*, ed. John Yolton (Cambridge: Cambridge University Press, 1969), p.68. Earlier that year in Scotland, L.C.S. member Joseph Gerrald invoked Locke, along with Hooker and Blackstone, in support of the right to agitate for reform. See E. P. Thompson, *The Making of the English Working Class* (New York: Pantheon, 1964), p.128.

3. Quoted in Dunn, "Locke," p.46. This may have added to Blake's dislike of the Hunts and *The Examiner*. More personal reasons for the animosity are discussed in David V. Erdman, *Blake: Prophet Against Empire* (Princeton: Princeton University Press, 1977), pp.454-61.

4. It is not certain that Blake was born into a Dissenting family. He was baptised in St. James Church, Piccadilly. See Mona Wilson, *The Life of William Blake*, 3rd ed. (Oxford: Oxford University Press, 1969), p.2; and Erdman, p.142.

5. See C. B. Macpherson, *The Political Theory of Possessive Individualism* (Oxford: Oxford University Press, 1962), pp.194-262.

6. Dunn, "Locke," p.77. See also Bernard Bailyn, *The Ideological Origins of the American Revolution* (Cambridge, Mass.: Harvard University Press, 1967), p.29.

7. Thompson, *Making of the English Working Class*, p.92.

8. *Anti-Jacobin* 1, 396, quoted in Lincoln, *English Dissent*, p.114.

9. I am indebted for much of what follows to Staughton Lynd, *Intellectual Origins of American Radicalism* (New York: Vintage, 1969).

10. Price, *Additional Observations on the Nature and Value of Civil Liberty*, 3rd ed. (London, 1777), p.17, in Lynd, ibid., p.58.

11. *A Review of the Principal Questions in Morals* (1758), ed. D. D. Raphael (Oxford: Oxford University Press, 1948), p.23, quoted in D. O. Thomas, *The Honest Mind: The Thought and Work of Richard Price* (Oxford: Oxford University Press, 1977), p.61.

12. Quoted in Lynd, *Intellectual Origins*, p.54.

13. See John W. Yolton, *John Locke and the Way of Ideas* (Oxford: Oxford University Press, 1956), pp.34, 62, 70.

14. *The Dignity of Human Nature* (London, 1754), p.171, cited in Lynd, *Intellectual Origins*, p.27. Burgh was an influence on, among others, Mary Wollstonecraft and H. D. Thoreau. See Eleanor Flexner, *Mary Wollstonecraft* (Baltimore: Penguin, 1972), pp.48, 161-62.

15. *Review of the Principal Questions*, p.19, in Lynd, *Intellectual Origins*, p.28.

16. Ibid., pp.63-64, in Lynd, *Intellectual Origins*, p.28, and Thomas, *Honest Mind*, p.52.

17. Blake and the Romantic poets often applied moral and political metaphors to the domain of sight and vision. See especially M. H. Abrams, *Natural Supernaturalism* (New York: Norton, 1971), pp.363-73.

18. Blake sometimes used the older term as synonymous with "conscience": "Innate Ideas. are in Every Man Born with him. they are [truly] Himself. The Man who says that we have No Innate Ideas must be a Fool & Knave. Having no Con-Science [or Innate Science]." Annotations to Reynolds, E 648.

19. *Review of the Principal Questions*, pp.23, 53, in Lynd, *Intellectual Origins*, p.28. For Price's criticism of Locke's empiricism, see Thomas, *Honest Mind*, pp.50ff.

20. Ibid., p.169, in Lynd, *Intellectual Origins*, p.29. Price could nonetheless say, perhaps as a rhetorical concession, that his own principles "are the same with those taught by Mr. Locke, and all the writers on Civil Liberty who have been hitherto most admired in this country." Thomas, *Honest Mind*, p.188.

21. *On the Conduct of the Understanding* (1697), in *The Works of John Locke* (London, 1812), sec. 2, p. 26, quoted in Sanford Lakoff, *Equality in Political Philosophy* (Boston: Beacon Press, 1968), pp.98-99.

22. *The Reasonableness of Christianity* (1695), ed. I. T. Ramsey (Stanford: Stanford University Press, 1958), p.66.

23. *American Independence the Interest and Glory of Great Britain* (London, 1774; Philadelphia, 1776), pp.32-33, in Lynd, *Intellectual Origins*, p.37.

24. *Works*, vol. 15, p.85, in Michael R. Watts, *The Dissenters*, vol. 1 (Oxford: Oxford University Press, 1978), p.478. Watts has a brief chapter on Price and Priestley, pp.471-78. See also Basil Willey, *The Eighteenth Century Background* (London: Chatto and Windus, 1940), pp.168-204.

25. Price's sermon takes as its text Psalm 122, the "second and following verses," which are about the love of country. "Our feet shall stand within thy gates, O Jerusalem, whither the tribes go up. . . ." Blake might have noticed that Price's text splices verses 2 and 4 (after "Jerusalem"), omitting all of verse 3, which reads, "Jerusalem is builded as a city that is compact together." Not very important, perhaps, and Price may have thought it merely redundant, or slightly obscure, but it is just the sort of line Blake liked, and wrote himself. The building of Jerusalem is the important thing, not the thrones and walls and palaces the psalm goes on to mention, and the city is compact or composed of people working together, in a spiritual "com-pact" or bond of brotherhood.

26. Price, according to one scholar, was roused (like Kant) from his slumbers by Hume's devastating extension of Locke. A. S. Cua, *Reason and Virtue: A Study in the Ethics of Richard Price* (Columbus: Ohio University Press, 1966), p.6.

27. One might also charge Price and company with a tendency toward solipsism, but they never doubted the reality of nature. They rather extended the definition of man to include a spiritual apprehension of it.

28. See H. M. Bracken, "Essence, Accident, and Race," *Hermathena* 116 (1973), 81-96.

29. *A History of Western Philosophy* (New York: Simon and Schuster, 1945), p.605. Russell, of course, is a case in his own point.

30. *Autobiography* (1873; rpt. New York: NAL, 1964), pp.192-93.

31. Karl Marx and Friedrich Engels, *The Holy Family* (1844), in *Writings of the Young Marx on Philosophy and Society*, ed. Loyd Easton and Kurt Guddat (Garden City, N.Y.: Anchor, 1967), p.395.

32. *Theses on Feuerbach* (1845), in *Writings*, ed. Easton and Guddat, p.401. To this passage Engels added, "as in Robert Owen."

33. *Reason and Revolution* (1941; rpt. Boston: Beacon Press, 1960), pp.19-29. The word "reason" here has a more inclusive meaning than Locke gives it, embracing man's total intellectual capacity. For an extensive discussion of many of the issues in this section see Ellen Meiksins Wood, *Mind and Politics* (Berkeley: University of California Press, 1972). See also my excursus on "Resistance Epistemology" in

The Resistance, by Ferber and Lynd (Boston: Beacon Press, 1971), pp.253-76.

34. Karl Polanyi, *The Great Transformation* (1944; rpt. Boston: Beacon Press, 1957), esp. chap. 7.

35. Eagleton, *Criticism and Ideology*, p.153. In his *Walter Benjamin* (London: New Left Books, 1981), Eagleton groups Blake and Milton as petty-bourgeois radicals (p.8), but later (p.177) he pays Blake a fine tribute.

36. Karl Marx and Frederick Engels, *The German Ideology* (1846), ed. C. J. Arthur (New York: International, 1970), pp.65-66.

37. Christopher Hill, *The World Turned Upside Down* (New York: Viking, 1973), p.307.

38. See Hill, "John Mason and the End of the World," in *Puritanism and Revolution* (1958; rpt. London: Panther, 1968), pp.311-23; Thompson, *Making of the English Working Class*, chap. 2.

39. Erdman, *Prophet*, pp.35-36; Morton Paley, "William Blake, The Prince of the Hebrews, and the Woman Clothed with the Sun," in *William Blake: Essays in Honour of Sir Geoffrey Keynes*, ed. Paley and Michael Phillips (Oxford: Oxford University Press, 1973). Thompson is at work on a book that will try to show the extent of Blake's affiliations with the plebeian subculture. On Brothers and Southcott, see also Clarke Garrett, *Respectable Folly* (Baltimore: Johns Hopkins University Press, 1975), chaps. 8 and 9.

40. Blake "was the greatest English Antinomian, but also the last." A. L. Morton, *The Everlasting Gospel* (London: Lawrence and Wishart, 1958), p.36. Burke, *Reflections on the Revolution in France*, ed. Conor Cruise O'Brien (Baltimore: Penguin, 1968), pp.99, 157-58, 166. See also Lynd, *Intellectual Origins*, p.27: "Dissenting radicalism reached back over the heads of Trenchard and Gordon, back even beyond Locke, to John Lilburne, Gerrard Winstanley, Richard Overton, and other religious republicans of the 1640s and 1650s."

41. *Aids to Reflection* (1825), p.381, cited in *Inquiring Spirit*, ed. Kathleen Coburn (1951; rpt. New York: Minerva, 1968), p.404.

42. Christopher Hill, with his unrivaled command of the contemporary pamphlets, traces quite a few points of resemblance between Milton and the "left," but they remain a miscellaneous set of gestures and not a consistently radical stance. *Milton and the English Revolution* (New York: Viking, 1978). For a more coherent attempt to place Milton ideologically, see Andrew Milner, *John Milton and the English Revolution* (London: Macmillan, 1981).

43. Marx and Engels seem not to have known of Winstanley, though they studied Thomas Münzer and the Anabaptists. Eduard

Bernstein and Karl Kautsky mention him in their *History of Socialism* (1895), and the first full treatment is in Bernstein's study of the English revolution (1908), translated as *Cromwell and Communism* (1930). See the "Bibliographical Note" in Hill's edition of Winstanley, *The Law of Freedom and Other Writings* (Harmondsworth: Penguin, 1973). See also George Woodcock, *Anarchism* (New York: Meridian, 1962), pp.44-49. The standard edition is George Sabine, ed., *The Works of Gerrard Winstanley*, (1941; rpt. New York: Russell and Russell, 1965); all Winstanley quotations are from this edition, with the pages cited in parentheses. I owe the biographical data to Sabine's and Hill's introductions.

44. *The Saints Paradice*, p.89, cited in Hill, ed., *Law of Freedom*, p.19; abstract only in Sabine.

45. Thomas J. J. Altizer, *The New Apocalypse: The Radical Christian Vision of William Blake* (East Lansing: Michigan State University Press, 1967), pioneers in adducing resemblances to Hegel, though sometimes he illuminates the obscure with the opaque. The same is true of Leopold Damrosch, Jr., *Symbol and Truth in Blake's Myth* (Princeton: Princeton University Press, 1980). The classic study of Blake and the English Romantics alongside contemporary German writers is Abrams, *Natural Supernaturalism*.

46. Hill, *The World Turned Upside Down*, p.141; Abrams, *Natural Supernaturalism*, pp.161-63, 223; Erdman, pp.11-12. See also E. J. Hobsbawm, *The Age of Revolution* (New York: NAL, 1962), p.294, on the preservation of archaic German intellectual traditions.

47. Isaac Kramnick quotes Walker in "Religion and Radicalism: English Political Theory in the Age of Revolution," *Political Theory* 5 (November 1977), 505-34. On equality, see below, p.68.

48. See Erdman, *Prophet* pp.80-83. Of course, some merchants expected profits from the American War and broke with the peace party of Wilkeite merchants and artisans. And the mercantile interest of the port cities did not always coincide with the manufacturing interest, which was more typically Dissenting.

49. See J 65.12f, quoted below, pp.131-32; Erdman, *Prophet*, pp.329-32.

50. See also J 27.85-88. The London Exchange impressed many liberals. Voltaire wrote, "Enter the London stock exchange, that place more respectable than many a court. You will see the deputies of all nations gathered there for the service of mankind. There a Jew, a Mohammedan, and the Christian deal with each other as if they were of the same religion, and give the name of infidel only to those who go bankrupt; here the Presbyterian trusts the Anabaptist, and the

Anglican honours the Quaker promise." Quoted in Roy Porter, *English Society in the Eighteenth Century* (New York: Penguin, 1982), pp.187-88.

51. Albert O. Hirschman, *The Passions and the Interests* (Princeton: Princeton University Press, 1976).

52. Geoffrey H. Hartman, *The Fate of Reading and Other Essays* (Chicago: University of Chicago Press, 1975), p.278.

53. But see the objections by Nancy Bogen and David Erdman to connecting the Birmingham Lunar Society to Blake's early satire, in Erdman, p.93, n.13; Kramnick, "Religion and Radicalism," 522f.

54. Abrams, *Natural Supernaturalism*, pp.210-211, 508, n.16.

55. Translated from an unnamed sans-culotte (May 1793), by Gwyn A. Williams, in *Artisans and Sans-Culottes* (London: Arnold, 1968), p.19.

56. Hannah Arendt, *On Revolution* (1963; rpt. New York: Penguin, 1977), p.245.

57. Its historian notes that "*fraternité* is more a term of the 'Left' than *liberté* or *égalité*." J. M. Roberts, "Liberté, Egalité, Fraternité: Sources and Development of a Slogan," *Tijdschrift voor die Studie van die Verlichting* 4 (1978), 329-69. I owe this reference to Jeffrey Merrick.

58. Albert Soboul, *The Parisian Sans-Culottes and the French Revolution, 1793-4*, trans. Gwynne Lewis (Oxford: Clarendon Press, 1964), pp.153, 154.

59. Arendt, *On Revolution*, p.264.

60. Albert Goodwin, *The Friends of Liberty* (London: Hutchinson, 1979), p.240.

61. Robert Darnton, "The High Enlightenment and the Low-Life of Literature in Pre-Revolutionary France," *Past and Present* 51 (May 1971), 81-115.

62. E 636. Here is poignant union of form and content. "I am hid" must have been hidden from virtually all eyes but his own.

63. One could make a parallel argument about the visual designs: they borrow but transmute the traditional "language" of attitude and gesture, even Greek and Roman forms, which stubbornly persist beneath the transmutations.

64. Jonathan Culler, *Structuralist Poetics* (Ithaca: Cornell University Press, 1975), p.244.

65. Culler has pointed out a few. Fredric Jameson has a fine account of the limits and contradictions of the critique of all privileged principles or models, in *The Prison-House of Language* (Princeton: Princeton University Press, 1972), pp.173-86.

66. See Leslie Brisman, *Romantic Origins* (Ithaca: Cornell University Press, 1978) and Brian Wilkie and Mary Lynn Johnson, *Blake's Four Zoas: The Design of a Dream* (Cambridge, Mass.: Harvard University Press, 1978).

67. Milton's Satan says "assume / Monarchy" with this latter sense, though he himself, as Abdiel immediately replies, has set himself "so high above thy Peers" (PL 5.794-95, 812; cf. 1.38-39).

68. Erdman, *Prophet*, p.31.

69. Goodwin, *Friends of Liberty*, pp.37-40; Erdman, p.34.

70. Christopher Hill, "Sir Edward Coke—Myth-Maker," in *Intellectual Origins of the English Revolution* (1965; rpt. London: Panther, 1972), quotation on pages 257-58. See also Hill's "The Norman Yoke," in *Puritanism and Revolution* (1958; rpt. London: Panther, 1968); "Before 1640," he says there, "antiquarian studies were dangerous" (p.71). Milton, *Areopagitica* (1644), in *Complete Poems and Major Prose*, ed. Merritt Y. Hughes (New York: Odyssey, 1957), p.725.

71. Burke, *Reflections*, pp.92; 181, 144; 92, 275, 117 (Burke's italics).

72. Paine, *Rights of Man*, ed. Henry Collins (Harmondsworth: Penguin, 1969), pp.87-88.

73. Burke, *Reflections*, pp.107, 276.

74. Raymond Williams, *Culture and Society 1780-1950* (Harmondsworth: Penguin, 1958), p.43.

75. I find it fascinating that the word "mystery" in Blake's day could mean not only a religious rite or truth or a secret of any sort, but also a skill or craft and even a guild of craftsmen. Two etymologies are conflated here, one from Greek (related to "mystic") and one from Latin (whence "ministry" and *métier*), and "mystery" in the latter sense may have been confused with "mastery." So Blake, in terms somewhat archaic in his day, was a member of a mystery of engravers and master of their mystery. Perhaps tradesmen wanted their own "trade secrets" and initiation rites to counter the mysteries of priestcraft and statecraft; if so, despite the puzzles of his own production, Blake seems to have wanted nothing to do with it, and "mystery" in his poetry is always pejorative.

76. Marshall McLuhan, *The Gutenberg Galaxy* (1962; rpt. New York: NAL, 1969), p.184.

77. Morris Eaves, "Blake and the Artistic Machine: An Essay in Decorum and Technology," PMLA 92 (October 1977), 903-27.

78. See Frank Kermode, *The Genesis of Secrecy* (Cambridge, Mass.: Harvard University Press, 1979).

79. Letter to Bernard Barton, 3 April 1830.

80. Cited in George Steiner, *On Difficulty and Other Essays* (New York: Oxford University Press, 1978), p.34.

81. Sidney, *A Defence of Poetry*, ed. J. A. van Dorsten (Oxford: Oxford University Press, 1966), p.37. Sidney's phrase refers in the first instance to one who feigns disloyalty to his prince the better to serve him (like Kent in *King Lear*), and then by extension to poetry, which serves truth by feigning.

82. Erdman, *Prophet*, pp.403-11.

83. Ibid., p.152.

84. Ibid., pp.153-54, has a judicious assessment of the matter. For evidence of Blake's prior self-censorship, see pp.153, 274 n.13, 279, 413-15.

85. "The Grey Monk," E 489.

86. *The Complete Poems of Emily Dickinson*, ed. Thomas H. Johnson (Boston: Little, Brown, 1960), #1129.

87. Walter Benjamin, "The Work of Art in the Age of Mechanical Reproduction" (1936), in *Illuminations*, trans. Harry Zohn (New York: Schocken, 1968); Blake, FZ 71.7-8. David Punter suggests that "Blake writes difficult poetry because to write with ease and facility is itself delusive in a situation where language is tainted with domination." His remarks on difficulty, though general, are in the same spirit as my own; he usefully invokes Hegel and Marcuse as examples of the struggle against positivistic, one-dimensional, or repressive modes of thought. "Blake, Marxism and Dialectic," *Literature and History* 6 (Autumn 1977), 219-42.

3. Brotherhood

1. Wilson Carey McWilliams has taken a step toward remedying the neglect in *The Idea of Fraternity in America* (Berkeley: University of California Press, 1973). For his account of the omission and possible reasons for it, see pp.2-5. In the five-volume *Dictionary of the History of Ideas*, edited by Philip P. Wiener (New York: Scribner's, 1968-1973), there is neither article nor index entry for either brotherhood or fraternity.

2. In his poem *about* the French Revolution, Blake has the liberal Duke of Orleans challenge the nobles to "learn to consider all men as thy equals, / Thy brethern" (*The French Revolution*, 193-94), but what impresses the Duke most is the unique individuality of every man, "the infinite labyrinth of another's brain" (190).

3. See Otto Gierke, *Political Theories of the Middle Ages*, trans. F. W.

Maitland (Cambridge: Cambridge University Press, 1922), pp.22-30 and 103-104 n.7, for the history of this idea. See also 1 Cor. 12:12. An interesting variant occurs in Eph. 4:25: "We are members one of another."

4. "Adoption" (*huiothesia*) is translated "sonship" in the Revised Standard Version.

5. McWilliams, *Idea of Fraternity*, p.4.

6. The immediately following lines seem to contradict my claim that the fatherhood of God is not the basis of Blake's idea of brotherhood: "Each shall behold the Eternal Father & love & joy abound / So spoke the Eternal at the Feast they embracd the New born Man / Calling him Brother image of the Eternal Father" (133.26-28). The "Eternal Father" here, almost a nonce creation, may mean simply the eternal *source* of our brotherhood; he is hard to distinguish from the Eternal Man Albion himself (except that there are "Many Eternal Men" in the preceding passage).

7. Karl Marx, *Grundrisse der Kritik der Politischen Ökonomie* (Moscow: Foreign Language Press, 1939), p.6; my translation. I owe this citation to Nancy Schwartz.

8. Max Horkheimer, *Eclipse of Reason* (1947; rpt. New York: Seabury Press, 1974), p.135.

9. On the other hand, the brotherly love we are meant to feel is closer to eros than *philia*, as the "cominglings" suggest. In an important but difficult speech Los turns from his higher realm to his fallen brother Albion, saying "pangs of love draw me down to my loins which are / Become a fountain of veiny pipes: O Albion! my brother!" (J 82.83-84). Whatever else this means, it sounds erotic, even phallic (not unlike Shelley's idea of universal love); it may, however, be a symptom of Los's descent.

10. I am developing an idea I owe to Irene Tayler.

11. See below, p.128.

12. And perhaps of Jewish liberty. See Arthur Waskow, *Godwrestling* (New York: Schocken, 1978), esp. the first four chapters (on brotherhood).

13. Cannot be saved qua elect, that is. There is always the possibility of seeing the light and ceasing to be elect. The elect is a "state," not an individual.

14. Sermon on Ephesians 1:3-4, in François Wendel, *Calvin*, trans. Philip Mairet (New York: Harper & Row, 1963), pp.272-73.

15. For a summary of the differences between Calvinism and the two currents of humanism and mysticism, see William Haller, *The*

Rise of Puritanism (New York: Columbia University Press, 1938), pp. 193-95.

16. For a careful account of Blake and the Swedenborgians, see Morton D. Paley, " 'A New Heaven is Begun': William Blake and Swedenborgianism," *Blake: An Illustrated Quarterly* 50 (Fall 1979), 64-90 (esp. 69-70).

17. *Man's Hope (L'Espoir), passim.* Malraux's fraternity, of course, is a product of the Spanish Civil War, and to the extent that it depends on hatred of a common enemy Blake would reject it. In this it is easy enough to dismiss Blake as a deluded utopian along the lines of Marx's sarcastic debunking of the 1848 slogan of *fraternité* as the "imaginary abolition of class relations" which, in Lamartine's priceless phrase, had been based on "a terrible misunderstanding" (*The Class Struggles in France: 1848 to 1850*, trans. Paul Jackson, in *Karl Marx: Surveys from Exile*, ed. David Fernbach [New York: Vintage Books, 1974], p.47). Class solidarity is possible; fraternity is a dream. Yet the mistake, surely, is to confuse the real with the ideal and announce the arrival of utopia, not to maintain an ideal utopia as a measure of the real. Whatever he may have thought about the means, Marx believed that the end of class solidarity is the classless society, and so, in his way, did Blake. I would add that, even if a Marxist found Blake's universalist thrust unassimilable to his own theory of revolution, he might still find Blake's ideas partly translatable into a phenomenology of revolutionary groups. See, for example, Sartre's use of Malraux's "apocalypse" in his account of the fusion of the Parisians in 1789 (*Critique of Dialectical Reason*, trans. Alan Sheridan-Smith [London: New Left Books, 1976], p.357).

18. In a note on Reynolds Blake writes, "Man varies from Man more than Animal from Animal of Different Species" (E 656), though here the context is the variability of human identity as expressed in art.

19. McWilliams, *Idea of Fraternity*, p.8 and *passim.*

20. "To Tirzah" (c. 1804), E 30. Blake almost always uses "sex" and "sexual" to suggest separation, as if he is reviving its probable Latin root *sec-*, whence "sect."

21. The Joseph motif continues at J 67.23, 68.1-2, and 81.11. Joseph's famous coat becomes the veil of generation, bloodied in the sacrifice of innocent soldiers in the Continental wars. I have left out any discussion of Blake and his own natural brothers, one of whom, Robert, certainly became a spiritual brother after he died. William and Robert are engraved in striking symmetrical poses on plates 32

and 37 of *Milton*, but Robert appears nowhere else in any of the texts.

22. *The Second Sex*, trans. H. M. Parshley (1953; rpt. New York: Bantam, 1961), pp.89-90.

23. Erdman, *Prophet*, pp.57, 550.

24. Ibid., p.365.

4. Nature and the Female

1. The phrase is from E. D. Hirsch, Jr., *Innocence and Experience* (New Haven: Yale University Press, 1964), p.61 and *passim*.

2. Damrosch has a thorough discussion of dualism in chapter five of his *Symbol and Truth in Blake's Myth*.

3. Northrop Frye, *Fearful Symmetry* (Princeton: Princeton University Press, 1947), p.74.

4. On the *Poimandres* see Hans Jonas, *The Gnostic Religion* (Boston: Beacon Press, 1958), pp.147-73. On Everard see Haller, *Puritanism*, pp.206-12, and Hill, *The World Turned Upside Down*, p.149.

5. Hazard Adams, *William Blake: A Reading of the Shorter Poems* (Seattle: University of Washington Press, 1963), p.60.

6. The politics of Isaiah 34:4 is made clear in Isaiah 24:21: "the Lord shall punish the host of the high ones that are on high, and the kings of the earth upon the earth." Revelation 6:15 is less political, for it includes "every bondman, and every free man," with the kings and great men who will be brought low. In paraphrasing it, Coleridge omits the bondman and free man, and thereby repoliticizes Revelation. I am amplifying the discussion in Morton D. Paley, *Energy and Imagination: A Study of the Development of Blake's Thought* (Oxford: Clarendon Press, 1970), pp.53-56.

7. Jonas, *Gnostic Religion*, pp.26-62; Jean Daniélou, *Primitive Christian Symbols* (Baltimore: Helicon, 1964), pp.111-15.

8. See Friedrich Engels's letter to Lavrov, 12 November 1875: "The whole Darwinian theory of the struggle for existence is simply the transference from society to animate nature of Hobbes's theory of the war of every man against every man and the bourgeois economic theory of competition, along with the Malthusian theory of population. This feat having been accomplished . . . the same theories are next transferred back again from organic nature to history and their validity as eternal laws of human society declared to have been proved. The childishness of this procedure is obvious, it is not worth wasting words over." Ronald L. Meek, ed., *Marx and Engels on the Population Bomb* (Berkeley: Ramparts, 1971), p.198.

9. *Enquiry Concerning Political Justice* (1798), ed. Isaac Kramnick (Harmondsworth: Penguin, 1976), p.138.

10. *A Discourse on the Origin of Inequality*, Part I, in *The Social Contract and Discourses* (London: Everyman, 1973), p.65.

11. *History and Class Consciousness*, p.130. One should note Alfred Schmidt's dialectical reply that society is a natural category; see *The Concept of Nature in Marx*, trans. Ben Fowkes (London: New Left Books, 1971), pp.69-70.

12. See Alfred Sohn-Rethel, *Intellectual and Manual Labour* (London: Macmillan, 1978).

13. *Grundrisse*, quoted in David McClellan, *Karl Marx* (New York: Harper & Row, 1973), p.301.

14. Aldous Huxley, *The Doors of Perception* (New York: Harper & Row, 1954); Milton Klonsky, *William Blake: The Seer and His Visions* (New York: Harmony, 1977), pp.7-8.

15. The quotations from the *Reflections* in this paragraph and the one following are on pp.90, 315, 156, 119, 120, and 120 again.

16. See now especially Morris Eaves, *William Blake's Theory of Art* (Princeton: Princeton University Press, 1982).

17. For Blake on mountains see Nelson Hilton, "Blake and the Mountains of the Mind," *Blake: An Illustrated Quarterly* 56 (Spring 1981), 196-204.

18. *A Philosophical Enquiry into the Origin of Our Ideas of the Sublime and Beautiful*, ed. J. T. Boulton (Notre Dame, Ind.: University of Notre Dame Press, 1968), p.57.

19. Burke, *Sublime*, p.59.

20. Paley, *Energy and Imagination*, p.41. Thomas Weiskel, *The Romantic Sublime* (Baltimore: Johns Hopkins University Press, 1976), has an interesting chapter on Blake.

21. Burke, *Sublime*, p.59.

22. See the Tate Gallery catalogue *Henry Fuseli* (1975), pls.87 and 92.

23. William Morris, *News from Nowhere* (1890), ed. James Redmond (London: Routledge & Kegan Paul, 1970), p.154.

24. Northrop Frye, "The Drunken Boat: The Revolutionary Element in Romanticism," in *Romanticism Reconsidered*, ed. Frye (New York: Columbia University Press, 1963), p.5; *A Study of English Romanticism* (New York: Random House, 1968), p.47.

25. Conclusion to *The Recluse*, quoted in the Preface to *The Excursion* (1814).

26. These passages, from *The Description of the Intellectual Globe*, *The Advancement of Learning*, and *The Refutation of Philosophies*, are con-

veniently gathered and discussed by William Leiss in *The Domination of Nature* (1972; rpt. Boston: Beacon Press, 1974).

27. Jean-Paul Sartre, *Being and Nothingness*, trans. Hazel E. Barnes (New York: Philosophical Library, 1956), p.578.

28. See, for example, Irene Tayler, "The Woman Scaly," *Bulletin of the Midwest Modern Language Association* 6 (Spring 1973), 74-87; Susan Fox, *Poetic Form in Blake's "Milton"* (Princeton: Princeton University Press, 1976), esp. pp.214-19; Diana Hume George, *Blake and Freud* (Ithaca: Cornell University Press, 1980), esp. chap. 6.

5. *Liberty*

1. Entry #3918, Volume 3 of the *Notebooks*, ed. Kathleen Coburn (Princeton: Princeton University Press, 1973).

2. A sense I would use, however. The burden of this book is that Blake's speculative philosophy had practical, social implications. But these do not comprise a moral doctrine in the usual (traditional and Blakean) sense.

3. Morton, *The Everlasting Gospel*, p.36. This was the first book to deal in any detail with Blake's relationship to his seventeenth-century forbears.

4. *Fearful Symmetry*, p.12.

5. Martin Werner, *The Formation of Christian Dogma*, trans. S.G.G. Brandon (Boston: Beacon Press, 1965), p.78.

6. See ibid., pp.77-94, for an account of this debate in the early Church.

7. Luther, *Commentary on Galatians*, in *Puritanism and Liberty*, ed. A.S.P. Woodhouse (London: Dent, 1938); see his Introduction, pp.65ff.

8. Wendel, *Calvin*, pp.203-206.

9. The words are Luther's, quoted in Hill, *The World Turned Upside Down*, pp.124-25.

10. *The Christian Doctrine*, Book I, Chap. XXVII, in *Complete Poems and Major Prose*, pp.1007b, 1010b, 1012a.

11. See R. A. Knox, *Enthusiasm* (New York: Oxford University Press, 1950), pp.9-24, for speculations on what prompted Paul's letter.

12. R. McL. Wilson, *The Gnostic Problem* (London: A.R. Mowbray, 1958), p.181.

13. Jonas, *Gnostic Religion*, pp.137-46.

14. Ibid., p.271.

15. Ibid., pp.273-74.

16. Norman Cohn, *The Pursuit of the Millennium*, rev. ed. (New York: Oxford University Press, 1970), p.310; see Hill, *The World Turned Upside Down*, p.254.

17. *A Fiery Flying Roll* (1649), in Cohn, *Pursuit*, p.329; cf. A. L. Morton, *The World of the Ranters* (London: Lawrence and Wisshart, 1970), p.80; and Hill, *The World Turned Upside Down*, p.254.

18. Cohn, *Pursuit*, p.296.

19. Gershom G. Scholem, *Major Trends in Jewish Mysticism*, 3rd rev. ed. (New York: Schocken, 1961), chap. 8, "Sabbatianism and Mystical Heresy."

20. Abrams, *Natural Supernaturalism*, pp.416-18.

21. Hill, *The World Turned Upside Down*, p.273.

22. Cohn, *Pursuit*, p.306.

23. Hill, *The World Turned Upside Down*, pp.141, 171. See also, for antinomianism in this period, Watts, *The Dissenters*, vol. 1, pp.179-86.

24. Cohn, *Pursuit*, p.314.

25. Ibid., p.313.

26. Blake explicitly identifies Satan, as we shall see, with the "Reactor." In the comments from which we have just quoted Blake defines Vice as a "Negative," an "omission of act" or of intellect. This privative definition of evil, though it has a respectable ancestry, seems to be essential to radical Protestantism. So Bauthumley: "Sin is properly the dark side of God, which is a mere privation of light" (Hill, *The World Turned Upside Down*, p.176). Pope Paul VI denied this view in 1972.

27. John Saltmarsh, *Free Grace* (1645), quoted in Morton, *Ranters*, p.51.

28. Hill, *The World Turned Upside Down*, p.133. The three classes are not explicitly called states, but Satan is called a state (FZ 115.23) and he is identified with the elect (M 11.19-21).

29. Cohn, *Pursuit*, p.290.

30. *Ranters*, p.112.

31. Knox, *Enthusiasm*, p.494. Cf. Rupert Davies, *Methodism* (Baltimore: Penguin, 1963), pp.88-89.

32. Eighteenth- and nineteenth-century antinomianism, and radical sectarianism generally, still await their historian. E. P. Thompson has been comparing Blake to the Muggletonians and other groups that descend from the seventeenth century. See Thompson's letter about the Muggletonians in *TLS*, 7 March 1975, p.253.

33. In *Political Philosophy*, ed. Anthony Quinton (London: Oxford University Press, 1967).

34. Cf. John Plamenatz, "On le Forcera d'Être Libre," in *Hobbes and Rousseau*, ed. Maurice Cranston and Richard Peters (Garden City, N.Y.: Anchor, 1972).

35. *Essay on the First Principles of Government* (1765), quoted in Lynd, *Intellectual Origins*, p.52. Italics omitted.

36. See Herbert Read, *Anarchy and Order* (1954; rpt. Boston: Beacon Press, 1971), pp.161ff.

37. I owe this example to C. S. Lewis, *Studies in Words*, 2nd ed. (London: Cambridge University Press, 1967), p.125.

38. Quotations are from Book V, ll.448-51, 486, 538-40, 545-46, and 763-64.

39. I have quoted ll.28 and 85-86. It would be interesting to compare Blake and Milton on the question of liberty. (Blake probably never saw Milton's *Christian Doctrine*, not translated until 1825, from which we quoted earlier.) Milton's stress on discipline and virtue as essential to Christian liberty was part of the selfhood Blake's character Milton must purge. The dichotomy we see in Cowper and Coleridge was Milton's as well. But as an active revolutionary and theorist of a republican polity Milton provides (at least until 1660) a collective or public inflection to his notion of Christian liberty. The *Areopagitica* alone could have given Blake much of his most characteristic imagery. See, on Milton and negative liberty, Hill, *Milton and the English Revolution* (New York: Viking, 1978), pp.262-67.

40. Ll.89-91, 140, 144.

6. Labor

1. Isaiah 2:4; also at Micah 4:3. At Joel 3:10 the order is reversed as a day of vengeance is proclaimed.

2. Since much of plate 65, including our passage, exists in draft in *The Four Zoas*, but plate 63 does not, it is possible that Blake first inserted place names into the existing material and then wrote the more allegorical passage about Druids and Jehovah. If that is true, he may have been prompted by sound more than sense. "Cheviot" and "chariot" rhyme with an odd clangor, and "summer in Annandale / And all . . ." seems to hum one sound softly, a little like a shepherd's flute. A few lines later Blake does it again: "O melancholy Magdalen behold the morning over Malden break" (65.38); no good reason for Malden has occurred to anyone, but it undoubtedly sounds very nice with "Magdalen" (pronounced maudlin).

3. E. P. Thompson, "Time, Work-Discipline and Industrial Capitalism," *Past and Present* 38 (1967), 56-97. See also George Woodcock,

"The Tyranny of the Clock," in *The Anarchist Reader*, ed. Woodcock (London: Fontana, 1977).

4. Michael Tolley notes that Ecclesiastes is present here in a note to a discussion in the *Blake Newsletter* 37 (Summer 1976), 36.

5. Adam Smith, *The Wealth of Nations*, ed. Edwin Cannan (New York: Modern Library, 1937), p. 734.

6. *Essay on the History of Civil Society* (1767), quoted in Abrams, *Natural Supernaturalism*, p.210. Abrams goes on to discuss Schiller's *Aesthetic Letters*, influenced by Ferguson. In the sixth *Letter*: "everlastingly chained to a single little fragment of the Whole, man himself develops into nothing but a fragment."

7. Paul Mantoux, *The Industrial Revolution in the Eighteenth Century* (New York: Harper & Row, 1962), p.306. See also Francis Klingender, *Art and the Industrial Revolution* (1947; rpt. Frogmore: Paladin, 1975), p.10.

8. It is interesting that the state of Israel has named its latest battle tank the *Merkava*, Hebrew for "chariot," an act almost as blasphemous as "christening" a Trident atomic missile submarine the "Corpus Christi."

9. S. Foster Damon's *A Blake Dictionary* (Providence: Brown University Press, 1965) has a useful summary under "Urizen's Sons."

10. *Theses on Feuerbach* 9 and 1, in *Writings*, ed. Easton and Guddat, pp. 400-402.

11. *The Poems of William Blake*, ed. W. H. Stevenson (New York: Norton, 1971), p.440. Cf. Erdman, *Prophet*, pp.352-55.

12. "Mould" can mean "earth" or "soil," but here it probably refers to the fungus; it would then be parallel to the weed and rust. "Fallows" are plowed fields left uncropped; cf. "weedy fallows" in Cowper's *The Task* 4.315. Blake is also invoking chapter 4 of Jeremiah: the prophet calls for Israel to repent and "Break up your fallow ground, and sow not among thorns." Blake's lions (124.16), winds (125.7), and kings and princes (125.10) are all in this chapter of Jeremiah.

13. Blake may have combined the imagery of the Parable of the Sower with that of the following parable, the Wheat and the Tares, where two kinds of seed are two kinds of people (Matt. 13).

14. Euripides, *Bacchae*, 66; 1 Thes. 1:3.

15. That this is not the fullest or fairest interpretation of Milton is not pertinent here. We are concerned with prominent aspects of Milton, of the sort Blake must have measured himself against.

16. David Punter's article, "Blake: Creative and Uncreative Labour," *Studies in Romanticism* 16 (Fall 1977), 535-61, is the only sub-

stantial discussion of labor in Blake I have come across. It should be read along with this chapter; I have tried not to repeat his points.

17. M. D. Chenu, *The Theology of Work*, trans. Lilian Soiron (Chicago: Regnery, 1966), pp.105-114. "Workshop" is *ergasterion* in Greek.

18. See *Paradise Lost* 12.18: "Laboring the soil."

19. *Jerusalem*, plate 9. Erdman plausibly suggests that through Hand Blake is attacking the English press that supported war; Blake unfairly included as his targets the Hunt (Hand) brothers who reviewed him critically in their journal. Erdman, pp.457-61.

20. "The forming [*Bildung*] of the five senses is the labor of all previous history." Marx, 1844 Manuscripts, "Private Property and Communism," my translation.

21. Lenin admired the American time-and-motion efficiency pioneer Frederick Taylor.

22. "Useful Work versus Useless Toil," in *Political Writings of William Morris*, ed. A. L. Morton (New York: International, 1973), p.88.

23. Frye, *Fearful Symmetry*, p.359.

7. *Time, Eternity, and History*

1. *Myth and Ritual in Christianity* (Boston: Beacon Press, 1968), p.71.

2. It is worth noting that the "recollection" here is of an imaginative act itself, a poem. Another example, perhaps, is the appeal of the Spectre of Urthona to Los to "unbar the Gates of Memory" (FZ 85.37), but the Spectre is an equivocal figure, always at least partly in error.

3. The fullest exposition of Blake on memory is Wayne Glausser's Yale dissertation, 1978.

4. *Natural Supernaturalism*, pp.385-90.

5. The old man says the supply of leeches has dwindled. No doubt the demand for leeches is drying up as well.

6. The Frankfurt School in general and Theodor Adorno in particular (partly under Benjamin's influence) have turned to the past and its obliteration. Guy Debord, *The Society of the Spectacle* (Detroit: Red and Black, 1970) and the other French Situationists carried to great lengths their critique of the closure and commodification of public (and private) life in the consumer society. More recently, see Russell Jacoby, *Social Amnesia* (Boston: Beacon Press, 1975), and Christopher Lasch, *The Culture of Narcissism* (New York: Norton, 1979).

7. Just why it should be *productions* is another question. It may

have to do with the creative or "Prolific" power Blake celebrates as the divine itself acting in and through human beings.

8. Bloom, "Commentary," p.906, cites this passage in connection with *Urizen* 3.13-17.

9. Blake would agree with Alan Watts's criticism of the orthodox Christian account of the Incarnation:

> Theological, as distinct from mythological, Christianity has always wanted to insist that such an Incarnation occurred only with respect to the historical individual called Jesus of Nazareth. It has confused the true uniqueness of the Incarnation with mere historical abnormality. For the Incarnation is unique in the sense that it is the only real event, the only occurrence which is Now, which is not past and abstract. It is thus the one creative and living act as distinct from dead fact, eternally happening in *this* moment.
>
> (*Myth and Ritual*, p.129)

The biblical passages important for the concept of the Holy Ghost are also important to Blake. The passages about the "Comforter" (*paraclete*) in John 14:16-18, for example, Blake mentions in MHH 5 and quotes at length in plate 17 of his Job designs, which shows Christ Himself as the "Comforter."

10. *The Human Condition* (Chicago: University of Chicago Press, 1958), pp.240-41.

11. *The Eighteenth Brumaire of Louis Bonaparte* (1852), trans. Ben Fowkes, in *Karl Marx: Surveys from Exile*, ed. Fernbach, p.146.

12. See also "The cut worm forgives the plow" and "A dead body. revenges not injuries" (MHH 7).

13. *Reflections*, pp.104, 108, 194-95.

14. Blake, who conversed with Milton and with his deceased brother Robert, to name but two, might have added that "the living" does not refer to those who now draw breath but to the spiritually energetic of all ages who have overcome the temporality of their lives. In this he is perhaps not so far from Burke after all.

15. I have not discussed Blake's series of drawings from English history, begun as early as 1779 but apparently included in a book advertised in 1793 (now lost). The subjects range from Brutus' landing in Britain through King John and the Magna Carta to a vision of England's future (see E 672, 693). It is difficult to extract from them a consistent vision of history, and Blake may have had none when he drew most of them. Six of twenty subjects listed in his notebook precede Julius Caesar, as if "British" or "Welsh" priority was important to Blake, as well as Britain's continuation of the "wes-

tering" of freedom we find in the *Aeneid*. Several concern cruel ty-
rants and God's chastisements (one is called "The Cruelties used by
Kings & Priests")—these well within the Miltonic and Dissenting
traditions of liberty, and some of them exemplary and "typological."
See David Bindman, *Blake as an Artist* (New York: Dutton, 1977),
pp.23-26.

16. On Blake's use of "revolution" see Aileen Ward, "The Forging
of Orc: Blake and the Idea of Revolution," *Triquarterly* 23/24 (Winter/
Spring 1972), 204-227.

17. Daniel 7:25: "and they shall be given into his hand until a time
and times and the dividing of time." Blake alludes to this passage in
FZ 25.35-36: "they shut & seald / The furnaces a time & times." See
also Daniel 9:27 and 12:7, and Revelation 11:4.

Another possibility is that 8,500 is a significant multiple of 200-
year Periods. The factor is 42½. Now 42 might be taken as six weeks,
that is, a "short" week of weeks; a "short" week is a week short of
the Sabbath, in this case a Jubilee Sabbath, so we have a sense of
incompleteness, a yearning for eternity. The number 42 is also the
number of months in the 3½ "times" of Daniel (and in the 1,260
days of Revelation 11:4). The remaining half may be that "half a
time" of Daniel. In any case, 8,500 has a lot of sevens in it as factors
(an Age, we should add, is a lunar month, or four weeks, of years),
and that may be the main point.

Blake's propensity for duplicating significant numbers reaches ab-
surd lengths in *Milton*; e.g., "Their numbers are seven million &
seven thousand & seven hundred" (M 28.22).

18. See Swedenborg's *Heavenly Secrets* (New York: Swedenborg
Foundation, 1967), vol. I, par. 483.

19. Short accounts of Joachim are in Cohn, *Pursuit*, pp.108-110;
and Morton, *The Everlasting Gospel*, pp.38-40. See also Morton
Bloomfield, "Joachim of Flora," *Traditio* 13 (1957), 249-311. On
Boehme, see R. M. Jones, *Mysticism and Democracy in the English Com-
monwealth* (Cambridge, Mass.: Harvard University Press, 1932),
p.128.

20. "Blake . . . postulates a historical process which may be de-
scribed as the exact opposite of the Hegelian one. Every advance of
truth forces error to consolidate itself in a more obviously erroneous
form, and every advance of freedom has the same effect on tyranny."
Frye, *Fearful Symmetry*, p. 260. Hegel has frequently been placed in
the Joachite tradition, which was strongest in Germany.

21. *The Class Struggles in France: 1848 to 1850* (1850), trans. Paul
Jackson, in *Karl Marx: Surveys from Exile*, ed. Fernbach, p.61.

22. *Fearful Symmetry*, p.205.

23. Hirsch, *Innocence and Experience*, p.52.

24. Ibid., p.85. Frye (*Fearful Symmetry*, p.202): "Such revolutions, while they cannot cause an apocalypse, may be symptoms of one."

25. Erdman, *Prophet*, p.428. On Orc generally, see Paley, *Energy and Imagination*, chap. five.

26. See Ward, "The Forging of Orc," 205-10; Frye, *Fearful Symmetry*, p.218.

27. Frye, *Fearful Symmetry*, p.217.

28. Hirsch, *Innocence and Experience*, pp.110-11. Ward agrees: "the revolution will be enacted not as a prophetic event occurring within some more or less foreseeable future, but as a Last Judgment or renunciation of error within the individual spirit" (p.225).

29. On this see Frye, *Fearful Symmetry*, p.217.

30. M 23.47. See Erdman, *Prophet*, pp.428-30.

31. Thomas Frosch, *The Awakening of Albion* (Ithaca: Cornell University Press, 1974). I am indebted for much of what follows to this interesting book. Quotations are from the following pages: 57-58, 59-60, 132.

32. Theodore Roszak, like Blake, has criticized the dominance of the "spectator senses" and urged us to recover a primordial tactile participation in the world: "In the sensory make-up of the human being, the eyes and ears (especially the eyes) predominate, vastly overshadowing the other senses. This is a distinctive feature of our sensory evolution. The senses that lend themselves to the illusion of distancing experience press despotically to the fore; the intimate senses recede and grow weak. . . . But it is clearly a violation of reality to forget that we permeate the experiences of vision and hearing, and that there is no more clear distinction between us and a sound or sight representation than there is between us and an odor." *Where the Wasteland Ends* (Garden City, N.Y.: Doubleday, 1972), pp.81-82.

33. See W.J.T. Mitchell, *Blake's Composite Art* (Princeton: Princeton University Press, 1978), especially pp.58-74 on multiple-sensory style.

34. *Negations* (Boston: Beacon Press, 1968), p.272, n.39.

35. *False Consciousness: An Essay on Reification*, trans. Margaret A. Thompson (Oxford: Basil Blackwell, 1975). Gabel is combining the approach of Lukács's *History and Class Consciousness* (1924), which argues that the mechanization and alienation of labor "degrades time to the dimension of space," with the method of existential psycho-analysis developed by Ludwig Binswanger and others, under the inspiration of Martin Heidegger.

36. *Fearful Symmetry*, pp.148-49, for example.

37. Trans. Jules L. Moreau (1960; rpt. New York: Norton, 1970), p.123. Further page references are in parentheses.

38. "We Europeans with our customarily spatial mode of thinking frequently think of temporal rhythms by means of the obvious image of a circle or cycle; the reason for this is the circular movement of the sun which from time immemorial has been used for temporal orientation, since the image of the circular movement of the sun was transferred to the corresponding time. The Hebrews, however, orient themselves temporally not toward the circular movement of the sun, but toward the regular change of the moon's phases, toward the rhythmic alternation of light and darkness, warmth and cold. . . . The use of such images as circles and cycles must be explained correspondingly. Human life runs its course as an eternal rhythm: earth—man—earth. If we depart a bit from our customary way of thinking and reflect quite dispassionately, we shall find in this alternation no trace of a circular line but purely and simply a rhythmic alternation." (p.134)

39. "The Social Context of Literary Criticism," in *Sociology of Literature and Drama*, ed. Tom Burns and Elizabeth Burns (Baltimore: Penguin, 1973), p.152.

40. Blake's dislike of harmony in music is perhaps a Protestant bias. Harmony is the "spatial" dimension of music. Blake's views on melody and harmony are very like those of that son of Geneva, Jean-Jacques Rousseau.

41. Michael Walzer, *The Revolution of the Saints* (1965; rpt. New York: Atheneum, 1970), pp.171-83.

42. "Song," in *Pictures from Brueghel* (New York: New Directions, 1962), p.15.

43. G.W.F. Hegel, *The Phenomenology of Mind*, trans. J. B. Baillie (1910; rpt. New York: Harper & Row, 1967), p.258. See also Frye, *Fearful Symmetry*, p.396.

8. *Blake's* Apocatastasis

1. Harold Bloom, *Blake's Apocalypse* (Garden City, N.Y.: Doubleday, 1963), p.425.

2. The phrase is from Walt Whitman, who continues the encyclopedic tradition in American poetry. For other lists in Blake, see the thirty-two nations at J 72.38-44; the weeds, bugs, and other vermin at M 27.11-29; the birds at M 31.28-45; and the flowers at M 31.46-63.

3. See Daniel Stempel, "Blake, Foucault, and the Classical Episteme," *PMLA* 96 (May 1981), 388-407, esp. 392.

4. If we take the number of Irish counties to be 32, as at J 72.1, 14, 17.

5. *The Complete Poems of Emily Dickinson*, #1234. Goethe's Faust may have something similar in mind when he assigns a district of the Peloponnesus to each Germanic tribe (*Faust II*, 9466-81).

6. Damon and others have pointed out that this list coincides exactly with the thirty-three Swedenborg endorsed as having the "internal sense," but only Blake would have thought to reduce them to *sixteen* books. See Damon, *William Blake: His Philosophy and Symbols* (1924; rpt. New York: Peter Smith, 1942), p.454; and Paley, " 'A New Heaven is Begun,' " 64-90, esp. 78.

7. See Peter Butter, "*Milton*: The Final Plates," in *Interpreting Blake*, ed. Michael Phillips (Cambridge: Cambridge University Press, 1978).

8. I am drawing mainly on the *Theological Dictionary of the New Testament*, ed. Gerhard Kittel and Gerhard Friedrich, trans. Geoffrey W. Bromley (Grand Rapids, Mich.: Eerdmans, 1964-1974); and on Origen, *On First Principles*, trans. G. W. Butterworth (1966; rpt. Gloucester, Mass.: Peter Smith, 1973). Quotations from the latter are on pp.53 and 57.

9. *A New-Year's Gift for the Parliament and Army* (London, 1650), in *The Law of Freedom and Other Writings*, ed. Hill, p.193. Spelling and punctuation are modernized. Winstanley asks his readers not to resent the eventual salvation of their prosecutors and enemies (in *The Mysterie of God*, 1648); see T. Wilson Hayes, *Winstanley the Digger* (Cambridge, Mass.: Harvard University Press, 1979), pp.10-11.

10. Law of Freedom, p.220.

11. Beginning rather like Winstanley's, quoting Colossians 1-26: *The Mystery Hid from Ages and Generations . . .*; subtitled *the Salvation of All Men . . .* ; see Conrad Wright, *The Beginnings of Unitarianism in America* (Boston: Beacon Press, 1955), chap. 8.

12. Notice in the *London Gazetteer*, 5 June 1790, p.2. I owe this reference to David Erdman. In an earlier draft I said it was doubtful that Blake had encountered the Universalist controversy; Erdman has convinced me that it was too prominent and persistent to miss.

13. Garrett, *Respectable Folly*, pp.137-38.

14. Quoted from Robert E. Davies, *Methodism* (Baltimore: Penguin, 1963), p.117. John Murray had been a Methodist, and was converted to Universalism by another Methodist, James Relly.

It is interesting that the leading American Universalist of the twentieth century, Clarence R. Skinner, wrote in *The Social Implications of*

Universalism (Boston, 1915) that "the most revolutionary doctrine ever proclaimed" is the Universalist idea of God, "a universal, impartial, immanent spirit whose nature is love." He frequently quotes Whitman. "A democratic people demand a democratic God, a robust deity who likes his universe, who hungers for fellowship, who is in and of and for the whole of life, whose sympathies are as broad as the 'rounded catalog, divine, complete.' "

15. In his comments preparatory to the 1975 MLA Blake Seminar, published by the *Blake Newsletter* in a pamphlet entitled "Blake's Visions of the Last Judgment."

16. Of course "hair" is not the same as "a hair," and the conglomerating tendency of dust and mud might defeat the indelible outline of any particle of it, but then maybe that is just the point. Plato would dismiss the masses *as* masses, without deigning to notice the unique constituent members. I owe the Parmenides reference to a suggestion by John Hodgson.

17. Donald D. Ault, *Visionary Physics: Blake's Response to Newton* (Chicago: University of Chicago Press, 1974), pp.72-74. Thomas Carlyle, "Characteristics," in *Critical and Miscellaneous Essays*, vol. 3 (Boston, 1840), p.87.

18. Walter Benjamin, "Theses on the Philosophy of History" (1940), in *Illuminations*, pp.254-55. The fullest commentary in English seems to be Irving Wohlfarth, "On the Messianic Structure of Walter Benjamin's Last Reflections," in *Glyph 3* (Baltimore: Johns Hopkins University Press, 1978), pp.148-212.

19. V. A. De Luca, "Proper Names in the Structural Design of Blake's Myth-Making," *Blake Studies* 8:1 (1978), 5-22; quotation on p.9.

20. See "Descriptive Catalogue," E 542, for a possible correlation.

21. See J 82.82: "I can at will expatiate in the Gardens of Bliss."

22. There are three or four counterexamples that prove the rule. With the spiritual sense of "converse" in mind, it seems all the worse for Theotormon to be "conversing with shadows dire" (VDA 8.12) or the fallen eye of man to be "conversing with the Void" (M 5.22). And "To / Converse concerning Weight & Distance in the Wilds of Newton and Locke" (J 30.39-40) is far worse than to talk about them.

23. The two Greek words, *anastrephomai* and *politeuomai*, which are each sometimes translated as "converse" in the Authorized Version, never become "walk," which represents a third term, *peripateo*.

24. Ed. Catherine Stimpson (New York: NAL, 1964), p.60.

25. See E. J. Rose, "Circumcision Symbolism in *Jerusalem*," *Studies in Romanticism* 8 (1968), 16-25.

26. Cf. Francis Bacon, of all people: "Words, as a tartar's bow, do shoot back upon the understanding of the wisest, and mightily entangle and pervert the judgment" (*Advancement of Learning*, II. 14.11).

27. Blake may have been struck by the fact that Satan invents the double-entendre immediately after he invents artillery (PL 6.609f.).

Appendix: The Seven Eyes of God

1. *Fearful Symmetry*, pp.128-34.

2. "Ode to the Departing Year," ll.76-77.

3. "Commentary," p.964. See also M 32.8 where Lucifer is called "Hillel," apparently for *helel* or *helal*, the "day-star" of Isaiah 14:12, first translated as "Lucifer" in the Vulgate. See Bloom, "Commentary," p.924.

4. C. G. Jung, in *Answer to Job* (Cleveland: Meridian, 1960), p.205, n.5, identifies Satan as one of the Eyes on this basis.

5. *Dictionary*, p.119.

6. Ibid., p.368.

7. *Fearful Symmetry*, p.361.

8. Jonas, *Gnostic Religion*, p.132.

9. Irenaeus and Origen are the sources. See R. McL. Wilson, *Gnostic Problem*, p.139, nn.46, 47; and Robert M. Grant, *Gnosticism and Early Christianity* (New York: Harper & Row, 1966), pp.46-51.

10. Grant, *Gnosticism*, p.59.

11. Scholem, *Jewish Mysticism*, pp.78-81. There is other evidence that Blake knew cabalistic tradition. See J 27 (E 171).

12. Leo Schaya, *The Universal Meaning of the Kabbalah*, trans. Nancy Pearson (Baltimore: Penguin, 1973), pp.66-67.

13. *The Kabbalah Denudata*, cited in Milton Percival, *Blake's Circle of Destiny* (1938; rpt. New York: Octagon, 1964), p.243.

14. Schaya, *Kabbalah*, p.21. Percival, *Circle*, p.247, says it is the seventh.

15. *Heresiography* (London, 1645), p.77, quoted in Morton, *The Everlasting Gospel*, p.39.

INDEX

Abrams, M. H., 122, 157
Adams, Hazard, 93
Adorno, Theodor, 3, 56
Aesop, 60, 62, 64
Althusser, Louis, 3, 9, 11, 45
American Revolution, 48, 88, 168, 174-75
antinomianism, 78, 116-26
antiquarianism, 49
apocatastasis, 124, 160, 175, chap. 8 passim
Arendt, Hannah, 40, 165-67
Aristotle, 72-74, 181
art, privileging of, 52-58
atonement, 76-80
Augustine, 171, 218
Ault, Donald, 200

Bacon, Francis, 14, 49, 73, 92, 108-109, 194
Ballou, Hosea, 190
Barry, James, 42
Basire, James, 49
Bauthumley, Jacob, 123
Beauvoir, Simone de, 86-87
Benjamin, Walter, 3, 65, 160, 201-202
Bentham, Jeremy, 22
Berkeley, George, 16, 48
Berlin, Isaiah, 127
Bible, 186-87, 197-99
    Old Testament, 11, 46, 78, 113, 121, 143-44, 155, 168, 173, 181-82, 189, 219; *Books*: Genesis, 47-48, 144, 215-16; Exodus, 105-106; Numbers, 186; Deuteronomy, 117; Joshua, 186; I Kings, 107; I Chronicles, 219; Job, 61, 214, 216; Psalms, 61,

206; Ecclesiastes, 61, 135; Song of Songs, 61, 173, 179; Isaiah, 28, 58, 93, 133, 214; Ezekiel, 58-62, 64, 137, 152; Daniel, 61, 214; Zechariah, 214; Malachi, 192; *Characters*: Abraham, 85, 118, 216; Cain, 120-21; Esau, 122; Isaac, 216; Jacob, 85; Joseph, 84-85; Moses, 60, 118, 126, 216; Noah, 85; Solomon, 60
    New Testament, 69-75, 77, 82-83, 86-87, 105, 121, 143, 173; *Books*: Matthew, 44, 61, 70, 82, 85, 118, 120, 140, 168, 197; Mark, 82; Luke, 61; John, 71, 73, 140; Acts, 74, 128, 130, 189; Romans, 69-70, 74, 117-18, 126, 188, 206; I Corinthians, 82-83, 86, 106, 118, 120, 188; II Corinthians, 87, 206; Galatians, 74, 117-18, 128; Ephesians, 70, 77, 188, 206; Philippians, 206; Colossians, 71, 189; I Thessalonians, 82; I Timothy, 87; I Peter, 70; Jude, 142-43; Revelation, 35, 42, 61, 93, 123, 129-30, 158, 191-93, 214; *Characters*: Jesus, parables of, 61-62, 140, 144, 167; Mary, 85; Paul, 69, 86-87, 90, 105-106, 113, 118-19, 126, 206
Blake, Catherine, 146
Blake, Robert, 194, 233-34
Blake, William
    Characters, places, and special terms: Ahania, 110, 138; Albion, 45, 63-64, 69, 71-72, 76, 84-87, 110, 128-30, 132-33, 138, 142, 145-47, 152, 155, 158, 163-64, 177, 179, 186-87, 192, 197, 202, 204-205,

LIBRARY OF CONGRESS CATALOGING IN PUBLICATION DATA

Ferber, Michael, 1944-
The social vision of William Blake.
Includes index.
1. Blake, William, 1757-1827—Political
and social views. I. Title.
PR4148.P6F4 1985   831'.7   85-522
ISBN 0-691-08382-7 (alk. paper)

Michael Ferber is Assistant Director of the Co-
alition for a New Foreign and Military Policy,
in Washington, D.C. He is co-author, with
Staughton Lind, of *The Resistance* (1971).